The Myth of Replacement

The Myth of Replacement

STARS, GODS, AND ORDER IN THE UNIVERSE

Thomas D. Worthen

THE UNIVERSITY OF ARIZONA PRESS

TUCSON

The University of Arizona Press
Copyright © 1991
The Arizona Board of Regents
All rights reserved
♾ This book is printed on acid-free, archival-quality paper.
Manufactured in the United States of America

96 95 94 93 92 91   6 5 4 3 2 1

LIBRARY OF CONGRESS CATALOGING-IN-PUBLICATION DATA
Worthen, Thomas D.
    The myth of replacement : stars, gods, and order in the universe /
Thomas D. Worthen.
        p. cm.
    Includes bibliographical references and index.
    ISBN 0-8165-1200-0 (acid-free, archival-quality paper)
        1. Mythology—Comparative studies.   2. Precession—Miscellanea.
    I. Title
BL313.W82   1991   291.1′3–dc20   90-20202
                                                              CIP

British Library Cataloguing in Publication data are available.

*Publication of this book is made possible in part by a grant
from the Provost's Author Support Fund of the University of Arizona.*

Title page: From many medieval sources we learn of a Teutonic idol holding a
wheel. This deity was identified with the Roman Saturn. The deity here stands
founded upon the fish, the home-sign of the spring equinox from late antiquity to the present. He carries a basket of fruit or produce, symbolizing plenty,
and bears in his left hand the wheel, signifying the right running of the universe. William Simpson copied the image from an early printed book entitled
The Restitution of Decayed Intelligence (*Buddhist Praying-Wheel,* 241). He reproduced the figure only because Jakob Grimm corroborated it in his *Teutonic
Mythology,* 1:248.

FOR ALL THOSE WHO WOULD
GLADLY LEARN AND GLADLY TEACH, ESPECIALLY
FOR MY STUDENTS AND MY TEACHERS.

CONTENTS

FIGURES

ACKNOWLEDGMENTS

Every author relies on the good will of friends and family whose patience under duress during the critical moments of authorship is a sine qua non to a live birth. To my friends and above all to my family, many thanks for your patience and indulgence. To my colleagues Norman Austin and Jon Solomon, who read this book in some of its many drafts, thank you for your patient and helpful readings. I owe special thanks to the several anonymous readers for the Press whose trenchant criticisms of the first submitted draft inspired me to persevere and to attempt surgery on the living being which is this book. And to the readers for this final version, again my gratitude for their imprimaturs, which induced the long-awaited birthing. Thanks to Margaret Rooker for her many helpful editing suggestions. And above all to Martha Sowerwine my deepest thanks for help that went far beyond editorship into the realms of a profound understanding of anthropology; you gave me invaluable insights into the nature and value of my own work. A special thanks to Raymond E. White, Jr., of the Steward Observatory, whose help, support, and encouragement over the years have meant a great deal. And thanks to all the library and college staff whose help I have relied on but who are too numerous to name here. A sabbatical leave that the University of Arizona granted to me for the academic year 1980–81 enabled me to lay the groundwork for this book.

The Myth of Replacement

CHAPTER I

METHODOLOGIES

C omparison of myths from very different times and places reveals
numerous similarities—some obvious and superficial, others not—
between myths about quite different characters or events. On the other
hand, a single myth often exists in a large number of written or spoken
variants. From its inception in ancient times, the science of mythology
has been attempting to explain this characteristic about its subject: similarity in the midst of variety.

Mythic narrative so resembles literary narrative that it is impossible
to make a rigorous distinction between them. Hence, according to one
school of thought, myth must have a philosophical or moral purpose.
Allegorical interpretation—which one might argue began with Plato,
or certainly with the Neoplatonists of antiquity—insists that myth is a
didactic parable that adumbrates current metaphysical or moral concepts and that its personae are symbols of natural phenomena or of
moral categories. Zeus was the universal principle, the primary fire;
Aphrodite was sumptuousness personified; and the myth of the labors
of Herakles was an ancient *Pilgrim's Progress* in which victory over sun-
dry adversaries represents the triumph of the enlightened soul over human passions.[1]

According to another system of interpretation, the characters of myth
are vested with human motives, and its sequences are diachronic; myth,

therefore, is an elaboration of history, and its gods are the apotheoses of famous human beings. In his spurious travelogue, *The Sacred Record,* Euhemerus (300 B.C.) purports to have learned the "real" facts about a prince named Zeus who was deified by ignorant natives. This kind of interpretation, which has seen periodic revivals, goes by the name of Euhemerism.

The resemblance of some pagan myths to certain stories from the Bible inspired in certain Church Fathers, a nineteenth-century Jewish prime minister of England, and a number of protestants in between the idea that pagan mythographers had plagiarized God's Revelation: the pagans of classical antiquity, in their depraved lack of grace, could not help but corrupt the "truth" in their attempts to imitate it. Antipodal to this idea, but still centered on the apparent similarity between pagan myth and biblical story, is the doctrine of condescension: God's plan calls for an evolutionary revelation; hence, pagan mythology represents the first faltering steps by fallible people in search of true religion. Analogous stories and rites recorded in the Bible reflect a stage in the more exalted religious evolution of the Jews, which would eventually culminate in the Good News of Christianity.

The exploration of foreign lands, first during the Crusades and later for purely mercantile purposes, prompted the publication of travel literature—advice and itineraries for the faithful, gazetteers for the greedy, and travel tales for the curious. Such works made a spate of ethnographic material on exotic "manners and fables" available to stay-at-home philosophers. The least bigoted of these recognized in these sources elements of religion and story comparable to those from classical culture. But unlike these simple tales and customs learned from afar, they thought, classical culture, especially its mythology, was encrusted by time and change, by generations of interpretation and exegesis. At its origin, our Judeo-Christian heritage must have been just as simple and straightforward. Encrypted through reinterpretation by newer civilizations, our common heritage needed deciphering, they thought, and the best available key to the truth about antiquity lay in the study of contemporary simple cultures—the more unspoiled by civilization and the influence of outside proselytizers, the better. Hence "primitive" acquired a new ameliorative meaning. The noble savage, uncorrupted by decadent civilization, was a model for study. People could be studied as specimens of their undeveloped selves. Abandoning the notions of natural law, which claims that the same moral sense is innate in everyone as a result of the gift of reason, Vico and other Enlightenment philosophers erected the structure of anthropological science. The impetus to comprehend "primitive" peoples as a prerequisite to understanding their "civilized" counterparts propelled hundreds of naturalists and ethnographers into the farthest reaches of the world.

In the nineteenth century, scholars tried to explain the patterns of similarity and variation in myth via analogy with language, embracing this philological approach to the study of antiquity with fanatic fervor. One such philologist, J. A. Wolf, went so far as to make the grandiose claim that philology could restore the ancient world in its organic totality so that we might understand it in every possible sense.[2] Another scholar touted etymology, philology's subdiscipline, as the key to the interpretation of myth: "All that one needs to understand myth is the names and epithets of the gods and their etymological interpretation."[3]

The science of comparative philology had discovered that Greek, Latin, and Sanskrit belonged together as siblings in a linguistic family whose parent (variously dubbed Aryan, Indo-Germanic, Indo-Aryan, and Indo-European) was missing. Of these, by far the senior heir was Sanskrit. Accordingly, myths told in the oldest documents in that language, the Vedas, were exalted as repositories of the archetypal cultural behaviors. Greek and Roman myth, ritual, and religion were held to be but cold and pale imitations.

Similarities in the languages set forth in a by-then growing apparatus of phonetic laws could explain the similarities in the very myths and ritual behaviors couched in them. Evolution and change in myth and ritual must follow, by analogy, evolution and change in language. All that was required was the discovery of the laws that governed these processes. The plethora of phonetic changes noted in the evolution of languages seemed to follow certain formulas. Could not mythological proliferation therefore be seen to have arisen from one common archetype and evolved according to some fixed principles? There was, among many nineteenth- and early-twentieth-century scholars, confidence that such laws could be found and given expression. Such a "scientific" mythology was eagerly pursued, and its reliance on linguistic—especially etymological—bases is evident in the rubric, Comparative Mythology, given it by its chief proponent, Max Müller, who above all others insisted that it be based on strict phonetic rules. Müller roundly criticized adherents of the anthropological approach (which he called "ethno-psychological") for pretending to study the folklore of savages without first learning their native languages.

Cross-cultural similarities in myth were thus found to be explicable. Comparative mythology would eventually incorporate all myth into a set of ur-myths indigenous to the Indo-Europeans, ancestors of the Hindus, Greeks, and Romans. Variation, on the other hand—the profusion of slightly different but recognizably similar stories—could also be accounted for with a philological model. Similar texts extant at one point in time resemble a hypothetical lost archetype. Similarities in their logic, vocabulary, and even syntax point to a common parentage. Their differences can be accounted for by the alteration wrought by accident or design. So, too, with myth.

But Müller's fixed principle was, in effect, derived from the approach of the anthropological school, that is, discovering the nature of the primitive mind. Müller may not have been aware of this teleological parallel. To his way of thinking, the peoples from the Indo-European parent culture (his Aryas) were noble and pure, not yet hobbled by the severe rules and ethnocentrism of an aged civilization. He invented the term *mythopoeic* to describe the nature of their mentality. This state of mind was characterized by pure poetic thought—thought without significant abstraction, conceptualization, or discursive reasoning. Before this stage, he theorized, language consisted of a limited number of verbal roots relating mainly to the Aryas and their social and economic world. But in the mythopoeic age, people were impelled to describe their experience of the phenomenal world. Natural phenomena were seen as the expression of divine activity. To effect such description, the limited language of the Aryas resorted to metaphor. This process expanded the basic vocabulary in two ways: by polyonymy, a term referring to the manner in which a simple verb like "to shine" could be extended beyond its primary human reference, "to be glorious or bright of mind" to a host of natural ones: to the appearance of sky, air, dawn, light, and to Dyaus, the supreme deity; and conversely by homonymy, the name for the semantic process by which numbers of different words might be used to refer to one central but complicated phenomenon, such as the sun with its diurnal and seasonal motions: *fingers* might be used as the word for the sun's rays; "Burning One" (Dawn) might be said to stretch her "fingers" over the "Bright One" (Sky). "The Concealing One (Night) gives birth to a brilliant child" might have been the standard way of saying that the sun was rising. "The Measurer looks at him who has put on the mountain for clothing" might have been a way of saying that the full moon rises with sunset. Such words and expressions are already quasi metaphors, called appellatives by Müller.

Then the Aryas dispersed and migrated. Owing to a lack of cultural cohesion, admixture with foreigners, and the vagaries of time and travel, the original meanings of the key terms in these metaphors were forgotten, yet the apellatives themselves remained. Hence "Bright One," Selene, became just a proper name for the Moon. So, too, the term "He Who Clothes Himself" became the name Endymion. This process, which Müller called a "disease of language," led to the creation of myth, a story confabulated in retrospect to explain the forgotten origins of these metaphors: "Endymion went to the home of the Night, where Selene discovered him and fell in love" might be the first elaboration of a myth designed to restore meaning to a dead metaphor about the rising of the full moon at sunset. Later Endymion was made a prince and given a territory. Still later the love affair was given a motive and a beginning, a middle, and an end. Müller and his adherents insisted that most myths grew up from forgotten metaphors about phenomena: the sun, moon, stars, and weather.[4]

"But surely this theory can't account for everything," insisted Müller's anthropologically minded opponents. If, indeed, Callisto was turned into the constellation Ursa Major, how does this account, based solely on natural phenomena, explain the existence of a bear cult centered around Callisto's mistress, Artemis? The anthropologists held to their dogma of cultural evolution, the idea that the human mind has evolved similarly no matter where a culture was located as the culture moved gradually from savagery to civilization. Explanations for similar myths, they claimed, should be traced by observing similarities in belief and custom stage by stage. Thus they believed that the survivals of primitive belief among the peasantry and aboriginal cultures, studied firsthand, constituted far better materials for the reconstruction of these stages than linguistic relics reconstructed from a narrowly circumscribed and hypothetical protoculture. The legend about Kronos swallowing his children is not a dead metaphor about some forgotten celestial event, they countered, but an antique survival from a era when cannibalism was practiced among the Greeks. Müller's critic, Andrew Lang,[5] argued in this vein at length, inspired by *Primitive Culture,* a landmark work in ethnography by E. B. Tylor.[6] Lang's approach was a precursor of the methodologies of folklore developed in this century.[7]

In the early twentieth century, anthropologists and historians of religion were preoccupied with the primitive belief in magic and other modes of dynamism—that is, the tendency to view and treat *things* as if they possessed personalities and powers that might be cajoled and that must be appeased. Ethnographers such as Bronislaw Malinowski spent (and still spend) a great deal of effort cataloging beliefs of this sort as they find expression in various cultures. In this, most of them concentrate on proliferation rather than on similarity. A few great synthesists—Paul Radin and Mircea Eliade, for example—have managed to create passable generalizations from this bewildering mountain of religious data. The effect upon the study of mythology has been to cause experts generally to admit that myth has an irreducible sacred dimension. In its very telling, myth validates the *reality* of an institution, personality, place, or object—a reality that the unvalidated events of mundane history do not and cannot possess.

At the same time that Malinowski's adherents were developing his functionalist theory of how myth functions to validate the social, moral, and religious systems of a culture, Freud and Jung were attempting to apply the results of their researches into the individual psyche to the genesis of cultural phenomena such as myth. "Certain psychic processes," Freud wrote, "tend always to be operative and to find expression in widespread human institutions."[8] In mythology, then, as in Kantian philosophy, we must account for a similarity of pattern by regressing, a priori, into the world of psychic categories. Consequently, in a sense, Freud devalued myth: to him it was simply data in which a clever interpreter can discover clues about the structure of psychic categories and about the manner in which they have been biased by individual or group idiosyncrasies. Nonetheless, Freud used his knowledge of the formation of antitypes from mythical types as the basis for his abstract theories about the life-and-death instincts. Jung, on the other hand, saw in myths and in dreams realities worthy of intensive study in themselves. From the regular appearance of images from ancient myth in the dreams of psychoneurotics who were ignorant of these myths, he developed a theory of "archetypes" divided into taxonomies. Here we have not only Freud's universal psychic categories but also the hypothesis that their modes of expression are universal. Myth has a social function. Chaotic experience from the outer world is categorized by the mind into paradigms derived from inner, psychic experience. Myth and dreams redramatize these psychic events as if they were human figures in real situations. No matter what culturally determined clothing these images wear, one can recognize behind them typical situations and archetypal figures. But despite the similarity of some dream images to images from myth, Jung's insistence that the meaning of any mythical image is the same as that of the dream that it resembles seems at its base to be dogmatic and forces his explanations into rounds of circular reasoning. Myths are like dreams whose messages are about conflicts in the psyche. Given such a hypothesis, it is no surprise that when Jung unlocked the "secrets" of a myth he found exactly the same messages. But no matter what we may find in the subconscious mind, there is nothing inherent in myths to lead one to posit that there are such secret messages encoded in them. Nevertheless, since myths in any given variant are told by individuals, not cultures, there is undoubtedly some psychic content to every story. Such content may well dramatize, in part, the teller's social conflicts, but this insight does little to explain the paradox of unity in diversity that we find worldwide and in diverse cultures whose imperatives differ.

Much of what Jung contributed on the subject of myth has an immediate appeal, especially as it is expressed in the mythological writings of his most articulate and mythologically learned adherent, Joseph Campbell. A session with a work of Campbell's never fails to be stimulating, seductively so, though one often comes away being informed and charmed by the experience but not convinced by the theory.

Almost directly contrary to these psychological ruminations, the sociological school, largely French in origin, asserted that culture determines all, and more particularly that the social structure, le système sociale, is the sacred dimension, which finds its symbolic expression in cult, totem, and myth. The school's founder, Émile Durkheim, rejected outright the attempt by Tylor and Freud, his near contemporaries, to ground social phenomena in the states of the individual psyche. The analysis of socially based ideologies, he insisted, will reveal a structure, a delicately balanced ecosystem, whose imperatives will find subtle or overt expression at every level of communication from the telling of myth to the telling of time. If myth has any function, it is to validate this system, its parts, and its interrelationships. Myths and the divine personalities that populate them are "collective representations" of important cultural factors. Belonging to a group, being a social animal, is necessary to man's survival, and we should look for the sources of religion in the joys and feelings of awe and dependence this embracing social framework evokes in the group.

Meanwhile, on either side of France, scholars were dealing with the data being gathered by anthropologists and folklorists in their different ways. The adherents of the Vienna school were historical ethnologists who claimed that an examination of cultural records from all times and all places would reveal an evolutionary scheme of cultural types, each stage of which is tied to economic status.[9] Hence myth serves an economic function—that is, the sacred dimension is the continued prosperity of the folk. The oldest primitive cultures were based on hunting and gathering, and a few such cultures remain—the southeast Australian aborigines and the bushmen of the Kalahari, for example. Next came the early food producers (primitive agriculturalists who lived in villages) and the pastoral nomads. There followed the secondary cultures, of which the ancient Egyptian, Mesopotamian, and Mayo-Aztecan cultures are examples. Each of these stages was characterized not only by its typical economic basis but also by its whole array of cultural facts, including myth.

Sir James G. Frazer and his largely British following developed the thesis that most rituals and myths (which are but spoken relatives of rites) are rooted in economic magic. The central and recurring drama concerns the rejuvenation, by means of a living sacrifice, of the natural order and of the social order, which is a microcosm of the former: the king must die—long live the new king! To this end, peoples in the mythopoeic age proliferated both formal ritual and myth and informal folk practices. Often surviving in cults beyond the rites that gave them birth, myths can be made to reveal their origins in a prescientific mode of thinking about the control of nature. The goal of such control was the prevention of death, decadence, and decay. Frazer's consideration of the cults of Attis and Osiris forms the center of gravity of his great tome *The Golden Bough,* and his followers have successfully extended his explanations to cultural data from the societies of the Near East. New Year festivals from Mesopotamia and enthronement rituals from Egypt have been analyzed for Frazerian components—the sacral king, ritual combat, and the dying-and-rising god.

George Cox, an early-twentieth-century follower of Max Müller, laid the foundations for a new approach to mythology. His treatment of the folktale of the master thief adumbrates type analysis and motif analysis. Most pan-Aryan legends, he maintained with Müller, cannot be accounted for by borrowing alone but must be related back to a common origin on the basis of comparable "phrases relating to physical phenomena," and if such phrases are absent, larger structural similarities may be analyzed for proof of a common source.[10]

Another advocate of comparative mythology, von Hahn, also sought a structural basis for the continuing search for Aryan antecedents. As early as 1864 he began listing formulas he had noted in folklore. Then, in *Sagwissenschaftliche Studien* (1876) he listed a "formula" of sixteen motifs by means of which he tabulated the biographies of fourteen Aryan heroes, including Oedipus. Underlying these sixteen motifs, von Hahn discerned two grand themes: expulsion and return. Most investigators who have followed von Hahn's lead have simply extended or altered this scheme *ad libitum*. Lord Raglan, for example, developed a set of twenty-two "incidents" that constitute the "hero pattern."[11] In his analysis, he did not emphasize the strict order of incidents, because his particular interest was not in mythic structure per se but in proving that the universal pattern reflects no actual historical hero but rather an underlying ritual whose phases predetermine the patterns of the later story.

The scholars Aarne and Stith Thompson developed structural analysis into an atomistic science. Collecting vast stores of material firsthand and from other ethnographers, Thompson categorized them into some seven hundred tale types. His analysis is based on an examination of all available versions of a tale for the minimal traits that still show variation. The distribution of the minimal variations allows the versions to be cataloged through the identification of ever-smaller groups of tales that share common variation in a given trait. A unique series is derived for each collected version. If a given version of a tale might exhibit variation 7 in trait A and variation 3 in trait B, place trait D before trait C, and exhibit variation 5 in D and variation 1 in C, its signature would be $A_7 B_3 D_5 C_1$. This procedure is called the historic-geographic method, and underlying it is the assumption that such variants are proliferated through many retellings diachronically interrelated and spread by diffusion across cultural boundaries. This implies that each story has a first telling and an archetype. Adherents of the method attempt to reconstruct this archetype by tabulating the frequency of the variations within a trait and by noting the presence or absence of principal and secondary traits.[12]

In contrast to this atomistic approach and in contradistinction to von Hahn's motif analysis, Vladimir Propp developed a system of pattern analysis that operates at a high level of abstraction. If I may use an example from a well-known myth, Propp's method would type Oedipus's need to consult an oracle to find out the truth (an incident ignored by Raglan and von Hahn) as an instance of "lack" and the final realization of the whole truth as "lack liquidated." Laius's warning would be typed "interdiction," his seduction into siring an unwanted child by Jocasta as "violation," and his death at the crossroads as "consequence." The thirty-one such elements, or "functions," that comprise Propp's morphology constitute elements for a dramatic plot in which the roles of the hero and other characters are constantly shifting from the beginning through the middle to the end. For example, a victim may become a persecutor, and a rescuer a new victim.[13]

By now it should be clear that scholars have staked out many claims in the lode that is myth, all of which have produced valuable ore. Some mythographers, like Campbell, thoroughly mined their approaches and continue to have a great following; others, once popular, have been consigned to oblivion, with their works long out of print. But each has contributed to a stimulating and continuing dialogue. Myth and mythology will never cease to fascinate. So far, we have discussed theorists whose approaches to myth are more or less unique, but since midcentury a number of eclectic approaches have been developed. Several of these have incorporated features in such a unique fashion as to be compelling, and one in particular has gathered numerous adherents. The *New Comparative Mythology*,[14] to cite a book that summarizes this approach's tenets and development, has roots in the Aryan etymologizing utilized by Müller, in the sociological interpretation promulgated by Durkheim and Mauss, and in structural analysis. Pioneered by a French scholar of comparative linguistics turned sociologist, Georges Dumézil, this methodology has elicited voluminous papers and monographs on the subject of Indo-European religion, mythology, ideology, and law, and their reflection in descendant cultures.

Dumézil's boldly titled 1924 doctoral thesis made his direction clear and revealed his antecedents. *Le Festin d'Immortalité: Étude de Mythologie Comparée Indo-Européenne* argued that the moribund Müllerian comparative mythology could be put on the sound footing of comparative religion rooted in social structure rather than in hazy notions about sky-gods, and that new and more scientifically based etymologies would again play a central role in the comparative method. To obviate the anticipated criticism from anthropologists that there are huge numbers of mythological themes in the world, some of which might be represented in the Indo-European cultures purely by chance, Dumézil restricted his analysis to complex sequences of themes found uniquely in the diverse Indo-European daughter cultures.

Many twentieth-century works that compare Indo-European daughter cultures have their roots in a classic of French historical writing, Numa-Denis Fustel de Coulange's *La Cité Antique* (1864). Dumézil's thesis is no exception. It expands upon de Coulange's discussion of ancestor worship and domestic religion by examining Indo-European myths concerning immortality and its origin, its objectification in rites involving a sacred drink (ambrosia and its congeners), and its loss through trickery. A foiled attempt by a trickster figure to secure the secret of immortality and bring it to earth dooms mankind to mortality and restricts the privilege of deathlessness to the gods. Dumézil called this sequence the ambrosia cycle.

Dumézil next expanded his interest in the ambrosia cycle to include common Indo-European myths and rites concerning spring and spring-time fertility. In 1930, however, Dumézil's work veered into a new and totally unpredictable direction. Observing that the four basic social classes of the early Persian Avesta are parallel in function (if not in ety-mology) to the Hindu castes—a conclusion seconded by the learned Iranist Emile Benveniste—Dumézil made the intuitive leap that the Indo-European culture must have had a tripartite social structure. The fourth and lowest class was created later to contain a foreign substratum of conquered "producers." He corroborated this hypothesis through arguments based on Scythian and Ossetic materials. This discovery set Dumézil on a new course and set in motion a scholarly regatta that he has steered ever since—correlating the mass of Roman, Indic, and Ger-manic myths (the Greek material proves more intractable) with the tri-partite structure and refining the concepts of tripartition into an Indo-European "ideology."

The sharpness of the change of direction can be detected in the sub-stance of a 1935 paper, "Flamen-Brahman."[15] Here we find the class of Indo-European priests, the basis of the first class, or "function," of Indo-European society. These priests create kings, their secular coun-terparts, by self-sacrifice. Gone and forgotten is Fustel de Coulange's domestic religion, centered on the sacred flame even to the point of ignoring the etymological significance of *flamen* ("blow" on the sacred flame) and the probable etymology of the Avestan word for priest, *ath-ravan,* in the word *athra,* "fire."[16]

Another French scholar, Claude Lévi-Strauss, roughly coeval with Dumézil and a sociologist become anthropologist become mythogra-pher, has taken a decidedly innovative and influential approach to the study of human societies. His structural principles are like other struc-tural analyses: all message systems encode their messages structurally, that is, in repeating elements found linked into bundles; the meaning of the series is to be found in the relationships among these elements; and each variation is a repetition that can be substituted for another with little gain or loss. In Lévi-Strauss's treatment, myth, like language as analyzed by Leopold de Saussure, is structured along two distinct axes. The narrative part of a myth can be analyzed into "themes" or "motifs," which, when strung together, produce a sequentially ordered narrative of events that allegedly took place "once upon a time." This feature of myth, however, which produces plots comprised of human or anthropomorphized actions, is its least interesting and least important aspect. The timeless element—whatever is universal about the myth, that which gives it "operative value"—is not to be revealed by analyses of sequentially ordered elements. Much as music must be analyzed in two dimensions (horizontally for melody and rhythm, and vertically for harmonic pattern), so myth has a second essential dimension that must be apprehended by noticing a less obvious "vertical" structure of "harmonically" repeated elements. In the Oedipus myth, for example, rape and incest recur through the generations of the family, as does a curious etymological element: Oedipus = "swollen-foot"; Laius = "left-sided"; and Labdacus, which possibly means "lame."

Lévi-Strauss calls such elements "gross constituent units," and their importance to myth is in proportion to the number of their repetitions, that is their recurrence in "bundles." But in order to discover whether such units aggregate sufficiently to be considered bundles—in order to distinguish the adventitious from the basic units—one must be careful to include in the analysis *all* versions of the myth, discarding all value judgments such as early vs. late, primitive vs. literary, pure vs. interpretive. If the Oedipus myth has been treated by Freud, Freud's interpretation becomes a version to be analyzed. If the Oedipus myth is part of the Theban foundation-and-destruction myth, then the stories of Cadmus and Europa, and of Creon and Haemon are to be considered as variants. In other words, individual stories cannot be made to reveal their meaning, which is entirely structural; myths must be interpreted only as members of a series.

Lévi-Strauss insists that myths exist *only* in partial versions, which are always in the process of positive or negative growth. In the analysis of myth, therefore, one must abjure the hope of identifying the "definitive" version; one can only hope to compare some myths with others, to point out similarities and differences, to find some that are not so obvious, and somewhat more grandly, to codify the process by which mythical variants are constructed and deconstructed. He derides the traditional mythographers' quest to reconstruct "whole," "pure," and "original" versions as an impossible ambition; archetypes and ur-myths exist only in the mind of the beholder.

When Lévi-Strauss himself goes to work on a myth, he arranges the constituent units into two columns. One column contains "mythologems" in which something is overstressed or overvalued; the other, those in which the same thing is understressed or undervalued. In the Oedipus myth, "underrating blood relations" is at the top of a column whose constituents are "The Spartoi kill each other," "Oedipus kills Laius," and "Eteocles kills his brother Polyneices." The choice of rubrics reveals Lévi-Strauss's sociological bias. A lawyer might have selected quite a different rubric to head the column. While Lévi-Strauss's chosen labels are always provocative and sometimes enlightening, they often seem arbitrary, lacking corroboration from other cultural elements.

Myth is a message system coexisting with other cultural message systems and exhibiting the same structures. But it is often easier to "read" than others, and by means of it we may find out how the culture seeks to mediate the paradoxical existence within it of two mutually contradictory or abhorrent viewpoints or institutions. Many cultures, for example, are torn between the contradictory perceptions that "man is a special unique creation" and that "man is created by sexual intercourse, just like the animals." Lévi-Strauss acknowledges the alleviation of these contradictory messages as the sole function performed by myth.[17]

Also germane to a search for sound method are the views of Ernst Cassirer, a philosopher of culture who has compared the discourse generated by myth with that generated by science and philosophy. The most elegant statement of this viewpoint is to be found in "Myth and Reality," H. Frankfort and H. A. Frankfort's introductory chapter to their anthology *Before Philosophy*. Calling on the distinction between I–Thou and I–It relationships, they vivify Cassirer's notions:

> The fundamental difference between the attitudes of modern and ancient man as regards the surrounding world is this: for modern, scientific man the phenomenal world is primarily an 'It'; for ancient—and also for primitive—man it is a 'Thou.'. . . Now the knowledge which 'I' has of

'Thou' hovers between the active judgement and the passive 'undergoing an impression'; . . . 'Thou' may be problematic, yet 'Thou' is somewhat transparent. 'Thou' is a live presence, whose qualities and potentialities can be made somewhat articulate—not as the result of inquiry but because 'Thou,' as a presence, reveals itself. . . . All experience of 'Thou' is highly individual; and early man does, in fact, view happenings as individual events. An account of such events and also their explanation can be conceived as action and necessarily take the form of a story. In other words, the ancients told myths instead of presenting an analysis or conclusions.[18]

None of the approaches to mythology surveyed here has given us the One True Hermeneutic to myth and mythology, and I make no claim that what follows does so either; siding with Lévi-Strauss, I doubt that any single methodology will do this. What I propose is a heuristic approach to comparative mythology beginning with an investigation of our state of knowledge in 1924 when Dumézil made his doctoral thesis public.

My first subject is a set of myths characterized by Dumézil as constituents of a pan–Indo-European ambrosia cycle. Instead of analyzing them in his way, however, I intend to treat each myth as a variant, in the manner of Lévi-Strauss, and then to analyze each one minutely for its gross constituent units—perhaps even more minutely than Lévi-Strauss. I hope to show through this atomization that certain atoms are wont to cleave together into elements—for example, motifs of eating, swallowing, and drowning are in my analysis the atoms that recur singly or in combination to form the element "hiding." Other elements admit of no reduction yet still display allomorphs; hence the element water has the allomorphs sea, river, milk, beer, Ocean, sky, and others. The variation and differentiation of variants often arise by allomorphic substitution for such simple constituents. The presence of these allomorphic constituents, the chief of which to be analyzed here is the element "replacement," comprise the "harmony" of the myth, and as in a harmonic scheme, in which musical triads must be present or implied, we will expect the elements such as "replacement" per se to be linked with other atoms and elements. These allied elements will recur in the presentation of the myth, though in no particular order, as its narration (the "melody") works through from beginning to middle to end in order to comprise a story.

The necessary recurrences of such elements in related myths enable us finally to demonstrate that a paradigm is present in a great number of myths, some of which superficially do not seem related at all but which embody the paradigm in concrete details and motifs that recur in a recognizable bundle, the salient feature of which is the theme of replacement. This bundle, which may not always be made up of *all* the elements that can be isolated from exemplary myths, we will then define as the Myth of Replacement.

As the result of this study, in anticipation of the subsequent studies to be done as part of a planned multivolume work on mythology, I offer the generalization that myths occur in typological series, the members of which bear sometimes close, sometimes very distant similarities to each other. Thus the process of defining these typologies will empower the reader to acquire a cogent understanding of the phenomena of similarity in difference and difference in similarity as they are found universally in myth.

Specifically, you may expect to find in what follows a search for congeners of the ambrosia cycle as identified by Dumézil. You will find a demonstration that adheres to Lévi-Strauss's principle that many variants and versions of a myth should be used in one's analysis and that in terms of their atoms and elements many myths that appear to bear no resemblance to the ambrosia cycle in sequence or in plot do in fact bear a great affinity to it and indeed are identical to it in import. An identity of conception lies behind the many similarities to be found in the variant myths, as evidenced by the recurrence of their many bundles. Finally, more in keeping with Stith Thompson than with Lévi-Strauss, we will discover embedded in the Myth of Replacement a conceptual archetype lacking any of the qualities of "story."

The archetype is constructed at only one remove from nature. Through it, nature is subjected to the constraints of culture. Culture seeks to bring nature into its own sphere, which is always regular and always prescriptive. Rituals are performed not to imitate the regularities in nature but to induce nature to imitate a culturally effected regularity. Beyond such rituals, many and varied myths are elaborated, and although the myths in question can be related to certain rituals, they are not merely verbalized echoes of their action. Myths have their own purpose (part of which is entertainment, to be sure), and it is to elaborate the ritual's archetypal acts, objects, and words into hierarchies of elements grouped into bundles and to place them into the framework of a narrative, a story that can be told. Rituals serve the culture in one central primary "message system"—that of defense, the protection of the group against its enemies, the central one of which is the irregularity and capriciousness of nature. As narratives, myths that grow from a given ritual extend the range of the ritual from defense to the other message systems of the culture—to recreation, for example, or to education, the exploitation of the environment (since they may encode information about the recurrence of the seasons), social interactions (the replacement of rulers, lovers, spouses), time and the keeping of time, and man's relationship to the divine. In fact, for a full understanding of simple rituals, one must have knowledge of the myths elaborated upon their archetypal actions. With respect to the Myth of Replacement, both the ritual of circular motion and its related myth of replacement function to express fear induced by the observation that noticed regularities in the heavens had failed and were no longer to be counted on.

CHAPTER II

THE RITUAL OF RIGHT RUNNING

A number of Hindu and Buddhist rituals involve movement about a sacred object in a clockwise direction (sunwise, as it was called by the ancients). A Shivaic ritual takes place annually about the city of Benares, a city so holy that the Hindus think every inch of soil within it to be hallowed, a city, in fact, which might be considered to be itself a temple since it is supposed to be built not upon the earth but in the sky, supported by the three points of Shiva's trident. The ritual involves circumambulation by pilgrims in the sunwise direction over a six-day span, a trek that amounts to some fifty miles.[1] On the last day of the pilgrimage, the devotees scatter barley grains along their path from a bag made for the purpose. Another such circumambulation of a city takes place in Bhuvanesvara in Orissa.[2] This circumambulation around the city is repeated three times, and certain mantras must be repeated in the process.

The purport of the mantras can be found by observing a parallel ritual among the people of Tibet. They construct dikes of stone from a few feet to a half a mile in length upon which, for good luck, they lay stone slabs engraved with "Aum Mani Padme Hum." The dikes are themselves called *manis,* and they are generally built along the center of public roads at the outskirts of the village so that a passerby keeps them always on his right, whether approaching or departing from town.[3]

This same mantra, whose meaning is "Om, jewel, lotus, Om," is inscribed on Tibetan praying wheels. It is uttered while the wheel is kept turning, always in the same sunwise direction. The wheels, whether driven by hand, wind, or water, are (or were) a ubiquitous sight in Tibet, where they are called *manis*, "jewels," and are thought, to produce good karma with their turning, since at every turn they reenact ritual circumambulation. They are also called *mani-chhos-khor*, "Precious Religious Wheels" and "Precious Wheels of the Law"⁴ (compare Sanskrit *dharma-chakra*, "Wheel of the Law" or "Wheel of the Foundation").

These rites derive from early Hindu practice. In the *Satapatha-Brahmana* we read of a religiously correct chariot race. Preparations for it must be ritually exacting, for the stakes are great:

> Now when they run a race, he hereby wins this same [terrestrial] world. And when the Brahman sings a Saman on the cartwheel set up [on a post] reaching to his navel, he thereby wins the air-world. And when he erects the sacrificial post, he thereby wins the world of the gods.
>
> Hence the threefold performance. The Brahman mounts a cart-wheel, set up on a post as high as his navel, with [*Vaj. S.* ix.10], "At the impulse [*sava*] of the god Savitri, of true impulsion, may I ascend unto the highest heaven of Brihaspati!" . . . Thrice he sings the Saman. Having sung it, he descends with, "At the impulse of the divine Savitri, of true impulsion, I have ascended unto the highest heaven of Brihaspati!"⁵

According to the medieval Hindu scholar Sayana, the wheel, after being mounted by the Brahman, is to be turned round three times in the sunwise motion, the pointed end of the post apparently being inserted in the nave of the wheel. In the Brahmanas, the turning wheel is compared with the Vajra, or disk-shaped thunderbolt. In its context the ritual hymn (Saman) itself has to do with a heavenly chariot ride, the setting forth of the solar charioteer Savitri on his daily ride: "The fiery steeds have gathered fiery mettle, the impulse of the god Savitri; win ye the heavens, O coursers!"⁶

In later times the use of wheel motifs to decorate or even construct the Buddha throne is ubiquitous and is found in all periods (fig. 2.1).⁷ Could the image of Buddha on his throne surveying all creation have been derived from the image of Savitri overlooking the earth from the

FIGURE 2.1

Drawings done by Simpson from the Buddhist sculptures found at Amarávati. Here we see depicted the empty throne of Buddha with its footstool onto which are worked the footprints of Buddha, given in detail on the right. Symbols of the wheel are in evidence both above the throne as a many-rayed solar disk and on the footprint. A child born with the "thousand-rayed wheel" on the soles of its feet is an elected one who will become either a Chakravarti Raja or a Perfect Buddha. According to Buddhist scripture, at birth the master walked to the seven steps along each of the points of the compass, and a lotus grew up in the print of each step. (Simpson, *Buddhist Praying-Wheel*, 42)

FIGURE 2.2
A bronze trisula from the Chola Period in India. (Ardhanarisvara Trident,
11th–12th century; courtesy of the Cleveland Museum of Art, purchase
from the J. H. Wade Fund, 69.117)

vantage point of his heavenly car? In any case, the throne has heavenly, even cosmic significance. A Chinese pilgrim to Buddha Gaya wrote down a myth about the origin of the throne there: "In the middle of the enclosure surrounding the Bodhi tree is the diamond throne [original: *vajrasana*]. In former days, when the Bhadra Kalpa [first millennium] was arriving at the period of perfection, when the great earth arose, this [throne] also appeared. It is in the middle of the great chiliocosm; it goes down to the limits of the golden Wheel [the gold circle], and upward it is flush with the ground."[8] Vajrasana means "thunderbolt throne," and indeed, a monument at the site, supposedly representing the absent throne, is decorated with a circle of thunderbolts. The depiction of the Vajra (the typical weapon of Indra) is much the same as that of the Tibetan Dorjé and of the trisula, or trident (fig. 2.2),[9] and although the pilgrim does not explicitly so report, we are safe in assuming that pilgrims to the shrine moved about it in the same way as Hindu worshipers circumambulate Benares, the city-temple, and walk clockwise in adoration around the Hindu Stupa (temple) outside, and then, once inside, around its central vacant point as if in imitation of the spokes moving about the hollow nave of a wheel.

A stationary throne around which the pilgrims move in the sunwise direction and a sun chariot that moves in the sunwise direction around the world which adores it—both are connected with the roots of being, with a post (or sacred tree) and navel (or hub), with lightning (Vajra) and the sacred trident, with the number three, and with bliss (good Karma, the world of the gods) or with plenty (the scattered barley).

This complex of ideas is associated not only with divine beings but also with the rulers of this earth. In the *Vishnu Purana* we read that the mark of Vishnu's discus is visible on the hand of one born to be a Universal Emperor (Chakravarti).[10] This title was accorded to anyone who conquered or obtained supreme power over a great territory, and it means, "He who abides or rules over an extensive territory called a Chakra."[11] Chakra, of course, means "wheel," and the question arises whether the territory was so named because it enclosed an area like a wheel or for some other reason. The discus emblem on Vishnu's weapon, and the wheel signs on Buddha's footprints (fig. 2.1)[12] should provide the answer. The elected one has claim to greatness only because he has turned the primeval wheel or has been associated with it. This deduction is corroborated by the title of the Buddha: Mahachakravarti Raja, "Lord, Revolver-of-the-Great-Wheel."

Ritual motion around a holy object in the sunwise direction was of such cultural importance that it bore a special name, *pradakshina,* "(motion) toward the right" or "toward the south (from east)," a term that survives in the Prakrits as Prudukshuna, a rite to Vishnu that involves circumambulation and the singing of a mantra.[13] Many sacrificial rituals described in the Vedas take place at dawn, with the observers facing the point of the sunrise, hence the connection of Pradakshina with sunwise motion from east to south (*dakshina,* "right," also means "south") to west.

On a higher level of abstraction, Pradakshina is therefore to be associated with two other Sanskrit words, *rita* and *ritu.* The concrete ritu means the round of the seasons and its related rites (our word "rite" is itself cognate with ritu and rita). Rita is more difficult. These nouns are both related to the verb *ri,* which has the sense of "to fit, join, fix" and then "to move fitly, to go on the path; the path followed in going." Hence it has to do with ritual correctness, which requires facing east, as we have seen.[14] Hence the sun is called "Bright Face of Rita."[15] But these motions are fixed, changeless; hence rita is conceived of first as the eternal foundation of all that exists, and then as law in general (compare *dharma,* law as foundation), and finally as "right, good, true." The two negatives of rita follow a similar semantic course: *nirriti* meant "going away," then "decay, destruction, death, the abyss" and "the mother of Hell, Naraka"; *anrita* was used to express whatever is false, evil, or untrue.[16]

In Hindu belief, the elixir of life is called *amrita,* "deathless(ness)," a word cognate with our word *immortal,* which is taken from Latin. While technically *amrita* is not unrelated to *rita,* "right running," discussed above, they must have been associated in the mind of mythographers by way of folk etymology. In the next chapter we will see that "right running" and immortality are indelibly connected in myth. In this chapter on ritual it is appropriate to explore some of the imagery and symbolism connected with amrita.

In the Vedas, amrita is described as being pressed from the sacred plant *soma,* and it is drawn from it in a secret rite. Soma, in turn, is a substance that is the earthly manifestation of Agni, "Sacred Fire." Both are referred to under a common name, *hiranyagarbha,* the golden "womb" ("germ, embryo"),[17] and hiranyagarbha leads us directly back to the mantra "Aum Mani Padme Hum," for the Mani Padme, "Jewel Lotus," is also hiranyagarbha.

Hindu and Buddhist art and iconography are a veritable thicket of lotuses, realistic and stylized. They appear as single flowers, in groups, or even as parts of flowers. Further, the lotuses are not merely decorative, they are symbolic. Representing dharma, "support, foundation," the lotus flower is the basic cosmic symbol.[18] Lotuses grow in ponds, where they float tranquilly upon the waters. As such, they symbolize the *maya* of the supernal god Vishnu, at once his beguiling consort, Lakshmi or Shri, and then that which deludes him into manifesting a world order. In the latter aspect she is addressed as *"prajânâm bhavasi mâtâ,"* "You are the mother of created beings," and simply as *ksamâ,* "Earth."[19]

Vishnu's lotus takes two forms in Hindu iconography. During the eons of nonmanifestation, it is the only thing manifest. Growing up from the sleeping god's navel, it forms the thousand-petaled, golden foundation-seat for the god Brahma, god of creation during the eon of material manifestation. Vishnu sleeping also holds a lotus in one of his two left hands, while the other hands hold his other symbols, the conch shell in the other left hand and the Vajra discus (*sudarsana*) and the scepter-mace in the two right hands (these weapons are shown with a standing Vishnu in fig. 2.3). But this whole image is reminiscent of the lotus, for the sleeping Vishnu is supported as is a blossom is on its infrastructure, the five- or seven-headed serpent Ananta-Sesha, which floats, its coils half-submerged in the supporting sea. Such iconography recapitulates objectively some of the motifs of the rituals examined in the chapter so far: a circle or wheel about a central spindle, thought of as a jewel in a golden receptacle.

Such images are found no earlier than the Gupta period (fourth century), but they are prefigured in the poetry of the Vedas. The deity that supports the earth and the heaven is referred to as hiranyagarbha and is personified under the generalizing name Prajapati (Progenitor).

Though not explicitly giving the name Vishnu, the language certainly reminds us of Vishnu as dharma:

> That which is beyond the sky, beyond the earth, beyond all the gods—what earliest germ (*prathamam garbham*) did the waters contain, in which all the gods were beheld?
>
> The waters contained that earliest germ in which all the gods came together. In the navel of the unborn the One was implanted in which all beings stood.[20]

In later myths about the creation of the gods, the Golden Germ assumes a different guise, that of a golden cup or an impregnable city.

1. Who knows that city of Brahman, invested with immortality. . . .
2. Within that impregnable city of the gods (*devanam pur ayodhya*) . . . there exists a golden receptacle (*hiranyayah kosah*), celestial, invested with light.
3. Those acquainted with Brahman know that living being (*yaksham atman-vat*) which resides in this golden receptacle.
4. Brahman has entered into this impregnable golden city, resplendent, bright, invested with glory.[21]

Again one thinks of gold, of circularity, and of circumambulation around sacred cities. But the similarities do not end there. Analysis of Hindu iconography has demonstrated that Padmamula, "The Jewel in the Lotus," generated manifold sculptural and pictographic forms: the bowl of plenty, the ball, the conch shell, the *chakra-vajra,* the trident (*trisula*), the sunshade, *lingam* and *yoni,* (phallus and vulva), the uprights of various structures (*stambha*), the shrine (*stupa*) thrones, palaces, the bole of the cosmic tree (*skambha*) and the base of the central mountain, Meru.[22]

Skambha, symbolized by the Padmamula, takes us back again to the motif of rita, "right running." In this conception the navel of the primeval waters produces not the delicate lotus but the trunk of the cosmic tree, at once the axis of the universe and the prop that supports the vault of heaven:

> Sprung from the Unmanifested (*avyakta*), arising from it as only support, its trunk is *buddhi,* . . . [23]

And quoting from F.D.K. Bosch himself:

> One of the oldest and most important elements in the Indian world system is the cosmic or celestial axis, *stambha* or *skambha* . . . a primeval

FIGURE 2.3
Vishnu with his panoply of weapons. Note especially the vajra-chakra and the axle-club. (Nepalese, ninth century; courtesy of the Brooklyn Museum, catalog no. 29.18, gift of Frederick B. Pratt)

being represented in a human shape, dwelling in the middle of the waters and from whose navel rises The One, the origin of creation and of all created things.

According to another Vedic notion, heaven and earth are both kept apart and joined by a support or pillar. So R[ig] V[eda] X, 89, 4 compares both hemispheres with cart wheels connected by an axle.[24]

And again:

I have dealt briefly with the representations which emphasize the function of the padmamula as main organ of the Tree and with its central position amongst the other parts of the plant. In this way the padmamula could be regarded as the centre of the cosmic Tree[,] and as the notions of cosmic Tree and universe run parallel[,] the idea was apt to lead to the notion that the Tree's central organ and the centre of the universe . . . are equivalent.[25]

But right running as represented by ritual motion to the right is not confined to Brahmanism and its offshoots. Among the Celtic peoples there existed a rite, now degenerated into a good-luck charm, the Gaelic word for which, *deasil* (variously spelled), is vestigially preserved in English. Deasil is cognate with dakshina, having the etymological sense of right or south. In fairly recent times it was performed as a charm for a safe passage, as we can see from Norman Macleod's *Reminiscences of a Highland Parish,* in which he recalls a rite performed by his father's parishioners on New Year's Day. They performed the deasil around the parish house, simply walking about it in the sunwise direction.[26] In Sir Walter Scott's *The Two Drovers,* Robin Oig, who is about to set forth on a journey abroad, is blessed by his aunt, who performs the deasil. This was done, in Scott's words, by "walking three times round the person who is the object of the ceremony, taking care to move according to the course of the sun."[27]

The antiquity and the sanctity of the ceremony can be seen in its undoing, as performed by witches. This unlucky, counterclockwise motion is also denoted by another relic in the English lexicon, *widdershins* or *withershins*. This Germanic word proves that the rite was not confined to the Celts (compare German *widersinig*). The Gaelic term was *cartua-sul*. Walter C. Smith (pseudonym, Orwell) has the witch Annaple Gowdie admit in her confession:

Hech! sirs, but we had grand fun
Wi' the muckle black deil in the chair,
And the muckle Bible upside doon,
A' gangin' withershins roun' and roun'
And backwards saying the prayer.
About the warlock's grave
Withershins gangin' roun',
And kimmer [godmother, midwife]
   and carline [witch] had for licht
The fat of the bairn they buried that nicht,
Unchristened beneath the moon.[28]

The child sacrifice in the latter lines is horrendous, given the recent recrudescence of such witchcraft as reported in the media. The lines make it clear that proper motion brought not only luck, but that the very heart of religion, well-being, and right doing were thought to depend upon it. Other ideas of good luck and prosperity involving right circular motion are preserved in English folkways: one sends the bottle around the table sunwise; one turns his chair around when playing cards to bring good luck; and at new moon one churns the coins in his pocket. In Ireland, a person who has fallen springs up and runs around three times to the right, and in former times one carried fire around persons and property to the right in order to protect them from harm or malignant influence. Boatmen row about to the right before proceeding on their direct course. Likewise, cairns and other holy stones were circled to the right; so too were consecrated places. In wedding ceremonies, brides were conducted to the right to encounter their spouses-to-be. Similarly, corpses were conveyed to the grave or pyre in the sunwise direction. Lighted torches were carried sunwise about the cornfields to secure a blessing on the crops. The deasil was traditionally performed on Maundy Thursday.[29]

There is a tradition from early Ireland about the sacred book *Catach,* a relic of Saint Columba. It was not lawful to open the book, but if it were sent to the right three times around the men of Cinel Conaill when they were going to battle, they would return safely with a victory.[30]

In addition to prosperity, we must add health as one of the benefits ensured by deasil. In *Waverly,* Scott described a scene in which a Highland physician comes to tend the wounded Edward. The first act he performs with his assistants is the deasil, perambulating the sickbed three times.[31] At a sanctified spa in Scotland known as the Holy Pool of Strathfillan, a curative ritual is performed in which each sufferer bathes in the pool, gathering there nine stones. Upon a nearby hill are three cairns, each of which he circumambulates three times in turn, depositing one of the gathered stones at each circuit.[32] Even the course of a disease might be predicted by spontaneous motions, somewhat like those supposed to take place on a Ouija board. St. Andrew's Well in the town of Shadar on the isle of Lewis in Scotland was known for its prescient waters. A tubful drawn up was used to float a small wooden dish in the yard of an ailing person. The dish was supposed to have begun a spontaneous rotation in one direction or the other; if clockwise, deasil, the patient would recover, but a widdershins motion portended death.[33]

The material remains of the early Celtic peoples, being much less abundant than those of the peoples of India, do not afford us a continuous record of iconography that reiterates and recapitulates the rite of circumambulation. Nonetheless, some isolated examples make it clear that the wheel and axle were sacred objects, and indeed that the wheel was connected with the lightning bolt, fertility, and the hammer. A Gallo-Roman statue found at Châtelet, Haute-Marne, depicts a bearded Celtic god with a wheel (fig. 2.4).[34] Like the Buddhist "wheel of being," this wheel has six spokes. The god has his supply of thunderbolts slung over his right shoulder, and in his right hand he elevates the cornucopia of ambrosia that he holds for his devotees. Another early Gallic deity, for whom the name Sucellos comes to us, has a pole in his left hand and a wheel of hammers above his right shoulder; he is here depicted as a manifestation of the power of his own world-creating, world-annihilating hammer (fig. 2.5).[35] Compare this with Sanskrit Vajra, "lightning [also diamond] bolt," the highest Hindu-Buddhist symbol of illumination, by which the world-illusion is destroyed and which itself is indestructible. In the right hand of Sucellos— whom the Romans identified with Pluto—there is the ambrosial cup.[36]

Certain pagan rites involving the sunwise rotation of a wheel persisted into the nineteenth century among the Celtic and Germanic

FIGURE 2.4
A bronze figure found in 1774 at Châtelet (near St.-Dizier, Haute Marne).
This small bronze (10 cm.) wears stockings or boots to signify firm footing
but is otherwise naked. His right hand holds the thunderbolt, and in his
left is a wheel with six spokes. (Simpson, *Buddhist Praying-Wheel*, p. 244,
from Gaidoz, *Le Dieu Galois du Soleil*)

peoples. These customs are recorded in Sir James G. Frazer's *Golden
Bough* and in other contemporary sources. I refer particularly to ceremonies of renewing the fire (*tein-eigen* "needfire" in Gaelic) which took
place in spring or early summer and which were often associated with
Christian festivals, particularly the feast of St. John the Baptist. The
general nature of the ceremony is reported to be as follows:

> The night before, all the fires in the country were carefully extin-
> guished, and next morning the materials for exciting this sacred fire were
> prepared. The most primitive method seems to be that which was used in
> the islands of Skye, Mull, and Tiree. A well-seasoned plank of oak was

FIGURE 2.5

A figure in bronze found at Vienne on the Rhomme in 1866. This figure
was dubbed Le Dieu Gaulois au Marteau. The image clearly has antecedents in the classical images of Herakles with a lionskin worn over the
head and tied at the shoulders, though Herakles's club has been replaced
by the hammer-wheel as though he were a many-Mjollnired Thor. The
staff in his left hand recapitulates the shaft of the revolving hammer,
and in his right hand—uncharacteristically for Heracles—the deity carries
a pot, which I take to be a variant of the magic porridge pot of myth
and märchen. (Simpson, *Praying-Wheel*, 247; originally published in the
Gazette Archéologique [1887], 306)

procured, in the midst of which a hole was bored. A wimble of the same
timber was then applied, the end of which they fitted into the hole. But
in some parts of the mainland the machinery was different. They used a
frame of green wood, of a square form, in the centre of which was an axle-
tree. In some places three times three persons, in others three times nine,
were required for turning round by turns the axle-tree or wimble. If any
of them had been guilty of murder, adultery, theft, or other atrocious
crime, it was imagined either that the fire would not kindle, or that it

would be devoid of its usual virtue. So soon as any sparks were emitted by means of the violent friction, they applied a species of agaric which grows on old birch-trees, and is very combustible. This fire had the appearance of being immediately derived from heaven, and manifold were the virtues ascribed to it. They esteemed it as a preservative against witchcraft, and a sovereign remedy against malignant diseases, both in the human species and in cattle; and by it the strongest poisons were supposed to have their nature changed.[37]

Rotation about an axis, prosperity, health, protection against malignant influences (witchcraft), the number three and its powers—all are linked together in this ceremony, just as they were in the Hindu Pradakshina and the Celtic deasil. These latter, however, did not seem to involve the production of fire,[38] though we do find ceremonies similar to needfire in Hindu sources. In the *Satapatha-Brahmana* a ritual is described, the purpose of which is to sanctify a cake for use as a sacrificial offering. Fire was carried around it in a circle. Eggeling's note amplifies its connection with other practices:

> The *paryagnikaranam* consists in performing a Pradakshina on an object whilst holding a firebrand, or burning coal; or according to the Paddhati in moving one's hand, which holds the burning coal, round the oblation from left to right. According to *Kâty* (ii. 5. 22), the Adhvaryu does so on the present occasion whilst muttering the formula, "Removed are the Rakshas! evil demons, removed are the enemies!" (*Taitt. S.* I. i. 8. l)."[39]

The same practices survive in other societies derived from the Indo-European protoculture. It is reported that in the last century the Poles of Masuria celebrated the feast of St. John by extinguishing all their fires and kindling new ones by friction in much the same way as described above, by fixing an oaken stake in the ground and making a wheel bear upon it with such force that it caught fire.[40]

These needfire ceremonies usually take place near the summer solstice (the Feast of St. John), as I have said, but they occur in several other seasons as well. The summer date of the rite and its accompanying festival have to do, among other things, with fertility, as can clearly be seen in a variant from the valley of the Moselle preserved for us by Jakob Grimm. Each household in the village was constrained to contribute a shock of straw to the nearby high place, Stromberg, where the males went at evening while the females went to a spring lower down on the slope. A huge wheel was wrapped with this straw. An axle run through the wheel served as the handles for those who were to guide it on its downward plunge. The mayor of a nearby town kindled the straw, for which office he was rewarded with a basketful of cherries. All the men kindled torches and some followed the burning orb as it was released downhill to shouts of joy. The women at the spring echoed these shouts as the wheel rushed by them. Often the fire went out of its own accord before it reached the river, but should the waters of the river extinguish it, an abundant vintage was forecast for that year.[41]

A very similar ceremony, called the burning of the Clavie, took place in Burghead on the Moray Firth on Yule night. A barrel half (instead of a wheel) was nailed to a long spoke of firewood, which acted as a handle. The nail could not be struck by a hammer but had to be driven in with a stone. The barrel was filled with tar-soaked wood. The lot was kindled with a piece of peat (no matches could be used), and the flaming Clavie was shouldered by one of the town lads. His duties were serious, for if he stumbled or fell, it would be a bad omen for him and for the town. Several boys took on the labor by turns until the Clavie had circuited the town; then it was carried to a local hillock, called the Doorie, where a hollowed stone received the fir spoke. After the Clavie had burned there a while, it was scattered down the western side of the hill, and the folk scrambled for possession of its brands and embers, for they were considered a sign of good luck and a safeguard against evil. Before mounting the hill, the bearers took the Clavie around to any ships that happened to be in the harbor, scattering grain, pouring libations of liquor, and offering humorous names to christen the vessels.[42]

Other such ceremonies took place in the spring on the first Sunday in Lent. In one example from Bavaria, after the wheel had been rolled down the hill, youths rushed about the fields with burning brooms to "drive away the wicked sower." In other localities an effigy representing "the witch" or the "old wife" or "winter's grandmother" was fastened to a pole, which was then stuck into the middle of a pyre. While it was burning, the youths threw blazing discs into the air. Charred embers from the effigy and from the discs were planted in the fields in the belief that they would keep vermin away from the crops.

In other places, a straw man representing Death was formally tried, shot, and then burned on a pyre.[43]

The seasonal nature of these fire rites and the burning of an effigy are interrelated. The effigy was not merely a scapegoat that magically assumed the sins of the community but was instead an old and defunct being that was replaced by a newcomer, as we can see from the practice of scattering the ashes of the old onto the growing crops. A wan vestige of this belief is to be seen in the figure of the spent old year being replaced by the babe who symbolizes the New Year at our now totally secular celebration.

In the ritual of the feast of St. John the Baptist, St. John himself seems to play the role of the old one who is replaced by a newcomer, and the event pertains to the seasonal apparitions of the sun. A description of one of the festivals of St. John survives in an early medieval *Summa de divinis officiis*:

> Also on the Feast of St. John are brands or blazing torches brought in, and fires are made, which signify St. John, for he was the light and the blazing lamp, the predecessor and forerunner of the pure light; . . . in some places a wheel is revolved which has a symbolic meaning because just as the sun has risen to the highest part of its orbit and is not able to rise higher, so was it the fame of John that although he was thought to be the Christ, he descended in accord with the testimony that he himself gave, saying: "I must be lessened, but he must grow."[44]

In Thuringia the midsummer festival called Sommer-Gewinn (Bringing in of Summer) or Leichnamsfest (Festival of the Corpse) was celebrated by disposing of the straw effigy of a defunct pagan deity by casting it into the river Hoersel with revelry and shouting. When dusk came on, a wheel, to which had been attached another straw effigy, was lighted and was sent rolling down from the summit of the nearby hill called Maedelstein (Maidenstone).[45]

These cast-out beings, deities that are replaced, were thought to represent the sun, which suffers seasonal decline, quasi death, and resurrection. This conclusion can be drawn from an examination of Hone's *Every-Day Booke* on the subject of the Feast of St. John:

> . . . .
> Some others get a rotten Wheele,
>   all worne and cast aside,

Which covered round about with strawe
  and towe, they closely hide.
And caryed to some mountaine's top,
  being all with fire light,
They hurl it downe with violence,
  when dark appears the night:
Resembling much the sunne, that from
  the Heavens down should fall,
A strange and monstrous sight it seemes,
  and fearefull to them all:
But they suppose their mischiefes all
  are likewise throwne to hell,
And that from harmes and daungers now,
  in saftie here they dwell.[46]

The sacred power of circular motion is a cultural phenomenon that we have located both in Europe and in the Indian subcontinent. The fact that motion to the right is beneficial in most of these cultures, while contrary motion is unlucky or harmful, and the presence in some of the languages of nearly cognate terms for clockwise motion (*dexratio,* deasil, and Pradakshina) and of terms that seem to refer both to the correct order of motion (ritu, rita, and Latin *ritus*) and to the incorrect (anrita, nirrita, withershins, and cartua-sul) lead me to propose the hypothesis that in the cultural milieu of the "original" speakers of the Indo-European tongue, circular motion to the right was considered sacred, and it was reenacted in a number of different rites. These rites involved the actions of circumambulation, of wheel rolling and wheel turning (the latter especially to produce fire). Three turns or phases of the action also seem to have been requisite for the correct performance of these rites. The actions were done to promote fertility, prosperity, good health, and good luck, which ends appear in various culturally conditioned ways, including victory in battle, happy marriage, good karma, and the production of seasonally propitious fire. Related actions also seem to involve the replacement of an outmoded ruler, deity, boogie, witch, sun, or Death himself with a new being and the selection or anointing of a chosen one (Chakravarti). Contrary motion is unlucky or disastrous and may be done on purpose as witchcraft to induce infertility or to weaken the established powers.

Numerous objects seem to be part of this ritualistic complex. These objects may have both cosmic and ordinary significance. They include a (six-spoked) wheel and axle, the sun and the circle of the seasons, a hub, navel, jewel, lotus, womb, phallus, serpent, serpent's coil, ocean (spring, pool, liquor), foundation, germ (seed, grain, fruit, money), city, cup or other receptacle, chariot, throne, ship, discus, conch, hammer or axe, lightning bolt, pillar, cairn, tree, egg, tortoise, ball, fire, Soma, trident (trisula), sunshade, monster, bird, mountain, mound, prayer wheel, swastika, book, (birch) wood, auger, and mushroom (*Amanita muscaria*). Frequently connected with the performance of the ritual was a chant or mantra composed of three parts, which had symbolic significance, like the exemplary "Aum Mani Padme Hum."

SUMMARY

William Simpson's book *The Buddhist Praying-Wheel* amply documents the existence of an Indo-European rite that involved imitating the lucky and productive motions of the cosmos: sunwise, to the right, clockwise. The prehistoric existence of the rite is corroborated by an associated vocabulary with at least three known reflexes: Sanskrit *dakshina,* Latin *dextratio,* and Celtic *deasil.* It is clear from many of the instances of this rite that it was seasonal, usually being celebrated at the summer solstice, and that it involved the getting of new fire while an old bogey was treated as a scapegoat, which act also ensured continuing fertility in the fields. The getting of new fire and the replacement of the bogey symbolize the death of the old sun and the ascendancy of the new. The importance of this ritual to Hindu society can be seen in that culture's artifacts and symbols from later Buddhist praying wheels, lotus blossoms with jeweled centers, and ritual circumambulation of Hindu temples and cities. Most of the evidence is Vishnaic and later, but traces are to be found even in the Vedas.

CHAPTER III

MYTHS EXHIBITING THE AMBROSIA CYCLE

Numerous myths from the various societies that descended from the Proto–Indo-European parent society can be related to the rite involving clockwise motion. This conclusion is based not solely upon the appearance within the myth of the motif of motion in a circle but also upon the pervasive presence there of constituent units, which are essentially independent of the myth's plot and which are reflexes of the action, objects, and incantations characteristic of the rites of right and wrong motion. These constituent units will be grouped together and presented here in paradigmatic form.

The previous chapter relied on the ethnological methods promulgated by Frazer, even echoing his conclusions in the fact that *dakshina* seems to lead to rejuvenation through replacement of one capital figure by another. This chapter continues the Frazerian pursuit of the intimate relation between myth and rite. Here, however, the methodology is refined and extended because "horizontal" plot analysis fails to reach the depths of the myths' structures. We must follow Propp and Lévi-Strauss into a structural analysis employing the "vertical" axis to explore and reduce to paradigmatic form the relations and patterns of our constituent units.

Dumézil's treatment of comparative Indo-European mythology must also be incorporated into our approach here. His dissertation included vital elements that he did not pursue in his later career, and our first materials for analysis will be the corpus of myth Dumézil analyzed to yield his paradigm, "the ambrosia cycle." Unfortunately, neither space nor the human attention span permit me to begin a true structural analysis where Dumézil began his "ambrosia cycle" thesis, with a section of the *Mahâbhârata* called the "Amritamanthana" (1.15–17),[1] which is loosely translated as "Churning of Ocean." I propose that instead we defer the "Churning of Ocean" to the end of the chapter and begin by atomizing a much shorter poem from the *Edda*—not "Hymir's Lay," treated by Dumézil, but "The Mill Song," which is quite parallel to the "Amritamanthana" and to "Hymir's Lay."

The etiology of the song sung in "The Mill Song" is given in Snorri Sterluson's *Skaldskaparmal,* in which Bragi responds to a series of questions by Ægir about why gold has acquired certain names, all of which are kennings (metaphorical names). In answer to the question, Why is gold called Frodi's flour? Bragi tells a story about the origins of this king and the mill he used to grind out gold and prosperity. Frodi inherited the kingdom from his father, Friedlief, during the Pax Romana instituted by Augustus. All was well in the world, and because Frodi was the most influential of the kings of Scandinavia, the peace was known there as Frodi's Peace. During a visit with King Fjollnir of Sweden, Frodi bought from him two slave women, strong beyond belief, whose names were Fenja and Menja. His plan was to have them grind on the Danish mill Grotti, whose stones were so massive that nobody in Denmark could turn them. The mill was of a special kind that when induced to grind would grind out whatever product the miller required of it. Frodi put Fenja and Menja to grinding out gold, peace, and prosperity. He was a harsh taskmaster, allowing the women to rest no longer than a cuckoo rests between its songs. Yet in these interstices, they composed their own song, called "The Song of Grotti."[2]

The Mill Song

> To the king's house came now the sisters,
> Fenja and Menja who foresee the future;
> to Frodi's dwelling, Friedlief's fair son
> these mighty maidens as his mean slaves.

To turn the milltree these two were forced,
to grind by turning the grey millstone,
not to leave turning, not for pleasure nor rest
before the song of their turning soothed Frodi's ear.

The din didn't daunt them dispensing still grist,
milltree in the eye, millstone on its nether.
Frodi gave them no rest; he forced them the harder.

Singing and slinging they shoved on the threadstone
till Frodi's farmhands fell fast asleep.
Then Menja came milling with a message to speak:

We're milling for Frodi good mirth and good wealth,
measureless means on our mill, our gladmill.
Gold be his throneseat and gossamer his quilting.
May he wake as he wills: now that is good milling!

In his state shall no one despoil another
nor plot any malice nor plan any murder
nor hack anybody with hatchet or sword
not even the bound killer of his brother, tied helpless.

But then Frodi first let fall them a word:
"Sleep may you sleep the same as a cuckoo;
no more than I take to make this verse."

"To 'buyer beware' you bowed Frodi not,
O king-over-kin, when our kind you bought.
You chose us for strength, you chose us for looks.
You deigned not to look in our pedigree books!"

Hrungnir was hard, harder his sire
and Thiazi owned more thews than they;
ilk to our race were Idi and Aurnir
rockberg-dwellers' brothers, our race's beginning.

This Grotti stone from grey feldspar,
this hard stone had not come from the earth,
no miller maids like us maid-mountain sisters
would be milling had he heard of our birth.

Nine winters long we denied any work.
Troll sisters we played, twins under the earth
trying our tricks, our tests of strength,
heaving the throne rock heist off its foundations.

Down the grey rock down out of their yard
onto flat earth so forcefully rolled
that it trembled and shook; we took from the giants
their ponderous quernstone for poor man. Will he take it?

Such were our deeds; then to Sweden we came
to fight among men—we fate-knowing sisters;
we sliced into hauberks, we shattered some shields.
We waded waist-deep through warriors in steel.

We laid low one prince and lifted another.
To Gjuki's son Gotthorm we granted the gain.
Round after round we sat, then skinned knuckles.

We held on to fighting a half-year and more;
Valkyries, Brunhildes, our fame became lore.
With sharpened spears we stuck our opponents;
the stabwounds ran blood, our swords blushed vermilion.

Now here we are only mean slaves not heroes at all,
in this king's hall without any kindness.
Frostbitten our heads, our feet are grimy—
We who've unseated the foe. Frodi's is boring.

"Now still our hands, stop turning the mill;
my share is done, my stint at milling!"
"Our hands must have pause; give them a rest
until Frodi nods that it has been well ground."

Our hands to their spears, hardpointed and straight.
Back to the struggle and blood. "Stand, Frodi, it's late.
Frodi awake! Frodi alarm!
Hear our sagas; heark unto our lore."

East of the castle my eyes see warfire.
Be warned by such fires. War news is afoot.
An enemy host is approaching; an enemy host soon will be here!
Our king will be burned, his castle, his dwelling.

"Hleidra (that's Leire) you shan't hold tomorrow,
nor gold rings' red luster nor gristmill's gold grinding."
"Hold tighter the milltree, turn faster the grindstone;
our grip's not yet slipping in gore from the slain."

My father's daughter kept forcefully grinding.
Baleful her visions: bane to great heroes.

Unseated the millstone, broken its braces,
its staunch iron bonds. "Yet stay at the grinding!"

"Stay at the grinding. For the son born of Yrsa
shall avenge Frodi's brother, avenge Halfdane's murder
at the hands of his brother. (Hrolf Kraki will come).
Yrsa's brother we know; he's Yrsa's son too."

So the mighty maidens maintained their fast milling,
Troll maidens inspired by Troll-strength to Troll-deeds.
The millhandle shivered, the milltree snapped;
two halves lay akimbo from a whole weighty millstone.

Then railed the daughters of the rockberg giants:
"For Frodi we ground; now freedom from grinding!
Our servitude's finished, these sisters are through."³

The next step is to analyze "The Mill Song" in terms of its gross constituent units. Strictly speaking, this cannot be done unless the entire series of myths is examined, and in what follows I do refer to other stories about Fenja, Menja, and Frodi. The important elements are italicized and are later grouped into bundles in tabular form. We are leaving behind the smooth horizontal groundline of plot, so what follows will seem strange indeed.

Fenja and Menja have *name types* that distinguish them as *twins*.⁴ As such, they are held *captive* at the *king's house*. They can foretell the future with *truth*. They use *rotary motion* to grind *plenty* (good fortune, treasure, joy, gold, and featherbeds) on the *mill*, which has an *axle* (shaft-tree) and a *socket* (millstone). *Wealth and happiness*, themes of their song's first part, require an interdiction of *internecine strife*. *Song* seems to be an accompaniment to their happy activity. But King Frodi ignores the women's message, and the song now becomes threatening. The women recall that they learned to grind by *rolling* boulders through the giant's *yard* and into the plain. *Below the Earth*, they had trained for *nine* years at mighty feats like moving the *throne rock*. As the throne rock rolled down, the *world trembled*. They went (*east*) to Sweden seeking a *fight*. They *overthrew one king* and set up *another king*. *Red blood* flowed. Now they are in a king's *house*, taken captive, and they are *dirty and cold*. Their grinding produces *song*—sagas and lore. *Premonitions* from the past are to become *truth* for Frodi. *Fire* will burn the *castle* with the king *inside*. He will not retain his *throne* or red *rings of gold*. The mill comes *unseated:* its iron *bonds break*, the *milltree* snaps, and the stone breaks into *two* halves. Frodi will be *replaced* by Hrólf Kraki (*Little Pole*).[5] He is *both son and brother* to Yrsa. The mill *grinds too fast*. The grinding *ceases*. The mill has earned its name, for instead of producing wealth, Grotti (The *Devourer*) now grinds out a song predicting *ruin*.

This story of Frodi and his demise is mentioned, as we saw, in the *Prose Edda*. Snorri Sterluson explains why "Frodi's grist" is a kenning for *gold*. Frodi ruled during a *peaceful and productive period*, contemporaneous with Augustus's Pax Romana and the birth of Christ; hence the kenning.[6] There were *neither thieves nor robbers* during this period, "so that a *gold ring* lay long on Jalang's heath."[7] Snorri continues his account with the legend of the mill beyond what is told in the song: The girls' grinding produced an *army hostile to Frodi*. On the very day of the girls' predictions, the *sea-king*, Musing (Son of the Mouse), landed on the Danish shore, *killed* Frodi, and *took away* Grotti and the women on his *ship*. The girls were bidden *to grind* out *salt* on the mill. At *midnight* they asked for further instructions. "Keep grinding," he told them. Then they ground with such vigor that the *ship sank*. Water poured into the *eye of the mill*, creating the *maelstrom* of the *sea*. Thereafter the sea was *salt*.[8] Incidentally, the mill was given a kenning, *Serpent's Couch*.[9]

Saxo Grammaticus tells us about the peaceful rule of a certain King Frodi, a reign that lasted *thirty years*.[10] To mark his reign as revolutionary in the annals of *peace and prosperity*, this Frodi forbade his subjects to have *sliding bolts* on their doors, and he hung a gold *necklace* on a *rock* in the public view to demonstrate that no *theft* would occur. The rock was known as Frodi's rock.[11]

Saxo tells a story about Frodi and a certain Erik, who had been sent by the king of Norway to seek the cause for Frodi's recent reputation as a tyrant. Before Erik and his *half-brother* Roller left on the mission, they were fed a *magic meal* by their mother, who had been seen *stirring* a large *pot* with a *rod* while *three suspended snakes* dripped *venom* into the porridge. On the way, Erik *sank* the *boat* of his Danish foe Od[12] by *boring holes* in the planks. Once in Denmark, Erik discovered an *adultery* between the *queen* and a retainer and divulged this fact to Frodi. Frodi put Erik to the *test* by asking him a series of questions about his route. His way stations had been *crags* and *stones*; he rested once by a large *tree trunk*, where *wolves, sated on human blood, licked* his *spearpoints*. There a *lancehead* was *shaken* from the *shaft of the king*; this lancehead was identified as the grandson of Friedlief (i.e., the son of Frodi).[13]

Now that we have collected the versions of Frodi's story and isolated its elements as they occur in the narrative, our next task is to look for Lévi-Strauss's vertical harmonies—that is, to abandon the narrative sequence and look for bundles of constituent items that reveal themselves by recurrence.

Circular motion of a *socket* and an *axle* is evidently salient. The mill Grotti itself, so structured, functions this way. Holes bored in planks and porridge stirred by a rod in a vessel are close repetitions of the same pattern. The stirred porridge repeats not only the circular action of the mill but also its product—agricultural plenty. The maelstrom created in the sea is closely allied. The mill gone awry (backwards?) produces not plenty but salt. The *gold* necklace hung on a rock repeats the structure if not the action of the mill. Grouping these items together can be justified through the intermediate term *gold*: the mill produces gold and plenty, and the gold necklace is a sign of peace and prosperity, the same result produced by the mill. The gold ring lying so long on Jalang's heath looks like a doublet of the similarly exposed necklace. The lancehead shaken from the king's shaft certainly repeats the structure of axle and socket; the significance of the action of its removal is parallel to the *destruction* of Frodi's mill when its stone fell from the shaft in ruin. The structure of axle-in-socket and the apparent significance of their function—*fertility*—lends a *sexual element* to the complex, which is repeated in the personal name given to the necklace's rock (Frodi's rock), whereby it becomes a phallic symbol. This idea is parallel to the king's lancehead. The removal of a lancehead, however, may be indicative of a broken marriage, castration, or adultery.

Fertility and its loss or destruction are certainly central motifs in this complex. The mill produces peace and prosperity, the porridge lends strength; the necklace on the rock is a sign of peace and prosperity, while its converse appears in the broken mill, in the holes bored to sink a ship, and in the ship sunk into a maelstrom by a malfunctioning mill, which breaks and then produces salt enough to make the whole sea saline. This countermotif is also found in the lancehead that is shaken off the king's shaft. If the proper marriage of shaft and wheel hub produces prosperity, the converse should be reflected in elemental divorce, and so we find the motif of incest and adultery in these texts. Hrólf Kraki is at once the son and brother of Yrsa. The Danish queen commits adultery.

Replacement of one king or regime by another is central here. Fenja and Menja have been party to such replacement before, and either Musing, the Mouse King or Hrólf Kraki will replace Frodi. Erik's mission, too, has elements of replacement in it. Frodi became tyrannical, just as he did in "The Mill Song" version of the story, a sure sign that a king needs replacing. As a result, Erik arrives to replace Frodi just as Musing did. The intention to replace is further corroborated by the symbols that surround Erik—his blood-anointed spearpoint and his mountains and crags destined to replace Frodi's rock just as Hrólf Kraki (Little Pole) came to replace both Frodi and the broken tree in his mill.

Internecine strife, including even the petty crime of theft, is absent when the mill works right. But when the throne rock is moved, replacement is at hand, and as a result, sexuality goes awry, the world trembles, war breaks out, a mill is wrecked, and a ship is sunk. The broken mill is replaced in the new regime by a functioning one, as promised by Hrólf's nickname, "Little Pole," and by the fact that Erik gets rid of his enemy Od by *boring* holes in his boat.

Strife takes place between characters *closely related*. The relatives-at-odds motif occurs in the story of Erik, who has a *half*-brother Roller. The replaced lancehead, sign of Frodi's downfall, is impersonated by his own son. The impaired pair is also to be seen in the two halves that result from the fragmentation of the mill.

Captivity and *concealing*, *freedom* and *revealing*, are also antithetical bundles germinal to the myth. The mill is bound with iron. The sisters were Frodi's prisoners. They had been below the Earth for nine years. Their ship sank with them on board as did Od's boat. Wolves devoured human beings, leaving blood as the only vestige. All these forms represent surrounding, swallowing, or hiding of some central thing. The truth is hidden, but it is revealed in the girls' song.

Snakes and *serpents* form their own bundle. The mill is a serpent's couch, and the stirred pot is watched over by serpents, which drip venom into it.

Numbers seem important: *three* serpents, *thirty* years of peace, and *nine* years of life underground have three as a factor. The importance of these and other numbers will become clear in later examples. Furthermore, etymologies seem significant: Frodi, Od, and Kraki are names with etymological meanings significant to the context.

Allow me here to attach a letter code to each of the elements found above. Let those elements that have to do with replacement—such as war, internecine strife, twins or other close relatives being at odds, and tyranny—be labeled A. Adultery, incest, and other illicit sexual relationships will be labeled B. The operation of the mill, I have argued, is in part a sexual metaphor, so let us label as C the female aspect of it—the hub or any hollow or circular object or container, especially if it occurs in context with a phallic symbol. The phallic counterpart—mountain peaks, crags, spearpoints, axles, and the like—will bear the sign D. When the two occur together, as in the case of the operating mill, we will use the sign C-D, and when they are broken apart or cease to function together, C/D. E will be the label for capture, binding, or concealment; F for lost fertility, disorder, ruin, upheaval, and monsters on the loose; and G for gold, fertility regained, order and order restored, release, a new regime, the death of monsters, stability, plenty, and prosperity. The etymology of names and key terms seems important too, for which the label H will be used. For future reference, let me present these codes more clearly in the following list:

A   elements that have to do with replacement, such as war, internecine strife, twins or other close relatives being at odds, and tyranny;

B   adultery, incest, and other illicit sexual relationships;

C   the female aspect of the operation of the mill, which, I have argued, is in part a sexual metaphor, thus a hub or any hollow or circular object or container, especially if it occurs in context with a phallic symbol;

D   the phallic counterpart—mountain peaks, crags, spearpoints, axles, and the like;

C-D   when C and D occur together, as in the case of the operating mill;

C/D   when C and D are broken apart or cease to function together;

E   capture, binding, or concealment;

F   lost fertility, disorder, ruin, upheaval, and monsters on the loose;

G   gold, fertility regained, order and order restored, release, a new regime, the death of monsters, stability, plenty, and prosperity;

H   names and etymologies.

Now we may turn to the "Lay of Hymir," another story from the so-called *Poetic Edda*, which Dumézil used in the construction of his Indo-European ambrosia cycle. Limitations of space forbid a complete reproduction of each myth, so I will resort to synopses with labels. Previously unencountered or doubtful elements will be designated with an asterisk.

In days of old, the Æsir (the benign gods of the Norse pantheon) were feasting together after a good hunt. There was plenty of game (G) but apparently no beer (F). They learn by divination from bloody (E*) branches that the giant Ægir ("Mr. Moist") has everything needed to brew beer: a vat, a paddle, and plenty of grain (G). Thor's imperious tone of command, "Beer here!" prompts Ægir to seek revenge (A). "Bring your own cauldron (C)" is his challenge. Nowhere can another such cauldron (C) be found (F). Then Tyr responds to Thor's request, saying that in the hall (C) of his father, Hymir, there is a kettle (C) of great proportions, which they may procure through guile (D*). On the way to Hymir's, they meet Tyr's uncle Egil, who promises to guard Thor's goats, their horns held on high (D). The two gods encounter Tyr's awful grandmother (F*), who has *nine hundred** heads (C* or D*). But Tyr's beautiful mother (C), dressed in gold (G), brings a cup of beer (G) and with it the advice to hide (E) under some cauldrons (C-D*). In giving aid to Thor, Hymir's wife (Tyr's mother) seems disloyal (B*, A*). Hymir returns late from an icy hunt. His wife reports that Hymir's son is *home* after a long absence (G) and that he has brought a companion named Veor (Friend of Man) (H*). She discloses their whereabouts, saying that they are hiding under the protection of a tall pillar (D). An angry glance from Hymir causes the pillar to fall to pieces (C/D), and from a cross-beam (D*) *eight* kettles (C) come crashing down (F). *One* remains unbroken, so there were *nine** in all. *Three** bulls are brought for feasting (G). Thor eats two of these and falls asleep. A hunt is proposed for more food to feed the *three.** Thor will row (C-D*) out to sea (place*) if Hymir will provide the bait for the hook (C-D). A black ox (G*)[14] is the bait. Thor kills it by seizing its horns (D) and wrenching off its head (C/D). Thor and Hymir engage in a rowing and fishing contest (A). Hymir pulls two whales from the water (C-D*). Thor baits the hook (C-D) with the ox's head (C). The hidden (E) serpent (F), which surrounds the world (C-D*, C/D), gapes open its mouth (C) to eat the bait (E). Thor pulls the venom(F*)-streaked (E*) serpent[15] into the boat (C-D*)[16] and strikes its head with his hammer (C-D). The monster roars, rocks crash, the whole world moves (F). The serpent sinks back into the sea (E). Hymir proposes another test (A): He will haul the whales to the house (C-D*) if Thor will tie the boat ashore (C-D). Instead, Thor hauls the boat (C) to Hymir's place (C-D*). Hymir remarks, "A man may look good after rowing on the sea but weep when he tries to crack a cup" (C/D). Thor hurls the cup at the tall pillar, which breaks in two (C/D), but the cup remains unscathed (C-D). Upon the wife's advice (B*), Thor tries again by hurling the cup (C) at Hymir's head (D). Hymir's head remains unscathed, but the cup cracks (C/D). Hymir concedes the loss (F) of the great prize. No more can he revoke his promise (F*): "Ale be brewed." But he proposes a *third** test (A): "Can you carry the cauldron outside?" Tyr tries to move it twice.* Thor tries the third* time and carries it easily, fitting it over his head (C-D); the cauldron's chains clatter about his heels (G, unbinding*). Hymir pursues them (A) from his lair (C) with the aid of many-headed (D*) giants (F). To kill these giants, Thor uses his hammer (D), Mjollnir (Mill) (H). Now, after every harvest the gods will drink beer (G). On the way home, Thor finds his draught goats (a sign of right running or stability, like the boat fastened to shore [C-D*]). One goat had been left with its horns (D) held high in the giant Egil's care, but the animal was now lame (F) in one leg (C/D). For his careless inattention to Loki's trickery (D*) in this matter, Egil is forced to pay Thor by giving up his own two sons (A) as recompense.[17]

The adventure took place where the sky ends, yet the contest was at sea. The Midgard serpent was caught at sea. In a variant story, Thor's feat raised the serpent up nearly to the sky. Somehow, sky and sea seem interrelated. The place in the east where the ocean meets the sky's end is the location of this great contest, which brings right running and fertility back to the world. Ocean and sky seem to be the locale for epochal contests (more of this in chapter 6).

The number three is associated here with trials, just as Thor's trials

with Utgard Loki in the "Deluding of Gylfi" (not discussed here) all
have three phases. Hence, we will incorporate the occurrence of the
number three into bundle A from now on. Three and powers of three
and their multiples by ten, one hundred, and so forth are included. The
number nine hundred occurs here, and in "The Mill Song" Fenja and
Menja said that they spent nine years in training.

Finally, there is the curious matter of Thor's hammer, Mjollnir, the
etymology of which is "mill." The mill in "The Mill Song" gave Frodi
his prosperity; porridge correctly stirred endowed Erik and Roller with
superhuman power; and so does the mill hammer for Thor. Obviously
the mill symbolizes more than just fertility and the wealth of plenty. It
symbolizes physical power and efficacy as well. It is a paradox that Thor
uses his "mill" against the serpent, for in Frodi's story the mill's kenning
is "serpent's couch." The mill of one primal enemy will replace the opponent's. Musing's mill replaces Frodi's. "Serpent's couch," moreover,
is cosmological (compare Ananta-Sesha), likely referring to the world
tree, Yggdrasil (not a mill but certainly somehow the central axis of the
revolving world); beneath it a knot of encircling snakes would devour
(F) it.[18] If Yggdrasil were devoured, the spinning world would crash
into ruins as did Frodi's mill. Yet in itself the phrase "serpent's couch"
couches no such threat of ruin. Whether and how the serpent is a symbol for good or for evil will have to await explication until chapter 6.

Yggdrasil, encircled at the bottom by snakes, lies thrice deeply
rooted: in the well Hvergelmir, in the spring Urd (Destiny), and in the
palace of the Æsir (Sky-Gods). In some sources it has a fourth root
extending into the void Ginnungagap. The connection of the world tree
to an axis is obvious—its deep roots signify its role as the supporter of
all that is regular and right running. As the world tree, therefore,
Yggdrasil has a cosmological significance. Does its structural counterpart, the mill of Frodi, as well? Millstones churning plenty or ruin, the
world running aright or awry, the axle being true or unseated—all seem
to form a complex, which again will be explored more thoroughly in
chapter 6.

Eight major bundles of constituents (A through H) have been isolated from these Icelandic stories. Some are more salient in one myth,
and others in another. Replacement (A) seems to be the central con-

stituent in "The Mill Song," while the lack of fertility (F) and its restoration (G), symbolized by brewing (C-D), are thematic in the "Lay
of Hymir."

It is important, therefore, to make the point that Dumézil's chosen
stories are not restricted to the ambrosia cycle; he selected the stories
because they emphasize and repeat the bundles that have to do with
circular motion and the restoration of fertility, including the brewing
of a sacred drink. This was itself a brilliant observation, and certainly a
point of departure for my work. But there are other features of these
myths, common to them all, which went unobserved by Dumézil.
These features have been set forth in the Replacement Paradigm.

We may compare Dumézil's analysis of "The Lay of Hymir" into its
thèmes étrangères in *Le Festin d'immortalité* (p. 52), with my paradigmatic
analysis. The *thèmes* include (1) a *council of the gods* in which (a) the
gods, menaced by death or famine, deliberate on how they might obtain the drink of immortality, and (b) a god provides the formulas:
churning or brewing the sea will produce it; and (2) *acquisition of the
vessel,* which (a) the gods have no means to provide, and which (b) is
the possession of a sea denizen whom a god must (c) petition or battle.
Dumézil's elements find their way into the paradigm given here but in
a completely different distribution and emphasis. His 2c is reflected in
my A; his vessel manqué is an example of my C; his 2b, a trip beneath
the sea, is an example of my E. His 1a is embraced in F; his 1b is C-D in
one form, and his B1, a *feast of the gods* (not presented above), is an
example of G. His B2, a *demon chained,* is my E, while B2b, an *earthquake,* falls into my F. His C, *the False Fiancée,* is my B. Notice that
other *thèmes étrangères*—(a) a trip by Thor to the land of the giants and
the extermination of the giants, (b) combat with the black ox, (c) combat with the serpent, (d) the cup broken over the giant's head, and
(e) the lamed goat—are all brought to account through the use of the
Replacement Paradigm in the explication of "Hymir's Lay" offered
above.

Here I must rephrase the observation made above: other myths,
which include all seven of the paradigmatic elements, may pass lightly
over the theme of brewing ambrosia only to emphasize a different
bundle. If we keep this in mind, we will soon discover that these seven

bundles of constituents appear in a vast array of stories that superficially bear no resemblance to each other.

Snorri Sterluson's account of Ragnarok, the end of the world, is a case in point: A horrible winter will come; the sun will be of no use (F). Three (A) such winters without any summer (G) will presage great wars in which brothers will fight with brothers and fathers with sons (A), and incest (B) will be rife. The wolf will swallow the sun and the moon, and the stars will disappear (F, E). All bonds will burst, trees will be uprooted and mountains dashed down, and the Midgard serpent, Fenrir,[19] will be on the loose (F). The unholy ship (C), Naglfar, will be launched. Garm (the hound of Hell) and a horrible eagle will rend the bodies of the numerous dead (F). The wolf Fenrir will make as if to devour (E) heaven and earth, one jaw against the sky, the other on earth; and the Midgard serpent will blow poison so as to spatter (E) the whole sky and sea. The demon sons of Muspell will be loosed from the sea (F), and Surt will set fire to the whole sky in his conflict (A) with the gods. Yggdrasil (D) will shudder (F), and the Bifrost bridge (C-D*) will break (C/D). Loki, Hrym, the frost giants, and all the family of Hell will join the sons of Muspell on the square Vigrd plain (C) to oppose the Æsir (A). Despite Freyr's effort with sword (D), Odin's with bow (C-D), Thor's with Mjollnir (C-D), and Vidar's magic shoe (C), the demons will win, and Surt will fire the whole world (F). But there will survive a fair hall (C), Gimli (Bright Heaven), thatched with gold (G), as Hoenir will foretell (G) from bloody twigs.* Barren fields will bear a man (G): earth will rise from the water (E, G). The Æsir will meet and discuss Odin's runes (G), and chessmen of gold (G), hidden (E) long ago, will be rediscovered (G). New lords, Vidar and Vali, will go forth unharmed and inhabit a new place (G), Idavoll, where Asgard used to be (F). The sons of Thor—Modi and Magni (twin names? A)—will come there to possess Mjollnir (C-D). Balder and Hoder will come from Hell (E-G). While Surt burns the world, two humans called Lif (Life) and Lifthrasir (Eager-for-Life) (twin names, A) will be hidden (E) in Hoddmimir's wood. They will eat the morning dew (ambrosia, G), survive, and repopulate the world (G). Before Fenrir swallows her (E), the sun will bear a daughter (G), the image of herself (A), who will follow the paths (G) of her mother.[20]

At this point our general rubrics for the bundles may be expanded. From the pan-cataclysmic effects of Ragnarok, we may add a ninth element, I, for cosmological significance.

A. Confrontation, war, deadly social or family conflict.
    1. Opposing generations, kinds of people, or gods.
    2. Twins, brothers, an impaired pair.
    3. The numbers three, nine, and nine hundred.
    4. Something that changes ownership: the cauldron, Mjollnir, a ring, a necklace, animals (goats, a whale).
    5. A place of battle: the ocean, the sky, a square plain, east.
    6. Help given to one side or the other by a trickster and/or a divine lady, often in disguise.
B. Incest, adultery, or other illicit sexual activity.
    1. A central female figure, usually disloyal, e.g., Hymir's concubine.
C. Symbols of sexual intercourse, with the female element predominant.
    1. A socket, a millstone, a vessel, a well, a whirlpool.
    2. A ship, a shoe.
    3. A necklace, a ring, a crown.
    4. A bow, a bridge.
    5.* The wolf's mouth, the eagle, a coiled serpent, a detached head.
    6. A residence, a throne.
    7. The moon.
D. Symbols of sexual intercourse, with the male element predominant.
    1. An axle, a stirring rod, a spear, an arrow, a bow, a tree, a mountain, a rock, a fishhook, a hammer, a horn, a pillar, fishing line, structural members, other weapons.
    2.* Wolf's teeth, an eagle, a head.
    3. The sun.
    4.* Trickery.
C-D. Fulfilled sexual activity, right running.
    1. Churning the mill, stirring a cauldron, brewing beer, hitting with a weapon, boring holes, wrenching off heads by the horns, rowing.
    2. Devouring.
    3. Tying a boat to shore, bringing booty to the house.
C/D. The abrogation of sexual activity, wrong running.
    1. The mill breaking down, pillars breaking, a weapon missing.
    2. Regurgitation.
    3. Theft, a loss of mooring?
E. Hiding, encirclement, disappearance into the dark or into the bright sky.
    1. Capture, detainment.

    2. Drowning, sinking.

    3.* Spattering the sky with blood or poison using bloody branches or golden boughs.

    4. Swallowing whole.

    5. Hell (the ultimate meaning of which is "to cover").[21]

    6. Where the sky ends

    7. Abnormal sleep or late return

    8. The number twelve, the number forty.

F. Destruction, death, human sacrifice, the loss of order, damnation.

    1. Earthquake, sky quake, mountain quake, the shattering of bonds and props, general catastrophe.

    2. Monsters on the loose, the devouring of stabilizing elements.

    3. Conflagration.

    4. The sun, moon, and stars dark or off their paths.

    5. Breaking of bones, laming.

    6. Loss of nourishment or fertility, plague, lack of means.

    7. Destruction of mankind, human sacrifice.

    8. Distortion or obscuring of the truth.

    9. A curse.

G. The Golden Age, a return to normality, restoration.

    1. Gold, precious objects.

    2 Abundance, fertility restored, a successful hunt.

    3. A magic drink brewed or recovered: ambrosia, beer, dew.

    4. Birth, salvation, or rebirth of gods and men; release of captives.

    5. The sun restored to its path.

    6. A new cosmological, natural, or civil order.

    7. Weapons restored, machinery restored to working order.

    8. Feasting, plenty, song.

    9. Truth revealed or discovered, or the future foretold.

    10. Thirty years, nine hundred years, or some other large total number of years divisible by three.

H. Names and etymologies.

I. Cosmological significance: the world beginning or ending; the structure or operation of the heavens.

This paradigm bears a close resemblance to the Monomyth developed by Joseph Campbell.[22] Campbell's Call to Adventure, with its Tokens of the Hero—a hart in the case of King Arthur; a golden ball in the case of the Frog King and princess—is related to my A4, and his category "Supernatural Aids" to my "Symbols of sexual intercourse (C and D)." For example, Campbell relates the Navajo spider woman, who lives in a subterranean chamber, to the Cosmic Mother, specifically the myth of Ariadne with her helpful, guiding thread. Exactly so. The nearly universal motif, which he calls too specifically The Belly of the Whale corresponds to my more general Hiding (E).

Like Campbell, I believe that the kinship among so many myths gathered from worldwide sources is not a fluke but a reflection of the processes through which they are created. Also like Campbell, I believe that a huge number of similar myths derive their similarities from an archetypal myth, which he calls the Monomyth but which I prefer to describe as a paradigm. The difference between our models lies in the cultural imperatives and the human capacities that we use to explain the formation of these grand myths.

Campbell, working in a Jungian vein, turns to the universals of human psychic experience—anxieties, desires, fears, aggressions, and so forth—which, when repressed because of social expectations, give rise directly to dreams and myths. Indeed, dreams may be generated directly from such psychic phenomena. Myths, too, as they are generated by any given storyteller, may be influenced by that individual's psychic temperament. To my way of thinking, however, the essential source of myth is not the single human self in its relation to a social context but rather the way our socially conditioned minds process our experience, especially of natural phenomena, in terms of social patterns and paradigms. He stresses the spontaneous emotive aspect of our minds, produced in the limbic system of the brain; I stress the cognitive devices, originating in and expressed by means of the cortex, by which we *order* our perceptions.

Myths—at least those examined in this book—were created by way of pathetic fallacy, if I may draw on a literary analogy. At the time of their creation, however, this mode of thinking was no mere poetic device. During the prescientific stage of human thought, the cosmos itself, in certain of its specific recurring aspects, was made directly to symbolize social facts. Universal cosmic events, therefore, are given different expressions in different cultures, but since these expressions are themselves based on the universals of human perception and the cognition of identical events, and since the fact of their expression is based on the all-embracing need for group survival, the result is great similarity in the extant myths from culture to culture.

The tale of Theseus's early adventures, which occupies some of

Campbell's first chapter, is a good vehicle to examine the difference between our two approaches. Campbell treats the story of Pasiphae, her illicit passion for the bull, and Minos's complicity in the affair as a story founded in psychology:

> Thus according to the ancient legend, the primary fault was not the queen's but the king's; and he could not really blame her, for he knew what he had done [by refusing to sacrifice the white bull sent by Poseidon as a sign of Minos's claim to primogeniture]. He had converted a public event to personal gain, whereas the whole sense of his investiture as king had been that he was no longer a mere private person. The return of the bull should have symbolized his absolutely selfless submission to the functions of his role. The retaining of it represented, on the other hand, an impulse to egocentric self-aggrandizement.[23]

Already we are deep in psychological terms and individual motivations. Yet Campbell does not *require* that the myth center only upon the individual psyche. Minos's motives were self-centered, but Campbell interprets his failure to sacrifice the bull as his refusal to submit himself *selflessly* to the demands placed upon him by society in his role as king. The imperatives of the culture are brought into Campbell's treatment of the story. In that regard, his conclusions have validity:

> And so the king "by the grace of God" became the dangerous tyrant Holdfast—out for himself. Just as the traditional rites of passage used to teach the individual to die to the past and be reborn to the future, so the great ceremonials of investiture divested him of his private character and clothed him in the mantle of his vocation. Such was the ideal, whether the man was a craftsman or a king. By the sacrilege of the refusal of the rite, however, the individual cut himself as a unit off from the larger unit of the whole community: and so the One was broken into the many, and these then battle each other—each out for himself—and could be governed only by force.[24]

But the point of the Minos story is not simply that refusal to sacrifice was an act of selfish dereliction of duty that resulted in a tyranny that must be overthrown. The refusal to sacrifice is not the cause of the call for Replacement; it is its sign. Further, Campbell's treatment here greatly oversimplifies a very complex myth that exists, not alone, but only in a constellation with many other myths, in fact—if one had the patience and the resources to follow every lead—with the whole corpus of Greek mythology. This sort of treatment, involving complex psychic motivations and rather glib conclusions, yields appealing but not very convincing results. I perceive less mire and more light when the myth is considered in the following outline, with the corresponding paradigm description given by rubric in the margin:

A1	Minos is involved in a dispute about succession to the throne.
A4	He prays to Poseidon for a token.
A4	A bull comes from the sea.
B	Minos's refusal to sacrifice the bull as promised angers Poseidon, who leads Pasiphae to conceive a monstrous passion for the beast.
E	She commissions Daedalus to make for her a cow disguise.
E1	Minos commissions Daedalus to build a labyrinth to confine the monstrous Minotaur, offspring of the union between the bull and his wife
H	but bearing his (Minos's) name (i.e., somehow it *was* his child he hid).
F7	The confined monster demands the sacrificial offering of seven youths and seven maidens.
F6	The sacrifice was demanded of the Athenians, who had to comply if they were to avoid the plague invoked on them by Minos, whose son was killed in Athens.
D	Theseus, one of the seven chosen,
A	disputes with Minos over
A1	whose paternity is true.
A	Minos's challenge is that the boy find a
C3	golden ring that
E2, A4	he had cast overboard.
A6	A divine lady or ladies help Theseus,
B	although they live in Minos's sea.
A4	Theseus's own paternity was proved by tokens exchanged between his father, Poseidon (Aegeus), and his mother,
H	Aethra, whose name means "the shining one."
D1	The tokens were a sword
C2	and sandals
C-D	hidden under a stone.
A6	Minos's daughter Ariadne, who is in love with Theseus, helps
D4	him with a tricky device—
C-D	a ball of thread.
G2	Minotaur is killed, and after him Minos's

H	son Asterius (Star Man). (In some sources Asterius is the Minotaur's name.)
G9	The labyrinth is solved.
G4	Theseus sets the others free.
G6	The old order is left behind as the hero escapes Crete.
A4	Ariadne changes hands again, becoming the consort of Dionysus
H	and/or the nymph of the grove Aridela (Very Conspicuous).
AI	Theseus assumes a new role at home, for he becomes king.
D4*	He has "forgotten" to change the color of his sails, and
E2	his father, Aegeus, thinking the boy dead, drowns himself.
E3	Theseus's early adventures are tripartite. They involve:
DI	(1) proving his paternity;
A	(2) replacing Minos; and
AI	(3) replacing his father.

Campbell does not see, or at least does not mention, that the Minos story and the story of Theseus are quite parallel in a very complex way. The similarities are best set forth in paradigmatic fashion. If we look at the histories of each hero, we find that each was born into a paternity that was questionable (AI). Minos had to discredit and replace his brother(s) who vied with him for the throne. He procured a token from the god that his was the true kingship (A4), that under him human affairs would run right (G). The token proved that the divine and the human worlds were "in synch." Theseus, too, had to prove his divine parentage by lifting the massive stone under which the masculine and feminine symbols of right running were hidden (C-D; add C-D4: finding, hitting the target). The truth is "uncovered" (G9). Theseus, too, is the legitimate heir to an ordered succession of kings. The sword token (DI) again proves who he is when he arrives at Athens to be recognized in the nick of time by his father, thus thwarting the machinations of the unfaithful (or at least ungrateful) Medea, who wanted her own sons to inherit (AI).

But there is something rotten in both kingdoms. All is not as well as it may appear. In both cases the wrong running is symbolized by a white bull sent by Poseidon (F). In Attica a white bull was causing havoc among the peoples of the Marathon district. Pausanias says (1.27.9) that this was the same bull that was let loose as a plague in the Cretan countryside by Poseidon for Minos's failure to sacrifice it. Herakles, as one of his designated twelve labors, was sent to Crete to retrieve it. He brought it back to Argos and released it there in the plain, but it got away (or was pursued by Hera) and wandered across the isthmus and into Attica. Others say the bull was the one that had taken Europa from Tyre to Crete. In any case, this monster on the loose originated in Crete and was visited upon Attica.

Theseus dragged it by the horns to Athens (C-D3, bringing the booty home; compare Thor's treatment of Hymir's black ox) and sacrificed it (contrast Minos's failure to do so) to Apollo or Athena. Meanwhile, it had killed Minos's own son Androgeus (Earthborn) on Attic territory, and for that reason Minos sent an armada of pirates to prey on Athens, until it was finally agreed that in recompense for the death of Androgeus, seven youths and seven maidens would be sent forth from Athens every "great year" (I) as sacrificial offerings to the Minotaur. Just how Theseus became a volunteer for the sacrifice during its third cycle (G10, A3) is disputed among the sources, but whether he volunteered or was selected by Minos, it seems that they struck a bargain about the Minotaur: should Theseus kill it with his bare hands (compare his treatment of the bull), the curse (F9) would be lifted. To this point, the life stories of Theseus and Minos are inextricably intertwined, and when Theseus reaches Crete the bundles are repeated all over again, as we saw above.

The issue of right running vs. wrong running is certainly at issue in these stories, which both belong to the Replacement Paradigm. Both kingdoms live under a curse. The bull and the bull's son, begotten through an adulterous and impossibly monstrous union, are the certifiable causes of the wrong adultery, the deaths, the curse, the forgotten sacrifice to Poseidon, and its gruesome surrogate offered to the Minotaur. The right and wrong running, furthermore, are not simply terrestrial in nature; the story presents bundles symbolic of the cosmos which are repeated. After the death of the Minotaur and the escape of Theseus, Minos vented his fury on Daedalus, the fabricator of both Pasiphae's cow disguise and the labyrinth. Daedalus and his son Icarus were imprisoned in the labyrinth, from which even its designer could not escape by landbound means. So he took to the sky, fashioning wings for himself and his son. Warning Icarus that the middle road was best, neither too low, where the moisture would soften the feathers' glue, nor too high, where the sun's heat would do the same. Exhilarated by flight, however, the hapless Icarus flew so close to the sun that the wax melted and the feathers came out, leaving him a plucked bird on high. The boy fell into the water and drowned, the sea being named after him. Compare this with Aegeus's unlucky fate, casting himself into his eponymous sea when Theseus forgot to change the color of his sails. The episode must also be compared to that of Phaethon related in the next chapter, a tale whose cosmic connections are unmistakable. Furthermore, the sacrifice of the fourteen children was offered every "great year"[25]—not an earthbound period but one discernible only by watching the heavens. Beyond this, we have the etymologies of names having to do with brightness and heavenly objects: Aithra, Ariadne (at least through her cult name, Aridela), Phaedra (Ariadne's sister, who becomes Theseus's wife only after the Cretan adventures are done), and Asterius (or Asterion), and also the names of one of Minos's human sons, his father-in-law, and according to some sources, the name of the Minotaur itself. As in the case of Frodi, a gold ring or necklace seems to recapitulate the product and the form of the right-running mill. Here, too, a golden ring cast into the invisibility of the sea's depths resurfaces in new hands, with divine aid given the hero who may now wear it. Finally, there are animals that change hands—the cursed bull on Crete becomes a cursed bull in Athens while its hideous offspring remains penned up in a cosmic cage, wreaking havoc upon both nations. Ariadne's bright aid is a clue that represents the cosmos in its right running, a ball with a string leading to the right place (compare the boat secured to the shore in "Hymir's Lay"). And Theseus, the embodiment of the new age of right running, has a father named Aigeus, (Goatman). These interrelationships and how they pertain to the cosmos are more fully explained in chapter 6.

THE ASTIKA

Now, indeed, we may approach "Churning of Ocean," still cognizant of Lévi-Strauss's injunction to include in our analysis not merely the story but also its context, which includes a whole book of the *Mahâb-*

hârata, [26] the book entitled *Astika*. This procedure will seem a bit tedious at this point, but I think it is necessary to side with Lévi-Strauss (who treats mainly Bororo and related myths from South America) that the stricture applies to all myth: myths may not be analyzed as isolated stories; they form nexuses and plexuses that enwrap themselves like the world serpent devouring its own tail. We have had an ample view of this in our quick look at the Theseus-Minos myths. Any treatment of these stories that ignores this injunction will produce ad hoc over-simplifications. The dictates of space demand that from here on the stories will be told by means of running synopses, with the rubrics from the paradigm inserted where appropriate.

The subject of the *Astika* is the son whom Vinata, the daughter of Daksha (The Right-handed One), bore to Kashyapa, the Old Tortoise Man, lord and progenitor of all earth's creatures. The name of this son was Garuda. He was the illustrious king of the birds, Vishnu's vehicle for travel through the skies (fig. 3.1). In this story Garuda purloins (E, F) the elixir of immortality, amrita (G3), produced during the "Churning of Ocean" (C-D). To procure it, Garuda had to do battle with the jealous Indra (A), besting him and smashing his thunderbolt. Among the many epithets, therefore, that Garuda bears is the title Vajra-jit (Lightning Smasher) (C/D). He is also known as Vishnu-ratha (Wheel of Vishnu) (C-D). Vishnu, it seems, has triumphed over Indra (AI). In its entirety, the story recapitulates these bundles over and over again, as we shall see in the following summary. (Bracketed numbers indicate the chapter number in the book *Astika*).

THE ASTIKA

Vinata and Kadru, who were sisters (A2) and who were both wives of Kashyapa, gave birth to eggs (C), Kadru to a hundred (G10) snake's eggs (F2), Vinata to two (A2) bird's (D2) eggs. Vinata unseasonably (F*) opened one of her eggs and from it a half-grown (F5) bird, Aruna (Red Dawn) emerged. Aruna cursed (F9) his mother to five hundred years (G10) of slavery (E1) for his premature genesis. Vinata allowed her other egg to grow to term, and its product was Garuda, destined to set his mother free (G3). [14]

The two sisters saw the horse Uccaihshravas, which had been churned from Ocean (G3).[15] Being unsure of its color,* the sisters made a wager (A), the terms of which were that the loser should be subject to the winner (AI, EI). Kadru asserted that the horse had a black tail,* while Vinata insisted that it was white.* Kadru planned to have her many (now counted as one thousand) serpent sons insinuate themselves into the horse's tail to make it black. When they refused, she cursed (F9) them to be sacrificed (F7) in the great snake sacrifice to be offered by the royal seer, Janamejaya. But the curse seemed too cruel to Brahma, who, though he approved of the curse so as to rid the earth of snakes (G) and the venom they might spread (E3) in vengeance, compromised by granting instead that the snakes should live but that Kashyapa should be given the power to heal snakebite (G). [18]

The sisters met at dawn (A6) to judge the color of the horse, and they saw the Ocean (E6) in its many splendors: home of all jewels (G1) blazing with submarine fire (E5); stirred by maelstroms (C-D); playground of sea serpents (C5); dungeon of the Asuras (E5*); spring of amrita (G3); concealer of earth in its muddy waters (E), which Govinda had recovered (G4); bed of Vishnu at the beginning of new eons (I) when he, god of the lotus navel (C1) sleeps the sleep of Yoga; sacrificer in the blazing flames of mare-head (C5) fire (C-D*); and mirror (A2*) of sky. [19]

Vinata lost the wager, but as she fell into slavery, her bird son Garuda emerged from his egg in due season (G2).[27] He was as resplendent as the god Agni (Fire), who averred that Garuda was his equal (A2). The gods refer to him as "redemption" (G4), "seer" (G9), "the future and the past" (I), and "sun that outshines the sun" (G5, G6). Yet he was also known as "the terrible dissolver of the eon" (I), who destroys creation in flames (F3) like the fire of sacrifice. [20]

At first, though, this mighty "eater of snakes" (C-D*) who devoured the Nisada serpents [24] lay in bondage (E1) to the snake sons of Kadru, and though Garuda had debilitated them with the power of the sun (F3), Kadru revived them with rainfall from Indra (G3). [21–22]

Garuda asked the serpents how he could win release (G4). "Bring us the elixir (soma-amrita)" (G3) was the answer. [23]

While devouring the Nisada, Garuda ate a Brahmin (E4) and then regurgitated him (G4) because the holy man burned in his stomach like a coal (D1*). [23–24]

Garuda, it seems, was destined to become the trickster (D4), the thief (C/D3) of soma-amrita, but to do so he needed more power. His father, Kashyapa, advised him to eat (E4, C-D2) two prophets (G9), two brothers who had become enemies (A2). They had cursed each other (F9) and had been transformed into animals (E*). One, a huge elephant, stirred up a large lake (A5) with its tusks, trunk, and feet (C-D1). In that very lake lived the other, transformed into a huge tortoise (C2). Garuda flew into a forest of very large trees with golden boughs (E3, G1). He alighted on a banyan tree only to break off a huge branch (C/D). There, certain visionaries (G9) called Valakhilyas dwelt upside down (C/D*). [25]

FIGURE 3.1
Garuda in his role as the avian steed of the god Vishnu. (Courtesy of the
Cleveland Museum of Art, purchase from the J. H. Wade Fund, 61.46)

To ensure that no Brahmins could be harmed by the branch, Garuda was instructed to drop it upon the highest mountain (D1). But the mountain began to shake violently (F1) under the blast of the huge bird's wings. Portents began to appear among the gods (F8*): Indra's thunderbolt (D1) began to blaze, and meteors came loose from heaven (F4). The weapons (C1) belonging to the several kinds of gods, the Vasus, the Rudras, the Adityas, the Sadhyas, and the Maruts, began to attack one another (A), an event never before seen, even in the war between the Suras and the Asuras (A2). The gods rained blood (E3), lights went out in the sky (F4), the gods' garlands (C3) withered (F6), and dust obscured (E3) the diadems (C3) of them all. [26]

Brihaspati gave answer to Indra's troubled question about the meaning of these signs (G9): Kashyapa, who was an honored Prajapati, desired a son (G6), so he had to offer up a great sacrifice.* The gods, the Gandharvas, and the seers came to help; Indra was sent out to fetch firewood with the other gods and with the diminutive sages, the Valakhilyas. Exulting in his superior strength at this task, Indra had belittled these latter, and so in their rancor they undertook a great sacrifice at which they prayed that Indra be replaced (A) with another, more powerful Indra (A2). Indra sought the help of Kashyapa, who deterred the prayer of the Valakhilyas with the proviso that this second Indra be an "Indra of the Birds." The Valakhilyas foretold that this "Indra of the Birds" would fulfill the wish of Kashyapa, for he was to be the longed-for son. [27]

The gods prepared to fight Garuda with weapons (D1) of every sort, some made of gold and beryl (G1). They formed a protective circle (C) about the Soma. But Garuda, coming on like the mighty bowman Shiva at doomsday (I), routed Indra's host. There was a general conflagration (F3), but Garuda quenched it by spraying water taken from all the rivers out through his ninety times ninety (A3) mouths. He arrived at the elixir's hiding place (E) in golden splendor (G1), and upon noticing that a revolving wheel (C-D1) set with scimitars (an image reproducing the Sudarsana; see fig. 3.2) of Vishnu (D1) was guarding the elixir, he synchronized his flight with the wheel and flew between the spokes (C-D1). There he found that two (A2) serpents (C5) were guarding the wheel. He threw dust in their eyes (E3*), killed them, and seized the soma (G3).

Then Garuda flew to Vishnu in the sky and procured from him two boons: ever to be higher than Vishnu (A1*) and to be ageless and deathless (G4*) even without soma-amrita.

Indra and Garuda made a truce (G6) after Indra's bolt (D1) merely knocked loose one of the bird's feathers. To seal the bargain, Garuda returned the soma undrunk (G3), and Indra granted to Garuda the office of devourer of snakes (E). They also played a trick (D4) on the serpents by pretending to turn over the soma to them in order to secure Vinata's

FIGURE 3.2

Bronze sudarsana, Vishnu's discus personified as a being with sixteen arms. Such images have a long iconographic history, beginning with the image of a chakra held in one of the god's four hands (compare figure 2.3), which evolved into images in which the chakra and the deity become one with the divine eight- or sixteen-armed deity standing in the center of the flame-emitting wheel. (Tamil Nadu, sixteenth century; copyright, The Archaeological Survey of India with permission) release (G4), but while the serpents were bathing (E2*), Indra and Garuda in collusion stole it back (G7). [28]

This rather lengthy and involved story is very important for the development of our understanding of the constituent bundles. Aruna, the first son of Vinata, born out of season from a pair of eggs, became the god of dawn. He cursed his mother to slavery. An eon later his brother, Garuda, was born from the other egg and in time freed his mother from the curse of slavery. Garuda, who was an enormous bird, took to the sky at his birth; at this moment he is compared to a kindled mass of fire. So Garuda is also the dawn, a newly *perfect* dawn born to replace that crippled dawn that led its mother into captivity. The story relates how one son came to replace his brother, and it has its basis in cosmology.

Replacement runs through the whole tale: Garuda was supposed to be a replacement for Indra and so is identified with Shiva, who, according to some Hindus, did vie for supremacy with Indra-Vishnu. It is clear from our previous study that upheaval followed by regeneration (F, G) and the replacement of one king, god, or set of gods by another (A) are the chief bundles in a mythic pattern of cosmic significance (I). Here we learn that this cosmic significance has to do with the end of an eon, and that the Fire of the Sun, rekindled in Dawn from the subterranean Ocean, forms a cosmic complex that is the locus or even the identity of the two gods who vie to replace one another.

The drink of immortality is not the real focus of the myth, as Dumézil's ambrosia cycle presumed. It is in part a token of the larger picture, the renewed eon, of *rita* and of *ritu*; and its theft and countertheft, for and by the alternating gods, repeat the bundle of replacement. The elixir is brewed from circular motion and is guarded by a rotary scythe, symbols of an eon that is running right, of a sun that is on its right track (G4).

The smaller story within the story, the "Amritamanthana," or "Churning of Ocean," repeats these bundles, which form its larger context, but with a different cast of characters and a different plot.[28]

THE AMRITAMANTHANA

Indra had been cursed (F9) by a saint named Druvasas. The god and his three worlds (A3) began to degenerate (F). Vishnu came on the scene and agreed to publish the recipe (G9) whereby the natural order might be restored (G6).

A great mountain (DI) rises to the vault (C) of heaven. It is populated by many animals, trees, and rivers. It is an ornament of gold (GI), which casts forth the splendor of the sun. Here the gods gathered and debated (A*) about how they might win amrita-soma (G3). Vishnu told Brahma that the bucket (CI) of Ocean (A5) had to be churned (C-DI) both by the gods (Suras) and by the demons (Asuras)(AI).[15]

Then the gods went to Mount Mandara (DI),[29] another august peak filled with living things (G2). This mountain is deeply rooted in earth (C-D3), but it had to be uprooted (C/D). Vishnu ordered the huge serpent Ananta to do so, for Mt. Mandara was destined to serve as a churn stick (DI). The churn itself was to be the fundament of ocean (CI), but Ocean agreed to suffer the disturbance of being churned only if a share of amrita would fall to him. The tortoise Akupara was asked to be the pivot point (CI), and Vasuki the serpent was to be the driving rope (C5). Once the action of churning began (C-D), its friction brought fire, smoke, and venom from Ananta's mouth (C5*). Shiva drank (E4) Vasuki's poison (E3). It singed his throat (F3). Lightning (DI) came, and rain; the gods were weakened (F5). Their garlands (C3) fell (C/DI, F6), and there was general ruin (FI). The friction (C-D*) of falling trees started general conflagrations (F3). Indra put out the fire with a great rain (G2), and the juices from herbs and trees flowed with gold (GI) into the ocean. This was to become the elixir (G3) of the gods' immortality (G4). The ocean ran with milk and ghee (G2).

But the elixir had not yet appeared (F6),[30] so Vishnu granted power to the weary gods. They again began to churn (C-DI), and from the ocean there arose the sun of a hundred thousand rays (G5) and with it Soma, the moon, to be a jewel (GI) for Shiva. A corresponding jewel, Kaustubha, was produced for Vishnu (A4). Sri Lakshmi came forth with ghee, and Goddess Liquor (G3). So too were produced Parijat, the tree of paradise (DI), and Surabhi, the magical cow (CI). They all followed the sun's path, and that is where the gods were standing (G5). Dhanvantari, the physician to the gods (G*), brought forth the elixir amrita (G3) in a white gourd cup (CI). But then the demonic Danavas seized the elixir, crying out that they owned it (A4). Vishnu assumed the disguise of a beautiful woman to trick them (D4), and out of their desire for her (BI) the Danavas willingly turned over the elixir.

Then there was a great battle between the Daityas and the Danavas on one side and the gods on the other (AI). Rahu, a Danava, disguised himself as a god (D4, E?) and began to drink the elixir, to which he now had access. But Sun and Moon revealed his disguise (G9) to Vishnu, who promptly cut off Rahu's diademed (CI) head (C5) before the elixir flowed down his throat (E4). Vishnu's weapon was Sudarsana, the sword-edged discus (see fig. 3.2) (C-D). Ever since, there has been a lasting feud (A) between Rahu's head (C5, D2) and Sun and Moon. Even today he sometimes swallows them both (E4, F4 expecting G5).

The blood ran so thick (E3) that the sunshine was blood colored (F3). Nava joined the fray with his magic bow (C-D), while Sudarsana, effulgent as the fire (F3) of Doomsday (I), felled foe after foe. After a great upheaval (FI), the gods gained the day, went home, and hid (EI) the elixir, giving it into the treasury (C6) of the new diademed god [the replacement for Rahu and left unnamed] (C3) for safety.

In this story the bundles "fertility lost" and "fertility regained" (F, G) are not emphasized. Yet the production of amrita by a method that imitates the rite of *pradakshina* is couched in images and terms suggestive of fertility and sexuality. There is the primary image of churning, which must be done according to formula. The sexual element is underlined by the manner in which Vishnu plays the tricksters's role disguised as a sexy courtesan and by the appearance of Sri Lakshmi and Surabhi. The emphasis here is rather on the bundle of internecine strife—one set of gods will replace another (AI)—and the possession of amrita is a token of the possessing party's ascendancy.

Gods vie with gods. The theme is of cosmic importance, a fact emphasized by the scale of the churning: the sea is its *mise en scène,* giant mountains its engines, the gods its motive power, and eons the time it takes to produce the three heavenly elixirs—the fire, the ghee, and the amrita itself (all three of which are but aspects of the one, a Hindu trinity, if you will).

SUMMARY

The myths singled out for treatment by Dumézil in *Le Festin d' im-mortalité* are centered on the ambrosia cycle as he described it. By examining closely the bundles recurring in the "Amritamanthana" and "Hymir's Lay" and comparing them with those that occur in the *Astika* and "The Mill Song," we found that the ambrosia cycle, in turn, fits into a larger pattern that underlies these myths and others such as the story of Theseus and Minos. Taken together, these bundles form the paradigm I call the Myth of Replacement. The constituents are: (A) replacement; (B) violations of sexual taboos; (C) symbols of female sexuality; (D) symbols of male sexuality; (C-D) male and female elements going together correctly in right running; (C/D) male and female elements dysfunctional in wrong running; (E) hiding; (F) disaster; (G) creation and re-creation; (H) etymological concurrence; and (I) cosmic significance.

CHAPTER IV

MYTHS FROM SOUTH AMERICA TO GREECE

The foregoing chapters have demonstrated that a certain array of gross constituent elements repeats itself across a wide variety of myths from the Indo-European tradition in stories so divergent in plot, character, and form that their structural similarity has previously been glimpsed—briefly and without consequent study and refinement—by only one scholar, Georges Dumézil.

My adoption of certain of Lévi-Strauss's principles has made it clear that this corpus of myths can be analyzed profitably and with interest by means of a structural methodology. I am quite certain, however, that had Lévi-Strauss himself done the analysis of the body of myth heretofore discussed, his procedures and results would have been quite different from my own. Despite this sense of unease that the application of like methodologies will yield somewhat different results when applied by different analysts, I cannot agree with some critics that the methodology is therefore totally flawed. I am positive that Lévi-Strauss has discovered one thing for us, namely that individual myths cannot be analyzed in isolation.

It misses the point to say that Lévi-Strauss gives us half an interpretation in his discussion of one myth, with obvious gaps and difficulties, followed by a series of other half-interpretations that fill in the gaps and difficulties of the first only to offer their own lacunas and so on through an indefinitely massive corpus of stories in a cycle that will never close. The myths, despite clear surface dissimilarities, are one and the same in their deepest structure. Often, however, their thematic tendrils are hopelessly snarled, as we observed in the discussion of the myths of Minos and Theseus. We can never hope to comb all of these myths completely free of their difficulties; so many cycles will never really be closed. On the other hand, it is more trenchant so say that Lévi-Strauss's mode of analysis secures beyond scrutiny a sufficiently vague privileged plane of meaning, the *esprit*, "which elaborates them [myths] by means of the world of which itself is a part."[1]

At this juncture I wish to depart from Lévi-Strauss. The brain does indeed react to the world about it. But it is not so clear to me, as he and his followers insist, that it always does so in a binary way, on vs. off, like a computer, so that the constituents can be placed in a Cartesian grid with two axes. Lévi-Strauss did his structural analysis of the Oedipus myth by placing its gross constituent units into two parallel columns in which one relation is overstressed or overvalued and the other understressed or undervalued, such as "underrating blood relations" vs. "overrating blood relations." The constituent units in the "underrated" group included the murder of brother by brother and father by son. This analysis was not very palatable to classicists; one friend expostulated to me that the analysis "was done with mirrors!" It is not surprising that Lévi-Strauss did not venture to try his hand at Greek myth again.

I would propose other ways of interpreting the manner in which the human mind encounters the outside world. One of these, mentioned earlier in the book, is somewhat akin to that proposed by Cassirer. Cassirer proposes that to the unscientific mind the world of phenomena presents itself to the mind as a "Thou." The Thou is a living presence— a person, perhaps fearsome and surely unknown and inscrutable. But this mysterious personality has qualities and potentialities that become known by the individual to some degree as the Thou reveals itself. All experience of this "person" is highly individual. The interactions between the Thou and an individual are conceived of as events rooted in action, action that is given the form of a story by the individual narrator. This, according to Cassirer, is the etiology of myth. My view is allied with this idea, but it is different. Phenomena are simply thought to have human motivations, personalities, and feelings. The prescientific mind is given to pathetic fallacy. The sun is harsh or it is kindly. The rain is gentle or it is angry. The seasons are on time or they are late or early. The ground welcomes the seed or rejects it, and so on. Such interactions with the Thou, however, are not personal; they are cultural. A given society perceives certain aspects of what we call "nature" as beings, beings that belong to an alien culture, possibly friendly, possibly inimical, but always having some power over the society's well-being, and that of its members, as in the case of any encounter with an alien. We still nurture these beliefs in our wonder about the cosmos; there may be hidden away in it alien denizens who could appear at any time and who may destroy us or benefit us but are beyond our control. We imagine these things of that unknown, and we tell stories about it. We may imagine them as benign, as in the world of *E.T.*, or hostile, as in the story of *The Alien*.

Stories are told, then, not so much to express the eventful encounter between the individual and the Thou but to relieve the tension, to give expression to the feeling states evoked from the tension arising between the foreign, the unknown "nature" and the familiar, one's own society and culture. Society wants to know; there is a need for cognitive order. It knows the explicit and implicit rules of its own culture, but what of that which is alien? Society wants to control; there is a need for a defense against all possible threats. Established mores deal with threats arising from within, but what of that which is alien?

The most comforting answers to these questions are that the alien is like us, and we can know the unknown by *knowing it as we know ourselves,* and we can defend against the alien by making it part of us, by enculturating it and giving it our values, by *adopting it and purging it of its otherness.* When it has become one of us, it is no longer threatening; if it misbehaves, it may be dealt with by means of the moral order applied to any transgressing member. I am reminded of Herodotus's story of Xerxes, furious with the storm that wrecked his Hellespontine bridge, giving the command that the nasty waters be given three hundred lashes.

One principle applied by all prescientific cognitive systems concerning similarity and difference, which I will invoke here and develop later, is germane to the modes of identification and adoption just mentioned: If something is like another in one way, it is like it in every way, even though some of those ways may not be immediately apparent. Hence, rituals are designed to bring what is alien into the order of knowledge and protection found in society. The ritual of right running is enacted so that what is alien (that which seems beyond our control) will be brought under the control of society, which, with its plethora of rules, *is* right running. Then we come to know "nature" as regular and helpful, just like one of us. This process survives today in the great enterprise that is science. I am writing a book so that the impossibly convoluted and complex corpus of mythology, so fascinating in its otherness, can be schematized and its ghosts laid to rest. Copernicus expostulated a theory of motion of the heavenly bodies so as to lay to rest the improbably complex rules of the Ptolemaic "science" of the cosmos, with its epicycles and other convoluted explanations. The cognitive imperative always was and always will be a fundamental of human nature, as Aristotle avers at the outset of his *Metaphysics*: "All men by nature desire to know."

Ritual and science regularize things, but myth and literature serve the needs of "what if" and "once upon a time." Our science and our rituals and religions do not really satisfy all of our doubts about the mysteries of life and the beyond. There is still the tension of the unknown, and chaos lurks behind every formula. Nature is irregular, and we shall never know all her rules and structures; indeed, in the final analysis there may be none.

The advantage of culture over life in a state of nature is that of control and regulation; the fewer things that are left to chance and the vagaries of nature, the more successful the culture. Culture will construct a predictable, orderly world. Yet the economic basis for man's existence is one of scarcity, even of vagary; economics *is* a dismal science. Nature is *not* predictable, but nothing is more regular and predictable than ritual; one ritual word misspoken anulls everything said before. Every threat nature offers to man's make-believe world of predictability is allayed (in his mind) by ritual: acts, words, and sacred objects.

Some myths are told to satisfy the same need: to allay or defuse the tension between regularizing culture and irregular nature by speaking of events, set in a cultural milieu, which threaten irregularity. The narratives so constructed often conclude with the reestablishment of regularity. On the other hand, some myths serve the dark side—once upon a time there was (or will be) a disaster. In their very telling, however, events conceived of as ultimate disasters (like Ragnorok) are in some sense regularized, because narration carries with it the regularities of sequence, syntax, and grammar, and of characters and things that, when described, become known and familiar, for all the terror we hold them in. So even those stories that leave us with horror and a chill, by giving syntax to the unknown purge us of its terror, at least for the moment, and the emotion, its physiological consequences once experienced, leaves our doubt and fear unanswered but at least allayed for the time being.

Thus ritual, myth, and other outer-directed cultural institutions are governed by a kind of structuralism: the tendency of the group to see every other group as having characteristics comparable to its own. Later in this chapter I expand on this idea with a discussion of the New Guinean tribes that hunt the dugong.

SOUTH AMERICAN MYTHS

The paradigm described in chapter 3 forms a system that pervades certain myths of Indo-European origin and that finds further expression in the rituals of several Indo-European–derived cultures. Two questions about the paradigm suggest the direction for this chapter's enquiry: (1) To what extent does the system pervade the mythologies of the Indo-European–derived cultures? and (2) Is the system culturally determined, or can it, or significant subsystems of it, be located in the myths of other cultures?

For an answer to the second question, let us turn to some myths from the Americas that are the raw materials upon which Lévi-Strauss erected the structure of the first of his three volumes of *Mythologiques: Le Cru et le cuit*. I use his own system of numeration, and the names following the numbers identify the cultures from which the myths were

collected. The versions of the myths come from the Weightman translation, *The Raw and the Cooked*. The names and references following
each story refer to the ethnographers who collected the stories and the
page numbers in their notes or publications on which the original tran-
scriptions and retellings may be found (see the bibliography in *The Raw
and the Cooked*). Since the repetition of the bundles of the paradigm in
these stories will be so apparent, so complete, and so pervasive, I do
not feel bound to follow Lévi-Strauss's principle of exhaustion; that is,
I will not discuss all the 187 stories he includes in order to demonstrate
that indeed my paradigmatic bundles and their repetition bind these
myths together as securely as—or more securely than—Lévi-Strauss's
structural principles. Let us first consider myths that are clearly of cosmic significance (I).

M_{138}. SHERENTE. "THE PLANET VENUS"

Venus (a masculine personage) was living in human shape among men
[E]. His body was covered with malodorous ulcers [F6], and behind him
was buzzing a swarm of bees [C/D*]. All the people turned up their noses
when he passed, and refused him when he asked permission to rest in their
houses [F*].

Only the Indian, Wainkaura, made the poor wretch welcome and gave
him a new mat on which to sit [C-D,* G*]. He asked his guest whence
he came and whither he was bound. Venus explained that he had lost his
way [F4].

Wainkaura ordered hot water to be brought to him so that he could
wash Venus' ulcers and, ignoring his guest's protests, insisted that this
should take place inside the hut [C6], and not outdoors. He even ordered
his virgin daughter to let Venus sit on her bare thighs [C-D], and washed
him in this position. Thus the visitor recovered [G4].

After nightfall the visitor said to Wainkaura, "What would you like to
have?" and as Wainkaura did not understand, he explained, "Do you
want to live or to die? Waptokwa is angry over the mutual massacring of
the Indians [AI]. They have even pierced little children [F7] with arrows
[C/D,* DI*]. So it would be better to destroy all of them at once [F7]. But
tell no one and quickly pack up your belongings."

He ordered Wainkaura to kill the juruty dove (*Leptoptila rufaxilla*).
When Wainkaura returned with the dove, Venus said that he had deflow-
ered his daughter [C-D, C/D], and offered to pay compensation. However,
Wainkaura refused to accept anything [G6*].

By means of the dove's carcass [G2], Venus made a large boat [C2] in
which Wainkaura took his place [C-D] along with his family. Venus took

leave and departed, a whirlwind [C-DI] lifted him up to the sky [G5]. At once a distant noise became audible. Then the flood came and carried them all away [FI]. Before long, all drowned [E2] or died from hunger [F6]. Only Wainkaura and his family escaped [G4]. (Nim. 6, pp. 91–92.)[2]

This story belongs to a type of folktale well known from European sources (inappropriately called "The Poor Man and The Rich Man" after the biblical version). A god disguises himself (E*) as a homeless (F4*) tramp and asks hospitality from a rich man, who denies it (F6). Then from a poor neighbor he asks the same and is treated well (G2). God gives the latter three wishes, which he uses wisely (G7). The rich man and others like him are ruined (F7). The best-known variant of this story from the Greco-Roman tradition is the story of Philemon and Baucis, told by Ovid:

> When Zeus and Hermes were wandering through Phrygia disguised as mortals [E*], they were refused hospitality in a thousand homes. At last they came to the poor hut [C6] of the old couple Philemon and Baucis. Baucis prepared a meal [G], but the table [C] was unsteady [C/D], for one of its legs [DI] was too short [FI]. During the meal the hosts noticed that the wine bowl miraculously kept refilling itself [G2, G3]. Realizing the presence of deity, the old couple kept trying to catch their goose [A4] so that they could sacrifice it [C-D*] to the gods. The gods revealed themselves [G9] and promised a wish fulfillment [G]. First they flooded [FI,[3] F7] the impious town and turned its inhabitants into fish [E*]. The old couple asked that they be made priests in the gods' temple [G6] and that neither one should outlive the other [G4*]. At their death they were transformed into trees [DI] growing outside the temple [C-D]. (*Metamorphoses* 8.620—720)

Even Thor Heyerdahl would not be able to convince us that the similarity between this Phrygian tale and that of the Sherente Indians is due to cultural diffusion. On the other hand, I am not willing to be placated by the invocation "common folktale type." Something in the physical world common to Phrygian and Sherente perception evoked a very similar cultural response in myths about the world gone awry, the parlous state of human morality echoing divine discomfort, a test, a disaster to destroy the wicked, regularity found, human culture rewarded, and the world put back on track.

Other myths cited by Lévi-Strauss concern the creation of the Pleiades:

M_{132}. WYANDOT. "THE ORIGIN OF THE PLEIADES"

Seven young boys [11+] were playing and dancing together in the shade of a tree [D1]. After a while they became hungry. One of them went to the house and asked for some bread, but the old woman would not give them any [F6]. They went on with their game, and then a little later another child went to the house and asked for some bread. Again the old woman refused. One of the children made a drum [C], and they began to dance around the tree [C-D1].

No sooner had they started the dance than they began to be lifted upward. They went on dancing, and still higher into the air they ascended [G4]. Looking around, the old woman saw them dancing high above the tree [C-D]. She now came running with food, but it was too late. They refused to listen. Now she was willing to give them food, but they would not even notice her and continued their dancing while moving upward [G6, C-D]. Filled with despair, the old woman started to weep [F].

The seven stars are the same boys dancing together. They were not given anything to eat: That is why they became Hutinatsija, "the cluster," which we now see in the sky [G5]. (Barbeau, pp. 6–7.)

These Native Americans did not use the wheel and axle as a practically applied, work-saving device. It is not surprising, therefore, that we do not often encounter in these stories the usual Indo-European symbol for right running. Circular motion is nonetheless symbolized in these American cosmological myths. Venus is carried into the sky by a whirlwind, and the Pleiades boys dance around a tree. The buzzing swarm of bees behind Venus may well symbolize that circular motion temporarily out of order. Instead of being deterred from their culturally charged play (a ritual dance?) by famine, the boys continue their circular dance, inventing a cultural implement to assist its efficacy. This regularity then infuses "nature" with the creation of the Pleiades, an asterism relied on as a seasonal sign-giver throughout South America and elsewhere.

Many tribes have stories about the origin of the Pleiades; they are extremely varied on the surface, but their deep structure reflects the paradigm.

M_{134}. ACAWI. "THE ORIGIN OF THE PLEIADES"

A man who coveted his brother's wife [B] killed his brother [A1] and presented his sister-in-law with her husband's severed arm [F5], as proof of his death. She agreed to marry him but, having been warned by the ghost's groans [F8], she soon realized the truth [G9] and rejected the criminal. The latter thereupon imprisoned [E1] the unhappy woman and her little child in a hollow [C] tree [D1] and left them there to die [F7]. That night the brother's ghost appeared to the man and explained that he bore no resentment for the crimes, because his wife and son had turned into animals [E9⁵] (*acouri* and *adourie* respectively) and were henceforth safe [G]. On the other hand, the ghost demanded that his brother give a proper burial to his maimed corpse [F5] and promised him an abundance of fish [G2], on the condition that he buried only the body and scattered the entrails [G11⁶].

The murderer did as he had been requested, and he saw the entrails floating through the air (G4) and rising into the sky, where they became the Pleiades. Since that time, every year, when the Pleiades appear (G5), the rivers teem with fish (G2). (Roth 1, p. 262.)⁷

The murder and dismemberment represents the disappearance of the Pleiades figure, who is then separated from his family—the culture, which needs what the Pleiades signify: rain. On the other end of the story, the rising of the entrails signifies the reappearance of the Pleiades figure, and abundance follows. The hiding of the family in the tree signifies the intensity with which the society expects the still-hidden sign. Again we find in this rather unusual myth the repetition of the bundles of replacement, fertility lost, and maiming, hiding, and restoration, in addition to the bundle, which we might expect in a story about the heavens—that is, right running, symbolized by the motion of the entrails and the seasonality of the Pleiades, which predicts the monsoon and an abundance of fish.

In this myth we find a curious reversal of the culture-nature opposition. Here the murderous brother represents the known as an unknown, unexpected evil. He shuts up the wanted sign in a hole in the tree. They will out nonetheless, but they have escaped the human world of murder, lust, and cruelty by being transformed into animals, people of a different "culture."

A discussion of one other myth about the Pleiades will complete the presentation of these interrelated myths:

M₁₃₆. ARECUNA. "JILIJOAIBU (THE PLEIADES) KILLS
HIS MOTHER-IN-LAW"

Jilijoaibu's mother-in-law used to feed her son-in-law on fish taken from her uterus [B,* G4, F2⁸]. When he discovered her trick, Jilijoaibu broke crystals [C/D] and threw the fragments onto the bank where his mother-in-law was in the habit of going, but took care to conceal them [E1] under banana-tree leaves. The mother-in-law tripped and fell [F4*]; the stones cut her arms and legs and the whole of her body [F5]. She died. The stones leaped into the water and turned into "piranhas" [E9], which for this reason have remained cannibalistic [F2]. The old woman's liver also fell into the water and floated on the surface [G4]. It can still be seen in the form of *Mureru brava*, an aquatic plant with red leaves, the seed of which is the old woman's heart [C1]. (K.G. 1, p. 60.)°

The broken crystal surely stands for the stars, the Pleiades themselves, which then become teeth in the mouth of the piranhas. The Pleiades appear in the sky in a significant way either at dawn (their heliacal rising) or at dusk (their heliacal setting). During their heliacal apparitions they are, as it were, amphibians, suspended between the brighter sky beyond the rim of the horizon and the darker sky toward the zenith. One could also imagine that they are caught in the maw of morning or evening, since the mountains on the skyline resemble teeth. Stars and planets would seem to be devoured or regurgitated, depending upon whether they were rising or setting into the "maw." In this case the brightness and ringlike structure of the Pleiades suggested the pearly whites of the piranha; the Pleiades have become the maw. The watery milieu of the myth is appropriate to the culture, because the Guianian Indians (of which the Arecuna are a tribe) assign to the disappearance of the Pleiades the beginning of the rainy season.[10] The suspension of such bodies in the sky between rising and setting, between being devoured and being vomited, belongs to the bundle of hiding and to the bundle of restoration (E2, G4). Amphibious beings are perfect symbols for such in-between states.

Hence, the creation of *Mureru brava* from the old woman's liver—a myth of etiology based upon a similarity in color between the plant and liver, and between this dusky red and the colored sky of twilight—has a more cosmic significance. The plant is an amphibian. It lives partly above the water (A6) and partly below, just as the Pleiades, during their moment of significance, are partly in the dark and partly in the light. In M_{132} the rising of the boys into the sky as they were transformed into the Pleiades recapitulates only the celestial facts; M_{136} recapitulates those facts with a transformed setting and objects, symbolizing the Pleiades with an amphibious plant, while M_{134}, with its transformed setting and objects, recalls as well the transformation into amphibians of the wife and son into rodents (amphibious in the sense that they live both above and below the ground). M_{134} somewhat illogically introduces the object to be transformed (intestines = Pleiades) into an untransformed setting (rising into the sky).[11] M_{136} has both object-to-be-transformed (the liver) and a transformed setting (the surface of the water = sky).

Amphibians are of great value to humans because they bring gifts to man by ferrying from their own realm those that are unattainable to men.[12] Hence the old mother-in-law in M_{136} (an amphibian, as we recognize from her transmogrified liver) brings forth fish from her womb. Giving birth, therefore, is quite parallel to appearing in the sky. In one expression of this mythologem, an unknown but expected visitor will come, bringing salvation to the family (or society). It will be a denizen of a watery world and therefore a creature of two realms (if not exactly amphibian, in that it cannot reenter once born). In another, a truly amphibious being (a planet or star), expected to reappear from the unseen world, becomes visible, with a period of transition between the two as in birthing.

These relationships are very clear in another myth, M_{55}, which also has a cosmic setting:

M_{55}. BORORO. "THE ORIGIN OF FIRE"

Formerly, the monkey was like a man; he had no hair on his body, sailed a canoe, ate maize, and slept in a hammock.

One day when the monkey was sailing back with the prea (*Cavia aperea*) [a kind of aquatic rodent; EIO[13]] from their plantation, he was alarmed to see the animal hungrily gnawing at the maize that was piled loose in the bottom of the canoe: "Stop," he said, "or you'll make a hole in the side, we'll spring a leak, we shall be drowned [E2], and you won't escape because the piranha fish will eat you [E4]."

But the prea went on gnawing, and the monkey's forecast came true. As he was a very good swimmer [EIO], he managed to slip his hand inside the gills of a piranha fish, and he reached the bank alone, waving his catch [G2].

Shortly afterward he met the jaguar who marveled at the sight of the fish and managed to get himself invited to dinner. "But," he asked, "where is the fire?" The monkey pointed to the sun which was sinking toward the horizon [EIO] and bathing the distant landscape in a ruddy glow. "Yonder," he said. "Can't you see it? Go and fetch it."

The jaguar went a long way, then came back to say he had not been successful. "But there it is," went on the monkey, "all flaming red! Run after it, and this time catch up with the fire so that we can cook our fish!" So off went the jaguar again.

Whereupon the monkey invented the method of producing fire by rubbing two sticks together [C-D,* G4], which men were to copy from him later. He kindled a good fire, grilled his fish, and ate it all up, leaving only the bones [G8]. After which, he climbed up a tree [E10]—some people say it was jatoba—and settled himself at the top [D1].

When the jaguar came back exhausted, he realized that a trick had been played upon him [D4], and he was indignant: "I'll bite that cursed monkey to death [A1, E4], but where is he?"

The jaguar ate what was left of the fish and tried in vain to trace the monkey's whereabouts. The monkey whistled [G9*], once, twice. Eventually the jaguar caught sight of him and asked him to come down, but the monkey refused, being afraid that the jaguar, in spite of his assurances to the contrary, would kill him. The jaguar then stirred up a strong wind, which caused the tree top to sway [F1]; the monkey clung to the tree as best he could, but soon his strength was exhausted [F5*], and he was hanging on by only one hand. "I'm going to let go [F4*]," he cried to the jaguar. "Open your mouth [C5]." The jaguar opened his mouth wide, and the monkey dropped into it and disappeared into the jaguar's belly [C-D2, E4]. The jaguar, growling and licking his chops, ran off into the forest [F2].

But soon he was in a bad way, because the monkey jumped about so much inside him [E1]. He begged the monkey to keep still, but to no purpose. In the end the monkey took his knife [D1], cut open the jaguar's belly [C/D2], and came out [G4]. He removed the dying jaguar's skin and cut it into strips, with which he adorned his head. He fell in with another jaguar, who had hostile intentions [A1]. He pointed out the nature of his headgear to this jaguar, who realized he was dealing with a jaguar-killer, and fled in terror. (Colb. 3, pp. 215–17, [*sic*]) [14]

Monkey is a culture hero who, being an amphibian himself (tree-animal/ground-animal, animal/man-animal), is able to release from its hidden world (in wood) fire, the most precious of all cultural possessions. Likewise, this amphibious being is a trickster who can go from the hidden world of the water to the land, to the tree, and back to the hidden world of the jaguar's stomach unscathed. By using artifact and ritual, he inverts the natural order of terror: jaguar now fears man. From the depths of jaguar's belly, monkey produced yet another gift of culture, the knife (unmentioned before he uses it). This parallels his production of fire after the sun had set or when it was setting. When nature defaults, culture may provide. The prea's gnawing is curiously similar to the holes bored in Od's boat, and though the theme of re-placement is not overtly expressed here, it is implied. Culture can make up for nature's deficits. The prea's action threatens to drown the mon-key man and destroy both him (as if by deluge) and his agricultural plenty with him. The prea drowns or is eaten (E) as a symbol of this instability in nature. But in those days monkey man was an amphibian, able to save himself by attaching himself to a piranha's mouth (the Pleiades, which are reborn from a watery womb, as we have seen), by procuring fire, and by using his knife—that is, by inventing culture. Culture seems to brag of itself in myth; putting one's hand in a piran-ha's mouth and baiting jaguars is culture with a swagger, not the stuff of ordinary experience.

Venus and the Pleiades are specific heavenly denizens whose appari-tions have cultural importance. Other myths treat star lore still as a personified entity but in a more general way.

M_{87}. APINAYE. "THE ORIGIN OF CULTIVATED PLANTS"

A young widower [F6], who was sleeping out in the open air, fell in love with a star. The star appeared to him first of all in the form of a frog [E10], then in the form of a beautiful young woman, whom he married [C-D]. At that time men knew nothing of gardening, and they ate rotten wood [F6] with their meat instead of vegetables. Star-woman brought her hus-band sweet potatoes and yams and taught him to eat them [G8].

The man carefully hid his tiny wife in a gourd [E1, C1], where she was discovered [G4] by his younger brother. From then on he lived openly with her.

One day, while Star-woman was bathing [E2 ¹⁵] with her mother-in-law, she changed into [E9] an opossum [E10; an in-between-animal in several ways, being arboreal/terrestrial and diurnal/nocturnal ¹⁶] and jumped on the old woman's shoulder until she drew the latter's attention to a large tree [C1] laden with cobs of maize [G2]. She explained that "the Indians were to eat this maize instead of rotten wood." As an opossum [E9], she climbed up and threw down quantities of cobs. Then she reassumed hu-man shape and showed her mother-in-law how to make maize cakes [G9].

Delighted with this new food, men decided to chop down the maize tree [C/D] with a stone axe [D1]. But when they stopped for breath, the

notch [CI] they had cut closed up again [C-D¹⁷]. They sent two boys to
the village for a better axe [DI]. On the way, the two discovered a steppe
opossum, which they killed and immediately roasted and consumed,
though this animal is taboo [F9] to boys. Hardly had they finished their
meal when they turned into [E9] senile [GIO*], stooping [F5] old men. An
old magician-doctor succeeded in restoring their youth.

When the men had finally felled the tree [C/D] with great difficulty
[FIO¹⁷], Star-woman advised them to make a clearing and plant maize
[FIO]. Star-woman, however, later returned to the sky [G5] after her hus-
band's death. (Nim. 5, pp. 165–7)¹⁸

Here the relationship between nature (the heavens) and culture
(agriculture) becomes clear. To get agriculture, people had first to love
the stars that revealed to them the regularities of planting and harvest-
ing by seasons, upon which successful crop production depends. Star
Woman is especially significant when she is amphibious (the frog) because the seasons are told by the rising and setting of the stars at twilight, as explained above in the case of the Pleiades. The younger
brother probably represents hunting culture, which coexists as a seasonal alternative with agriculture among these Indians (AI). This explains the taboo against the boys' eating the steppe opossum during
reaping time. Boys hunted opossums, but opossums are not hunted
when it is time to reap. This transgression of the cultural imperatives
with respect to the amphibious opossum made the boys move through
the seasons, many seasons, and become old men. In this case, however,
old age is seen as reversible, for just as the opossum is amphibious—
moving about at night and in the day too—the seasons renew themselves by moving from long days and short nights to the reverse and
back again. Agriculture takes advantage of this recurring process and
would have control over it, just as the shaman is thought to be able in
this case to reverse old age.

Here, too, we learn the meaning of the impossible task (FIO). Culture
provides the means to carry on agriculture just as it provides the means
to carry on hunting culture. But the methods of agriculture are extremely labor-intensive: after much effort at chopping, a dent is hardly
made into the maize tree; the tree is felled only with great difficulty.
And the chopping down of this single tree (representative of the great

tree of life), which symbolizes both the productivity of agriculture and the knowledge of the heavens, merely recapitulates the chopping down of the many trees necessary to clear a plot of land. Chopping down the maize tree in another sense seems to be a foolish crime (compare the killing of the goose that lays the golden egg), which would symbolize wrong running. But this act was a forerunner of digging into the earth and sowing seed, a taboo act, evil but necessary, as discussed in the next chapter in connection with Pandora.

Nature is not always dependable in her half of the partnership. Labor can make nature amenable to man's needs, but sometimes, despite his best efforts, his labor and valuable seed corn are spent in vain. Culture can fail only through human inadequacy, through the failure of individuals who do not (or will not) fit. Therefore, since culture will have nature in its camp, whenever nature fails or seems irregular, man attributes it to his own error. Thus, many tribes have elaborate taboos designed to avoid "committing a crime" against nature. This idea is well represented in one variant of a Kraho myth about the origin of cultivated plants (M_{89}), which is similar to M_{87} except at its ending, which goes like this:

> During all this time, Star-woman and her husband remained strictly chaste (c-D, c/D*). One day while her husband was away hunting, an Indian raped (B) the young woman, and she bled (E3). She prepared a philter with which she poisoned the entire community (E3, F7). Then she went back up into the sky, leaving cultivated plants to the few survivors.[19]

One is tempted to interpret chastity-in-marriage as waiting for the due season;[20] then the rape is perpetrated during the husband's absence for hunting (to the neglect of agriculture) during the wrong season. The taboo of due season in the culture-nature partnership has been upset, a fact represented on the societal level by a heinous crime. The next chapter includes a more fulsome discussion of the crime of rape vis-à-vis agriculture. Man's fault is the cause of nature's failure, symbolized here by Star Woman's bleeding (E3) and returning to the sky (F4, F6, since she no longer helps man). The poison philter recapitulates Star Woman's blood (E3), and man is destroyed (F7) because he broke the taboo. Since the broken taboo here and elsewhere is symbolized by an illicit sex act (rape), we could augment the infidelity-incest bundle in item B of the paradigm with a general rubric: breaking of a taboo having to do with the earth-mother figure.

The last myth in this series brings together the origin of agriculture and the invention of fire (necessary, too, to hunting culture), both delivered to man by another amphibian, the goatsucker, a nocturnal swallow. Birds are always amphibians, and nocturnal birds are ambiguous in more ways than one.

M₅₄. TUCANA. "THE ORIGIN OF FIRE AND OF CULTIVATED PLANTS"

Once upon a time men had neither sweet manioc nor fire. An old woman was given the secret of the first by the ants [E10]; and her friend, the nocturnal swallow (a goatsucker, *Caprimulgus* species), would obtain fire for her (keeping it hidden in his beak) [E1], so that she could cook the manioc, instead of heating it by exposure to the sun or by putting it under her armpits.

The Indians found the old woman's manioc cakes excellent and asked how she prepared them. She replied that she simply baked them in the heat of the sun. The swallow, amused by this falsehood [D4], burst out laughing, and the Indians saw flames coming from her mouth [G4]. They forced it open [B] and took possession of the fire. Since then nocturnal swallows have had gaping beaks. (Nim. 13, p. 131.)[21]

Lévi-Strauss's note here is important to our understanding of the forcing open of the jaws as a sexual act: "In *lingua geral*, the *Caprimulgus* (*Mae de lua*) is called *urutau, yurutahy*, etc., 'big mouth.' An Amazonian version compares this mouth to a vagina (Barbosa Rodrigues, pp. 151–2), which gives the key to the equivalence with certain Guiana myths about the origin of fire, which state that an old woman kept it in her vagina."[22]

The acquisition of fire is sometimes considered to be a violation of nature, the rape of "nature" by "culture," and therefore there must both be a price attached to it and stringent taboos affecting its acquisition, distribution, and misuse. The same is true of the acquisition of agriculture, as we have seen and will see again.

In the next group of myths, we learn of the ways in which the Indians thought of mortality and immortality. Immortal beings are all amphibious creatures, for they can imitate the stars' ability to sink into the gloom and then be reborn. Man is not amphibious; therefore he is consigned to a mortal existence.

M_{65}. MBYA. "THE ORIGIN OF FIRE"

After the first earth had been destroyed by a flood [F1], which had been sent as a punishment for an incestuous union [B], the gods created another [G6] and placed on it their son, Nianderu Pa-pa Miri. He created new men [G4] and set about obtaining fire for them [G7*]; at the time it was the sole possession of vulture-sorcerers.

Nianderu explained to his son, the toad [E10], that he would simulate death [E9], and that the toad must seize the burning embers as soon as Nianderu, having recovered consciousness [G4], scattered them.

The sorcerers approached the corpse, which they found suitably plump. Pretending that they wished to revive it [G4], they lit a fire. The hero moved about and shammed death alternately [E9], until the sorcerers had brought together enough embers; the hero and his son then took possession of the latter and put them inside the two pieces of wood [E1, E10] that would henceforth be used by men to produce fire by a process of rotation [C-D1]. As a punishment for their attempted cannibalism [F7], the sorcerers were doomed to remain carrion-eating vultures "with no respect for the big thing" (the corpse) and never to achieve the perfect life [C/D]. (Cadogan, pp. 57–66) [23]

Vultures are great amphibians, for they spend most of their time circling in the sky (like the stars), where they have access to fire (the sun). In M_{67} we are told that the birds know how to get fire from friction (by wheeling in the air). In M_{56} (not included here) the jaguar is the possessor of fire. He is bilked out of it by the trickery of the prea and must thereafter eat raw, bloody flesh. The jaguar, being terrestrial/arboreal/aquatic [24] and diurnal/nocturnal, is amphibious like the vulture; he transfers fire to another amphibian, the prea, who learns how to rotate sticks to make it. It seems as if the Indians needed to explain to themselves how two superior creatures, the vulture and the jaguar, lack fire, while inferior, unamphibious man possesses it. Both the vulture and the jaguar violate cultural taboos (they eat human flesh) and therefore lose their former privileged status in nature, a punishment symbolized by their loss of fire, the highest cultural gift.

A word must be expended here to extend to the vulture what happened to the jaguar. Notice that before Nianderu's theft of fire the "sorcerers" were building up a fire, ostensibly to revive a corpse (which was within their power as sorcerers; the next chapter discusses fire as a means of revivification) but in fact to eat it—"they found it suitably plump." This implies that the vultures were going to cook Nianderu (which is corroborated in M_{66} and M_{68}). But like the jaguar, the vultures in their current depraved state must eat raw, bloody flesh. Therefore, we must surmise, Nianderu's theft caused a permanent loss of fire by the vultures.

Nianderu in this story seems to be an immortal kind of human being—immortal owing to his amphibious capability; he alternately moves about and then shams death, that is, he can go from one state to the other and back again. In the parallel myths, M_{64} and M_{67}, the figures corresponding to Nianderu are a "civilizing hero" and "the demiurge." Furthermore, Nianderu and the demiurge both have toads (amphibians) as allies. There is some indication in these myths that man was thought to have had amphibious capabilities at one time or was able to cross from one realm to another under the guidance of certain amphibians such as the hummingbird but that he lost it through some mistake or through the violation of some taboo. Hence, in M_{78} a shaman seeks the secret of immortality. He is actually empowered to go into the Beyond (an amphibious mobility typical of shamans), but he is warned by its several denizens not to partake of tobacco or look at the creator's daughter. He gets some cultural implements (resin and a comb) that are supposed to be able to confer immortality on dead trees and men. But he violates a taboo by looking at the toes of the creator's daughter, and doing so makes her pregnant. So the creator arranges for him to die upon his return so that he would be summoned back to the Beyond to care for his family. Henceforth all people die[25] (that is, they are amphibious, capable of living in both the realm of the living and that of the dead), but unlike the shaman, once they go across they cannot come back; their movement between realms is restricted to one direction and one instance. The realm beyond is an alien culture where no human can live. At death, humans are transmogrified so that they can accept the new and totally repulsive way of life to be found there. This idea is brought home clearly in M_{93}, which is about a young man who falls in love with Star Woman (Jupiter). She tries to live in a gourd on earth but their secret is discovered; so he accompanies her to the home of her star parents. There the food is human flesh, and taking a bath is done in and about human corpses. He cannot abide this life, so he returns via the tree trunk he has climbed. But soon afterward he dies for good and goes back to live among the stars.

Culture is unable to provide a means to achieve immortality; indeed, the violation of some cultural norms seems to doom humans to death. Insofar as culture constrains one to live here in this world, to provide for one's family, it disallows life in any other world. Most animals and the "people" of the heavens, being fully amphibious, are able to put on new cultures as they change realms. But man has no such gifts. Agriculture and fire, the cultural artifacts that enable naturally weak man to be a kingly animal, are too good to give up in exchange for immortality. Surrogate immortality, through one's offspring, alone remains possible, an idea to be further explored in other contexts.

The notion that culture is a boon gained only with the loss of immortality is expressed in the following story.

M$_{76}$. SHIPAYA. "HOW MEN LOST IMMORTALITY"

The demiurge wished to make men immortal [G]. He told them to take up their position at the water's edge [A6] and to allow two canoes to go by; they should, however, stop the third [A3] in order to greet and embrace the spirit in it.

The first canoe contained a basket full of rotten meat, which was extremely foul smelling. The men ran toward it but were repelled by the stench. They thought that this canoe was carrying death [F], whereas death was in the second canoe and had taken human form [E9]. As a result, the men greeted death warmly, with embraces. When the demiurge arrived in the third canoe, he had to accept the fact that the men had chosen death—unlike the snakes [E10], the trees, and the stones, who had all awaited the arrival of the spirit of immortality. Had the men done likewise, they would have sloughed off their skins [E9, E10] when they grew old, and would have become young again [G4] like snakes. (Nim. 3, p. 385.) [26]

Humans are eager to embrace their own kind, which is death. Culture, which demands social living and caring for others, induces death. Death goes with being human. Snakes, trees, and stones do not spend effort caring for one another. Lacking this feature of culture, they enjoy immortality. The first canoe represents hunting culture, which makes living things dead in order to provide sustenance for mankind. By partaking of this culturally gained sustenance, humanity condemns itself to death. The canoes in the water, like the Juruty-dove boat taken by Wainkaura and his family on their voyage of immortality, symbolize the heavenly bodies on the edge of the sky, which—like the Venus-person, Starlady, or the Pleiades—make voyages into the beyond. Snakes are immortal because they are amphibious in several ways. They retain their pristine glory by entering any number of new skins, and they live on land, in the earth, up in trees, and in the water.[27]

The same ideas find quite a distinct expression in another story:

M_{49}. MUNDURUCU. "THE SNAKE'S WIFE"

A woman had a snake as her lover. Pretending to be going to gather the fruit of the sorveira tree (*Couma utilis*), she went into the forest every day to see the snake [D1], who lived in one of these trees [C5* C-D]. They would make love [C-D] until the evening, and when the time came to part [C-D5], the snake would shake down [C-D] enough fruit to fill [G2] the woman's basket [C1].

Becoming suspicious, her brother kept watch on the pregnant woman. Although he could not see her lover, he could hear her exclaiming in his embrace: "Don't make me laugh so much [G9], Tupasherebo! You are making me laugh so hard [C1, open mouth], I am urinating [G3]!" In the end, the brother saw the snake and killed it [A1, F6, killing the provider]. . . .

Later the son that the woman bore the snake avenged his father [A1]. (Murphy 1, pp. 125–6.)[28]

The snake that lives in or about the tree of life is a worldwide folktale element. The amphibious snake, which lives in holes, "knows" Mother Earth intimately; he encircles and guards the tree, which produces food without labor. But man fell from the grace of Eden by coveting knowledge beyond that possessed by the animals, that is, by substituting culture for nature. Therefore he is constrained to do labor of two kinds: hunting, fishing, and agriculture, and bearing and rearing children. Not only is the curse of labor brought into the world, it is divided labor. Many myths, including the Eden story, are in part etiological accounts of the origin of the division of labor.

A corollary of this belief among the Indians is that woman is Mother Earth while the man's penis recapitulates the role of the amphibious snake. Snakes satisfy the longing of Mother Earth for intercourse, which, when attempted with her by mankind, results in catastrophe. Among the peoples of Europe, plowing was seen as the rape of Mother Earth, and sexual intercourse was a type of plowing. The first plowing broke a taboo (B), which resulted in man's fall from Eden to husbandry east of Eden, where survival came only by labor, and immortality only by procreation. The original Golden Age, then, was that pristine condition of ignorant bliss in which all was provided; right running was taken for granted, because the world was without seasons and without labor or cultivation. No knowledge of the right season was needed; there was no fear of the alien other, for all was one cultureless fairyland. Then sin came into the world, taboos were broken, the heavens went awry, and man was destined ever after to a lot of labor and worry, mitigated only by the culture gained at the price of paradise lost.

The following story illustrates the deep-seated ambivalence man feels about this necessary communication with Mother Earth.

M_{50}. TOBA-PILAGA. "THE SNAKE'S WIFE"

There was a girl who had a continual flow of menstrual blood [G3–F6]. "Does your period never finish?" she was asked. The girl would answer, "Only when my husband is here [C-D–C/D]." But nobody knew who her husband was. Moreover the girl laughed incessantly [CI, G9].

It was eventually discovered that she spent all her time sitting in her hut just above a hole occupied by her husband, the python. A trap was laid for the latter, and he was killed. And when the girl gave birth to six little snakes [A3], all spotted, they too were killed. The girl changed into an iguana [E9, E10]. (Métraux 5, pp. 65–6.)[29]

The girl and her "husband" represent at once Mother Earth in her fertility and mystery, and mankind the way people would like to be—able to play all day and yet have plenty (the laughter, the menstrual flow). Culture cannot so enable them; it constrains them to work. Idleness is taboo, yet digging in the earth for plenty (here symbolized by copulation) is incestuous. The snake is put to death and the woman exiled from humankind for breaking this taboo. But the death of the snake is also the end of plenty (cf. M_{49}). That the archetype of this typical opposition between nature and culture is to be found in the heavens is beautifully illustrated in another story:

M₇₉. TENETEHARA. "HOW MEN LOST IMMORTALITY"

A young Indian woman met a snake in the forest. The latter became her lover, and she bore him a son who was already a youth at birth [G4]. Every day the son went into the forest to make arrows [D1, culture] for his mother [C1, C-D,], and every evening he returned home to her womb [C-D, B, nature, with a cultural taboo violated]. The [woman's] brother [A1] discovered her secret and persuaded her to hide [E1] as soon as the son went off. When the son returned that evening to enter the mother's womb, the woman had disappeared [F6].

The snake son consulted his snake grandfather, who advised him to hunt for his father [A3, three generations]. But the boy had no desire to do so, so that evening he transformed himself [E9] into a ray of lightning [E10, sky to earth] and climbed into the sky [C-D], taking his bow and arrow with him [C-D, culture]. When he got there, he broke his weapons in pieces, which became the stars [nature]. Everybody was asleep, and no one except the spider saw this take place. For this reason spiders (unlike men) do not die when they grow old, but change their shells. Formerly men and animals also changed skin when they were old, but from this day until now they die when they are old. (Wagley and Galvao, p. 149.)[30]

This myth has it all. In his Golden Age (G), remembered now only by the spider, man was like a snake, an amphibious skin-shedder. Like the snake, he renewed his youth every night from intimate contact with earth (represented by the Indian mother who mated with a snake and harbored her snake son in her womb). The snake son symbolizes man in his first condition, a hunter with the simple culture of arrow making. The woman's brother represents agricultural culture, which vies (A) with hunting culture. Seen from the point of view of agriculture, the hunter's appears irregular: Mother is induced to vanish, to deny her hunting son the benefits of renewal and sustenance. She favors her own kinsman, agriculture, over exogamous marriage with a hunter. The abandonment of one culture for the other is symbolized by the son's refusal to hunt (for his snake father) and his destruction of the hunting weapons. These weapons are, for the hunting culture, the artifacts par excellence. They are transformed into stars, and knowledge of the stars' motion is the cultural gift par excellence for the agricultural way of life. The transformation of the boy into lightning expresses his serpentine, amphibian nature. Lightning is shaped like a serpent; moreover, it is amphibian, coming from the sky to earth, bringing its dangerous gift of fire. The cost of man's adoption of agriculture is high. It makes him guilty of a crime against Mother Earth. The nightly incestuous union (the return to the womb is an ambiguous symbol in the story), brings punishment (effected by brother agriculture). The boy is caught between the two economies of agriculture and hunting, which are seen as incompatible, alien cultures. Enjoying his old way of life—which allowed both the creation of hunting arrows and the nightly vegetable renewal in the bosom of Mother Earth—he refused to give up one for the other. His transformation into lightning and the arduous climb into the sky, the breaking of his outmoded hunting tools and his use of them to make the stars—the tools of seasonal time telling—symbolize the irretrievable nature of the past world in which the two cultures could coexist. Hunting is dead and lives in the sky, the realm of the dead. Climbing to the other world is unusual; one can do so and return only with the help of a special amphibious assistant such as a hummingbird.[31]

South American myth seems to confirm the inferences we made earlier from some Norse tales, the Hindu "Amritamanthana," and the myths of Theseus and Minos: owing to some condition or other (the failure of culture or the necessities of nature), the usual store of plenty or abundance vanishes, is exhausted, or is interrupted. This fact may be symbolized by the failure of some artifact or technology. The upheaval on the human plane may be symbolized by internecine strife, a contest, maiming, or by a sexually based crime. Human sacrifice may be called for in order to redress the great imbalance. Before order can be restored, monsters or monstrous humans may have to be dealt with. The gods may interfere directly by giving man a new cultural gift (fire or agriculture), or they may recreate order by themselves by subduing the gods of disorder and/or by imitating order's circular motions (churning of the ocean or brewing beer, creating the Pleiades), or by finding their way back to their proper station in heaven (via a whirlwind). A magic food, drink, or drug (tobacco) may be produced. Good men are often invited to share in this bounty; evil men are destroyed by fire or by flood. This (good) outcome is often symbolized by the appearance of a new heir, the immortality of the hero (implicit or explicit), or the timely or regular appearance, reappearance, or transformation of the hero as a celestial or amphibious being. A new order is established.

Furthermore, these myths have provided the data for adding to the paradigm the vital element of amphibianism. This element belongs to the bundle of hiding (EIO), for the amphibian can disappear from one realm and reappear in another. The notion of the amphibian was elaborated from the myths about the origin of the Pleiades where it was argued that the phenomena of the heliacal rising and setting of heavenly bodies recapitulates the migration of the amphibian from one of its realms to the other. These considerations will be important to what follows.

The isolation of the empirical category of amphibianism calls back to mind Lévi-Strauss's notion of structural oppositions. Are the oppositions that Lévi-Strauss evokes from the myths "merely heuristic devices to order the symbolism," or are they "categories of the native mind which evoke the myths by their interplay?"[32] The answer is that they are neither. The idea of "opposition" is rooted in the notion that things alike in one key category are alike in all others. Hence jaguar and prea are both "amphibians," jaguar being diurnal/nocturnal and arboreal/land-dwelling/water-adapted, while prea is a rodent that lives below the earth in a burrow or out on its surface. Vulture, too, is an amphibian in that it inhabits the sky, the ground, and the trees. All of these creatures come to possess fire, which is amphibian too, coming as it can from sky to earth or from within rubbed sticks, where it was latent. Naturally, then, vulture and jaguar can have sky fire, and fire can be given to prea, who then learns to produce it from the sticks that are part and parcel of its rodent's way of life. But men, not being amphibious, had to steal fire to get it. They were able to do so because vulture and/or jaguar violated a taboo. Since these are beings who have a well-defined and observed way of life, they are like human beings, who have a cultural way of life, and cultural norms are violated by jaguar and vulture, who ate (or were tempted into eating) human flesh. Breaking taboos brings punishment; vulture and jaguar were punished with loss of fire. Losing fire brings a loss of cultural amenities, and whereas before they cooked with fire, from the time of its loss vulture and jaguar are condemned to eating raw, bloody flesh. They loose their privileged status, and poor unamphibious man, who before was their victim, now becomes the victor. Men, who were confined to eating rotten wood and raw meat and who were strictly diurnal, now—because of the indiscretions of jaguar and vulture—possess the cultural tool that makes them able to cook and to light the night, and to terrify jaguar. They have gained a tool that makes them, in a sense, amphibious.

The summation of these stories leads us to a glaring realization. Opposition is not itself the basic category of the prescientific mind, as Lévi-Strauss would have it. Opposition is a category evoked by the tendency to think by identities: things alike in one key respect are alike in all respects; things that are unlike in some key respect are unlike in all respects. In these stories the key "concept" is the idea of amphibianism. Indeed, this is the most important idea that runs through these myths. There are others, but we may extend observations about amphibianism to almost every corner of the Bororo culture.

Cultivated plants are all amphibians, for the seed must be sown—"hidden"—in the ground before it can sprout into the air. Culturally important wild animals are all amphibians; most of the animals, like hummingbird, that are singled out for mention in these stories are amphibian. Domesticated ungulates, on the other hand, though economically important, are not mentioned in the stories. Tobacco is amphibian; it was discovered inside a fish's slit-open belly (M_{27}). Smoking it produces a reversible high leading man into a new realm of consciousness, while the smoke itself, winding heavenward, is "amphibious," living hidden in the tobacco, being liberated by fire and then inhabiting the air, whence it may migrate to heaven. Failing to let the smoke free to go to heaven is taboo—too much intoxication produces quasi blindness, and those caught in this crime (like to like) are transmogrified into tiny-eyed animals.[33] Fire produces amphibianism in other things. Considered by itself, fire, as noted above, is amphibian, for it comes from sky to earth or appears magically from rubbed sticks. It transforms raw food into cooked food, an irreversible amphibianism that imitates nature's process of decay, with the softening but without the stench. In fact, fire is the child of decay, for it is drawn by friction from rotten wood (tinder). Decay is a one-way amphibianism: sound but green and inedible things become ripe and edible and then rotten and inedible. Death is like decay, conceived of as a one-way amphibianism except in the case of special heroes who have the help of birds or supernatural animals, who do "the dance of the ancestors," or who marry into the clan of the stars (but they find the realm of the stars unbearable because of its reversal of culture, cannibalism, stinking corpses lying about, and other things). The immortality of the stars is accounted for by their similarity to fiery sparks. The fiery stars live for a time on high and then move out of sight only to return again. Fire itself may go out of the ember only to be recalled with tinder and blowing or by rubbing sticks anew.

Dead animals may be cooked and made soft and edible, but without cooking, their flesh rots, stinks, and slowly disappears. The key feature about death unmitigated by fire is its stench. Old people, on the threshold of death, stink with intestinal gases, which may poison the young around them. Eating rotten food may do the same (M_5). Funeral customs are carried out in order to reduce this odor and thus render the dead the service of letting them dwell where they belong, in the other world, rather than remaining and stinking in this one. For a time the corpse lives in two realms, or between two realms, and funeral practices hasten the departure of the amphibian corpse on its one-way trip to the realm of the dead. Among these Indians, funeral rites are accomplished by burial in earth but especially underwater. The Bororo bury their dead in a shallow grave and water it copiously; this cuts down on the odor while hastening decomposition. After several weeks, the corpse is exhumed and the last remnants of flesh washed away. The bones are adorned with red paint and brightly colored feathers, rendering the remains ready to inhabit the other culture, the abode of souls, which is thought to be at the bottom of a lake. The bones are sent there in a basket weighted with heavy stones.

At one time, the aboriginal human lived in an underground place or under the water (the abode of the souls), then one moment, responding to the call of a savannah bird, this person seized the opportunity to become amphibious and climb out onto the surface of the earth. The bird led him to dead or rotten wood (in some versions the rotten wood calls him directly). The wise man of the underground realm, upon seeing what is brought back from above, concludes that earth is a beautiful, fertile place. But the Indians are better off where they are, since the presence of dead wood on earth proves that everything is destined to perish, whereas in his current status man is immortal. A number of "children" refuse this wise counsel and go abroad on the earth, where they and their descendants lead happy but brief lives (M_{70}). So in the end, by exercising the possibility of being amphibian in one direction, these "children" are doomed to close the circle and become amphibian in the other direction and return to the world of souls. The rotten wood represents not only itself in contrast to sound wood but as tinder it also symbolizes fire, the amphibian-maker par excellence.

The basic mode of thought that governs the formation of "concepts" like amphibianism is universal and is current even today among the superstitious, and the not-so-superstitious. Universal categories are created on the basis of what would appear to a scientist to be superficial similarities. The snake is considered immortal because it can go below the earth and come back, just like the planets. Other creatures that share the trait of living in the earth and above it (e.g., ants) must be immortal too. The category is also extended to include those that shed their skins, like snakes, spiders, and insects. The most beautiful extended example of such thinking I have encountered is among the dugong-hunting tribesmen of New Guinea.

The Papuan hunters of the dugong (Kiwai) have a myth and a related ritual about the dugong. The dugong has bristles on its snout (a superficial feature); it is also difficult to catch (or used to be before the advent of Western technology), but it is a very important source of protein for these people (an essential feature). An elaborate ceremony surrounds the butchering of a dugong and the distribution of its meat. A land-dwelling animal called the echidna (a kind of porcupine) is not much valued. It is easy to kill and hard to make use of, but its quills resemble the bristles of the dugong. This makes them similar, and their similarity is understood as extending to other, "secret" dimensions. Their similarity is authenticated by the telling of a myth: A great flood came once and drowned many creatures. Echidna, too, was swept out to sea, but it was transformed into the first dugong and became aquatic. Now the dugong-echidna pair-made-one is amphibious.

The ritual associated with the myth takes place in canoe building. Echidna quills are ceremoniously installed in the prow of the boat. Landgoing, easy-to-catch echidna will lead the boat to his seagoing, hard-to-catch brother. Culture wants regularity in nature—that is, what is hard to catch or difficult to procure should become prey-according-to-formula. The feeling state of wanting (control) is translated into a myth and ritual based upon what seems, in scientific thinking, to be a superficial similarity.[34] Thinking such as this is, I believe, the basis for the establishment of native taxonomies.

GREEK MYTH

Every mythology gives special place to amphibian beings, real and imaginary. Some examples from ancient Greek myth would be serpents, dolphins, swans, kingfishers, eagles, Pegasus, Thetis and the other Nereids, Attis, Persephone, Aphrodite, and Hermes. This is also the notion that being baptized in a stream or being bathed in fire can render one immortal (Achilles and Demophon, for example). Throughout the discussion of Greek myth, I invite the reader to pay special attention to this proposition, although a complete discussion of this feature will have to await another volume.

Now that we have observed the presence of the Paradigm of Replacement among the native peoples of South America and elaborated upon the paradigm by observing the manner in which the ideas of these myths are interrelated in the native mind, we may be girded for the Herculean task of slashing our way through the multiheaded monster that is Greek myth, one made especially difficult by our ultimate goal: the interrelationship between these myths and other myths from Indo-European cultures, some of which we have recounted, while others will be told farther on.

We shall not begin immediately with the kind of Gordian knot we found encumbering the myths of Theseus and Minos but will instead begin with a tale that is rather simple in the telling, the story of Phaethon, son of the sun god, Helios. In the longer versions of the story, Phaethon is doubtful that he is really the son (or grandson) of Helios. Seeking reassurance from the god himself about his paternity, the boy extracts from Helios a promise (the gods' promises cannot be forsworn): to guide, for one day, Helios's steeds in their diurnal journey across the sky from sunrise to sunset.

One can see, however, from the number of sources extant for this simple story, that the reference to a Herculean task was not idle: they include Hyginus, Plato, Euripides, Ovid, Aratus, Nonnos, Orphic fragments, Virgil, Solinus, the scholiast to Pindar's *Sixth Olympian Ode*, Apollonius Rhodius, Lucian, Diodorus Siculus and Apollodorus, and several works of art. Ovid's version is too prolix for our purposes, so we will choose two variants from Hyginus for our telling: [35]

PHAETHON
(Fabula 152A)

Phaethon, son of Sol [the sun god] and Clymene, who had secretly mounted his father's car and who had been borne too high above the earth, from fear fell into the river Eridanus. When Jupiter struck him with a thunderbolt, everything started to burn. In order to have a reason for destroying the whole race of mortals, Jove pretended he wanted to put out the fire; he let loose the rivers everywhere, and all the human race perished except Deucalion and Pyrrha. But the sisters of Phaethon, because they had yoked the horses without the orders of their father, were changed into poplar trees. [36]

PHAETHON OF HESIOD
(Fabula 154)

Phaethon, son of Clymenus, son of Sol, and the nymph Merope, who, as we have heard, was an Oceanid, upon being told by his father that his grandfather was Sol, put to bad use the chariot he asked for. For when he was carried too near the earth, everything burned in the fire that came near, and, struck by a thunderbolt, he fell into the river Po. This river is called Eridanus by the Greeks; Pherecydes was the first to name it. The Indians became black, because their blood was turned to a dark color from the heat that came near. The sisters of Phaethon, too, in grieving for their brother, were changed into poplar trees. Their tears, as Hesiod tells, hardened into amber. They are called Heliades. They are, then, Merope, Helie, Aegle, Lampetie, Phoebe, Aitherie, and Dioxippe. Moreover, Cygnus, King of Liguria, who was related to Phaethon, while mourning for his relative was changed into a swan; it, too, when it dies, sings a mournful song. [37]

There are several strange features about these variants. Notice, first, that the name (H) of his mother is not certain. Helios (Latin, Sol) and Clymene are the usual names given Phaethon's parents, as in 152A. In other sources Clymene is the name of one of Phaethon's sisters. The name Clymene appears in other stories too. In the story of the Titans, she was wife of Iapetos, daughter of Tethys and Ocean, and mother of Atlas, Prometheus, Epimetheus, and Menoitios. Ovid took this Titanic Clymene to be the same as Phaethon's mother. Elsewhere the name was given to the mother of the ill-fated charioteer Myrtilus, to the mother of an unwanted daughter, Atalanta, and to a granddaughter of Minos.

Clymene, the granddaughter of Minos, had two sisters, Aerope and Apemosyne. These two were exiled in response to an oracle that fore-told the death of their father, Catreus, at the hands of kin. Aerope was destined to cuckold Atreus, and Apemosyne to marry Nauplius the navigator. Nauplius was destined to avenge his son's (Palamedes') death upon the Greeks by inducing three of their leaders' wives to cuckold them. He also put a false beacon on Cape Caphareus, luring several Greek captains to their deaths. Apemosyne was kicked to death by her brother after he discovered that she had been lying with a man she claimed was the god Hermes.

The Clymenes, it seems, are mothers/wives of those who (1) run right (C-D): Atalanta, Atlas as sustainer of the world, Nauplius (as navigator), and Myrtilus (as winning charioteer); or (2) run wrong (C/D): Nauplius (as wrecker), Myrtilus (as wrecker of Oenomaus's chariot), Phaethon, and Atlas (when he shirks his duty, trying to pass off the burden of sustaining the world onto Herakles). Furthermore, Clymenes are relatives of sexual deviants or of those who cause sexual deviation (B). Ovid tells us that Clymene was married to Merops, yet she bore children to Helios. Clymene therefore belongs to a type that includes Alcmene, Danaë, and Antiope—women illicitly pregnant from having consorted with deities. Such illicit offspring, begotten by deities, are often featured in stories in which the son is destined to replace the father (A). Such children are rejected, either being exposed, as in the case of Zethus, or being sent on impossibly dangerous missions, as with Herakles, or a combination of the two, as in the case of Perseus. Only after completing a perilous mission to the west could those heroes come home to be recognized for who they really were, sons of the gods. Such are the main features of paradigmatic hero myths as described by von Hahn.

We would expect that Phaethon, too, as a son of a Clymene (or, as in one variant, a son of a man named Clymenus), would fit into this hero pattern. Indeed, the attempt to guide the sun's steeds on their fiery course is a perilous journey to the west, but unlike the other heroes here mentioned, Phaethon fails in that undertaking. Nevertheless, he fits the hero pattern outlined by von Hahn and Lord Raglan. Does his story fit the Replacement Paradigm as well?

Some elements of the myth follow the pattern transparently: Clymene's adultery (B), the chariot as symbol (C), Zeus's lightning and the poplar trees as symbols (D), wrong running as the chariot crashes or careens too near or too far from the earth (C/D), drowning (E), the ruin of the earth (F), and the creation of a new generation (G). Nonetheless, in order to satisfy the strict tenets of the paradigm, we would like to find some indication of Phaethon's intention to replace Helios (A). Perhaps the reader is satisfied with the replacement of Helios for one day in the chariot and his inability to control the horses, but I would like to argue the point a bit further.

There is a clue that element A is present in Hyginus 152A in the reference to "Phaethon, son of Sol and Clymene, who had secretly mounted his father's car." Why *secretly* if, as in most variants, the boy had been given the right to drive the chariot because of the father's indiscreet promise? We know that the stealth could not be due to the father's having reneged on the promise, for in myth a solemn promise given by a deity, no matter how indiscreet, cannot be retracted. We must conclude that Phaethon wished to usurp his father's place or prerogative. Notice that the actions of the Heliades repeat this theme: they "yoked the horses without orders from their father." Usurpation of an elder's position (A) turns out to be a common motif in Greek myth, whether done unwittingly, as in the case of Oedipus, or with mischievous forethought, as in the case of Hermes and the cattle of Apollo.

Furthermore, conflict between the older and younger generation is to be found repeatedly in other information we have concerning characters named Phaethon. Citations exist in which Helios himself is given the name Phaethon.[38] Phaethon becomes an alter-ego of the sun-god, and these stories may be versions that allude to another story in which the sun-god himself goes awry and brings about the destruction of the world. The name Phaethon is also applied to one of the horses of Helios, likely the wayward one.[39] The name is applied, too, in later times at least, either to the planet Jupiter or to Saturn,[40] whose divine namesakes, Zeus and Kronos, had warred with each other, son against father, Kronos having before replaced his own father, Ouranos. In a different myth, the name Phaethon is equated with Apsyrtos, son of Aëtes. He is thus by genealogy the *grandson* of Helios, as he is said to be in Hyginus 154. Apsyrtos tried to interfere with his sister's lover, Jason, and was killed by him. Or, as in other variants, he was taken along during the escape of Jason and dismembered into the water of the Danube by his own sister Medea to slow down her father. Aëtes was in hot pursuit of Jason and Medea, as Jason with her help had stolen the Golden Fleece. Apsyrtos's death and bloody dismemberment into the waters of the Danube compares with Phaethon's fiery crash and descent into the river Eridanus (Po). Finally there is the variant of the Phaethon story told on Rhodes, in which Phaethon did not meet his death by falling from the sky but at the hands of his six brothers, who were therefore exiled from Rhodes.[41] The evidence is clear. Replacement (A) is a characteristic feature of stories in which the hero is named (H) Phaethon.

The remainder of the story fits the established paradigm, as we noticed before. Its outcome is of cosmic importance (I), involving the end of one world by fire and flood. In one of the variants reported by Hyginus, this destruction gives rise to new creation in the persons of Deucalion and Pyrrha (G). Furthermore, in other variants the structure and operation of the heavens are altered at the myth's denouement. One Roman writer suggested that the Milky Way is the burned-out track the sun used to follow before the fateful career of Phaethon.[42] In most variants Phaethon was catasterized as the constellation Auriga, his cousin as Cygnus, "king of Liguria," is turned into the constellation Cygnus, the Swan, and the river Po is turned into its heavenly counterpart, the celestial river Eridanus.[43]

The chariot itself represents bundle c; being a solar chariot, its departure from the accustomed path (C/D) is an instance of the sun being off its path (F4), while the destruction upon earth occasioned by that fall (F6), is followed by Zeus's destruction of all mankind (F7). Phaethon himself fell into the Eridanus/Po (E2) while his seven forlorn sis-

FIGURE 4.1

The Death (Fall) of Phaethon. *Drawing of an Arrentine Mould of a Bowl.* (Greco-Roman, turn of the era; H. L. Pierce Fund, courtesy of the Museum of Fine Arts, Boston, no. 98.828)

ters, transformed (E9) into poplars or ash trees, sit in sad array beside the river, weeping amber (G1) tears (E3*).

Instances of bundle D seem to be missing from the extant written versions, except possibly Zeus's lightning and the trees into which the Heliades are transformed. But a pottery mold (fig. 4.1), contemporary with Hyginus and depicting Phaethon's fall, provides phallic elements in superfluity: there is a pole, a ladder propped against it at an angle, and a tree being hacked at by a youth (Phaethon's alter ego?) wielding a hatchet. The pole, as we will see in chapter 6, represents the celestial pole; the tree represents the agricultural abundance that the right running of the heavens ensures; the ladder symbolizes the communication between earth and the heavens; and the boy with a hatchet symbolizes in different terms the result of Phaethon's ride, wrong running. (Did this boy keep secrets from his father about the destruction of the tree, as Phaethon did about the chariot ride?)

In Ovid's recounting of the story, Helios expostulates in a coda about the frustrations he has known as god of the sun:

and the Sun-god,
All this long while, remained in deepest mourning,

Gloomy, without his brightness, darkened always
As in eclipse, and hates himself and daylight,
Gives way to grief and grief adds rage, refusing
His duty to the world. "From time's beginning
I have had no rest," he says, "and I am weary
Of all this thankless toil, this endless labor . . ."[44]

The theme of eternal labor and the sisters' number, seven, lead us quickly into one of many "secret" passages in the mansion of Greek myth, avenues whose gatelatch is the story of Phaethon. The seven Heliades suggest another group of seven sisters, also dependents from a heavenly connection—the Pleiades. Seven they were in number, but only six shine in the sky, for one alone of all the sisters married a mortal and so hides her face in shame. She shares the name Merope with the mother of Phaethon, and the man she married was known for his eternal labor of rolling a stone uphill in Hades only to have it roll back again. Sisyphus is a Helios gone awry, the Helios of Hades, who shares the never-ending toil but none of the apparent and daily glory.

The whole career of Sisyphus on earth was marked by contention. Upon the death of their father, Aeolus, Sisyphus vied with his brother Salmoneus over the Thessalian throne (A1). Salmoneus himself dared to rival Zeus in name and power, transferring Zeus's sacrifice to altars set up in his own name and even claiming that he was Zeus (A). In a striking parallel to Phaethon's career, he drove his chariot, dragging a bronze cauldron behind and hurling torches in the air to simulate Zeus's thunder and lightning. His hubristic charioteering ended when Zeus blasted him with real lightning, destroying his chariot and him and setting afire his eponymously named city, Salmonia.

Unlawful imitation of his father also brought Phaethon to ruin. In his case, the whole world was destroyed, not just a city. Salmonia's inhabitants were cremated, not all mankind; an earthbound deviant charioteer was brought to ruin, not a celestial one—yet these parallels make it clear that the stories of Salmoneus and Phaethon are versions, one of the other, and both derive from an archetype likely closer to Phaethon's story than to that of Salmoneus.

One of Sisyphus's other brothers, Athamas, had two children (Phrixus and Helle) by his first wife, Nephele (Cloud Lady). Athamas's second wife, Ino, jealous of the children and of Nephele, planned to replace them all with her own children (A). She parched the seed corn, causing a famine (F), and caused it to be foretold that Phrixus would have to be sacrificed (F7) in order to restore fertility (G). At the last moment he (and Helle) were saved from this fate by a miraculous airship (C2)—a golden (G1, A4) ram supplied by the gods. It flew them eastward (A6) to Colchis, where, as some say, Helios stabled his horses. But poor Helle got dizzy, lost her grip (F1*, F4*), and fell into the sea (E2). The straits where she fell thenceforth have borne her name (H, "fawn-colored?").

In the sequel, Athamas and Ino were punished by Hera for once having given refuge to Ino's nephew, Dionysus. Athamas, maddened by Hera, shot his son by Ino, Learchus, with an arrow (A1, D1) and tore his still-living flesh into pieces (F7). Fearing the worst, Ino picked up her younger son Melicertes and ran. While the distracted Athamas was whipping a she-goat (A4,* E9*) in his stead, Melicertes was carried to his death in the sea by Ino (E2), who had jumped from a cliff in a mad attempt to save herself and her son. Other variants claim that she put him into a kettle of boiling water before jumping into the sea. She was changed into the white goddess of the sea, Leucothea (H, White Goddess). Most variants report that Zeus changed Melicertes into a dolphin (E9, E10), which later swam to the Isthmus of Corinth, where it was plucked from the sea (G4) by Sisyphus. Others say that Melicertes, like his mother, underwent an apotheosis into the god Palaemon and that a dolphin carried the drowned boy's corpse to Corinth. Athamas's last son, Leucon (H, Whitey), sickened and died. Wandering aimlessly (F4) without food and drink, Athamas came to a pack of wolves (F2) feeding on a flock of sheep; he frightened off the wolves and ate what remained (A4, G2). In this act he recognized the fulfillment of an oracle (G) that he should find a settling place where he was entertained by wild beasts. The town was called Alos, meaning "threshing floor" (C1). Returning in his old age to Orchomenus, Athamas adopted his grandnephews (of Sisyphus's line) Haliartus (Loaf-from-the-sea) and Coronus (Crow), who continued to reign there until Phrixus returned from Colchis with the Golden Fleece. Then the two gracefully surrendered (A4) Orchomenos to Phrixus, and each established a city named after himself (G6).

Athamas's life, beset by disaster (F), ended on a peaceful note, his descendants reigning in his city (G).

Hyginus (Fabula 4, after Euripides' lost play *Ino*) tells a version of the story so different that only some names and the repetition of bundled elements seem alike. A hunting expedition undertaken by Ino led to her loss and disappearance (E). After she failed to return, a search revealed only a bloodstained tunic (E3). Athamas, after a proper period of mourning, married a second wife, Themisto, who bore him twin sons (A2), Sphincius and Orchomenus. But Ino returned. She was secretly installed in the nursery, but Themisto soon learned who she was. Themisto planned a trick to get rid of Ino and her children (A). She told the new nurse to dress her children in white and those of Ino in black, having arranged for the murder of the black-garbed children. But Ino switched the garments so that her own were dressed in *white* (E9), turning the tables on the threatened and threatening Themisto. The name Leucon in the genealogy is therefore no surprise, nor is the fact that Ino received the divine name Leucothea after her leap from the cliff. The meaning of these color terms will be discussed later.

The story of Athamas exists in many versions and variants; so does that of his brother Sisyphus. In particular, the nature of the crime for which he eternally atones is variously defined. He is said (1) to have revealed the secrets of the gods (simply divulging to a grieving father the whereabouts of a girl whom Zeus had abducted [G9]), (2) to have bound Hades (A1, E1), or (3) to have returned from the dead by means of a lie (G4, D4; more on this later). His most execrable crime was the way he took vengeance on his brother Salmoneus. In order to get his kingdom back from this usurper, Sisyphus was advised by the Delphic oracle to seduce his niece Tyro and have children by her. When she realized that the seduction was done not out of love for her but out of hatred (A1) for her father, Tyro murdered the two sons she had born Sisyphus (F7). She then fell in love with the river god Enipeus and haunted his banks every day, weeping bitter tears. This evokes the tears Heliades spent by the banks of the Eridanus. Their tears were tears of amber, the Greek word for which, *êlektron*, refers more to the color (morning-gold) than to the substance.[45] Tyro's name could also be a color term because it means "cheese."

Tyro had another seducer, Poseidon, to whom she also bore two sons. For these we have the names Neleus (of uncertain etymology) and Pelias (Black-and-blue). Compare the names of Coronus (Crow), who appears in the story of Athamas as Sisyphus's grandson, and contrast the name of Athamas's last son, Leucon (Whitey). The theme of black versus white in connection with children played a major role in the story of Ino-Themisto. Pelias and Neleus behaved like Sisyphus and Salmoneus. Pelias stirred up a bitter opposition between Neleus, his half-brothers, and himself (A1). Pelias drove out most of his male relatives, but he could not prevent his own inevitable replacement by his half-nephew Jason (A1).

Jason first appeared wearing only one sandal (C2, F5). Recognizing in this the fulfillment of a dire oracle, Pelias sent the youth on an impossible task (F10): to procure the Golden Fleece (G1) from distant Colchis. Only thus could the gods be appeased, and only then might Jason petition for the right to his father's throne (C) and scepter (D). There Jason enlisted the aid of a disloyal female (B1), Medea. Her witchcraft (D4) enabled him to yoke two fire-breathing (E3) bulls to a plow, sow dragon's teeth in the earth (E2), and vanquish the armed men who grew up (E9) by throwing a boulder (D1) among them, precipitating internecine strife (A1). But Jason had undertaken some ritual preparations of his own: sacrificing to Hecate, waiting for the proper moment (C-D5) (i.e., when Ursa Major had declined from the zenith [1]), putting on black clothing (E9), bathing in the Phasis (E2) at dawn, and digging a pit (C, E). Upon their return to Iolcus, Jason took his revenge (A1) upon his uncle for having rejected him and for having sent him on the perilous mission. Medea convinced Pelias's daughters that she could rejuvenate (G4) the old man (F6), offering a magical demonstration of her power by transforming (E9) a goat (A4) into a kid, cutting it into pieces, and boiling it (E2) in a cauldron (C1) of magic liquor (G3). Alas, the dismembered (F5) Pelias remained hidden in the pot (E1) because the brewmistress (C-D) went off duty (C/D) without working the required magic for the rejuvenation.

The marriage of Sisyphus and the Pleiad Merope (note both her name and ancestry) yielded a son named Glaucus. Repudiating the claims of Aphrodite, Glaucus did not allow his mares to breed (F). He believed that such sublimation would make them more spirited in the traces and further his all-consuming obsession of chariot racing. When Glaucus went so far as to feed his mares some extra vitamins in the form of human flesh (F7), Aphrodite complained to Zeus. The goddess fed the mares a drug plant, hippomenes, which grew at the edge of a well (C1). True to its name, the herb caused the mares to go mad during the celebrated funeral games of Pelias near the seashore of Iolcus. They bolted (F2), turned the chariot over (F4), dragged Glaucus who was entangled in the reins (E1), and then ate him alive (F7, E4). Other variants say that he drowned (E2) in grief for Melicertes, or indeed that Glaucus was the name given Melicertes after he drowned. In any case, Glaucus's ghost was called Taraxippos, Horse-scarer, with which we may compare the affrighted horses of Phaethon. Glaucus's name is a color-brightness term (Gleaming grey-green). We began with a disastrous chariot ride, moved to a blasphemous one, and here have found one with elements of each.

Greek tradition knew of at least one other Taraxippos—Myrtilus, another charioteer, employed by king Oenomaus of Pisa in Elis. Myrtilus was the son of Hermes and the nymph Phaethousa (whose name is simply the feminine form of Phaethon). Others say that Myrtilus was the son of Zeus and Clymene. Either way, a connection between Myrtilus and Phaethon himself can be established on the grounds of genealogy and name typology, as well as upon the disastrous denouement of their last great chariot rides. Myrtilus's master, Oenomaus, was himself the son or husband of one of the Pleiades: Asterope, Asterie, or Sterope, as her name is variously given. Hence Myrtilus can be connected with the Pleiades on two counts because his grandmother was Maia, the Pleiad. Another Pleiad, Merope's son Glaucus, shares with his cousin Myrtilus the sobriquet *taraxippos*.

The story of the chariot-driving contest for the hand of Oenomaus's daughter Hippodameia (Lady Bronco Buster) is as follows: Oenomaus had received an oracle that his son-in-law would replace him (A1), or else he was himself in love with Hippodameia (B) and did not want her married. Since the girl was so beautiful and her race so noteworthy, she had many suitors. Oenomaus's reluctance to give her up to any man took the place of a challenge: a successful suitor would have to win against him in a rather lengthy chariot race to the Isthmus of Corinth. Oenomaus himself had the aid of the god Ares, special armor, and selected racehorses. Twelve suitors (E8) had met this challenge to race, knowing full well that the loss meant not merely the loss of a chosen bride but the forfeit of their lives. On each occasion, Hippodameia (A4) rode in the current suitor's chariot (C1). In each case the suitor lost, and twelve heads (F7, C5) had Oenomaus nailed to his gatepost (D1). When Oenomaus began boasting that he would build a temple of skulls (F5, C6), the gods decided that his time was up, so they assisted the thirteenth suitor, Pelops. Poseidon had given Pelops a winged chariot (C1) with which he might challenge the immortal mares of Oenomaus, the gift of Ares, because the two gods were at odds (A1).

Myrtilus was induced by Pelops to betray his master (A1) with the promise that he, Myrtilus, would receive a share of the bride (A4), the right to deflower her on the wedding night (B). Some say that Hippodameia had fallen in love with Pelops and offered herself to Myrtilus with the proviso that he find a way to betray her father (A6, B1).

Yet this advantage was not enough. Myrtilus, true to his heritage as a son of Clymene, caused a wreck. He replaced (A) the axle pins (D1) of Oenomaus's chariot with waxen ones (D4) so that the wheel (C1) would fall off (C/D) in midcourse (F4*). Just as Oenomaus was poised to throw his deadly spear (C1), the chariot veered because of the loss of its wheel, and he fell entangled in the reins (E1) and was dragged to death. (Just how Myrtilus was saved from being killed in the wreck is made clear by no source.) The racecourse's beginning was the altar to Olympian Zeus at Olympia. Oenomaus stopped there to sacrifice a light-colored ram,[46] whereas Zeus should be offered a black ram (opposition of color*). The finish of the race was at Poseidon's altar by the Isthmus (A1, Zeus-Poseidon). Yet others say that the race took place in the hippodrome at Olympia. In this variant, the divine help given Pelops was a magic object, which he buried near the *taraxippos* so that Oenomaus's horses bolted there (or one of them did) and wrecked his chariot. Before expiring, Oenomaus laid a curse upon Myrtilus for his perfidy (F9).

The way in which this curse effected Myrtilus's demise is the subject of a number of variants. In one, Hippodameia complained of extreme thirst (F6) while the three victors were riding together in the winged chariot. It was sunset (C-D5), but Pelops nonetheless went to fetch water on an island. When he returned with his helmet (C1) filled (C-D) with water (G2), Hippodameia complained that Myrtilus had tried to rape her (B). This was the wedding night, and Myrtilus reminded Pelops of his agreement to share the bride: would the oath be broken (F8)? Pelops replied with a blow to his face (C-D*). Then, taking the reins from the charioteer (A1), he drove out over the sea near Cape Geraestus, sacred to Poseidon, where he ejected Myrtilus from the chariot (C/D). He fell into the sea and drowned (E2). The Myrtoan Sea, some claim, is named after him and his fall there. In any case, the name Myrtilus seems to be invested with a three-way significance (H): (1) clearly its main kinship is to the word for myrtle or myrtle berry in Greek—a symbol of harmony in marriage, sacred to Aphrodite, and the berry reminiscent of the female pudenda; (2) *-tylos* refers to anything knobby and was used particularly as a word referring to the male organ (C-D); (3) if the word be divided myr-tylos, as in (2), then the first element, probably non-Greek, must refer to the sea, as in the name Myrto, Myrtea, and Myrtoan Sea,[47] and the name may be a local cult-title of Poseidon. A longer form of this name, Myrtoessa, was a cult title of Aphrodite, perhaps in her role as Aphrodite Anadyomene (i.e., rising from the sea).

Oenomaus's palace was destroyed by a thunderbolt thrown by Zeus, according to a variant recorded on a bronze tablet in the precinct of Zeus at Olympia, as reported by Pausanias. Whether this destruction of the palace was an insult added to Pelops's injury of Oenomaus's person, or whether the fire from Zeus was the sole mode of punishment suffered by Oenomaus for his crimes against his daughter's suitors is not made clear by our source for this variant.[48] But in the aftermath of the ruin (C/D) there remained one pillar standing (D1), bound up in chains (E1, C-D?), which boasted on its inscription to the passerby that it had survived (G) the conflagration.

At this juncture it may be well to summarize the pattern that is beginning to emerge from our study of certain Greek myths. The primary determinant of the form of a number of myths whose superficial features also bear numerous similarities to each other is the Replacement

Paradigm. The reader will wonder at this point why I chose these relatively obscure myths to illustrate the theme of replacement when the chief stories of Hesiod's compendium about the Greek pantheon, the *Theogony,* are the stories of the replacement of Ouranos (Uranus) by his son, Kronos (Cronus), and of Kronos in turn by his son, Zeus. The reasons are that Hesiod is fraught with pitfalls, and the material he uses is best deferred until the next chapter, where the reader may well capitalize on his or her greater familiarity with stories of this family and of the wars between the races of gods.

Here also we might pause and reexamine what we have developed and to call upon another analogy to illustrate the operation of the paradigm. We might well compare elements of the Replacement Paradigm with the base phrase markers in Chomsky's generative grammar, which, when strung together, constitute myth in the deep structure. A competent mythmaker transforms such basic forms into myths on the surface level, in which elements such as name, plot, and accoutrement would correspond to the phonological component of Chomsky's surface structure. In most of the stories we have just examined, however, the surface structures reflect the pattern of the deep structure almost item for item so that we can say that not much transformation has taken place. These simple myths would correspond to kernel sentences. Right running reverting to wrong running (C-D becoming C/D and G becoming F) in the deep structure is manifested at the surface level as a disastrous chariot ride in the stories of Phaethon, Glaucus, Myrtilus, and Salmoneus. In the story of Sisyphus, this ride is transformed into the eternal but fruitless labor of rolling a stone uphill. Wrong running is also reflected in the wayward horse found in several of these stories. It is also symbolized by a horse-frightening object secretly placed on the course. The restoration of right running (G) is a kernel myth expressed by (1) the creation of mankind anew through Deucalion and Pyrrha in the Phaethon story, (2) the rejuvenation of a goat (but not of the enemy Pelias) in the Jason story, and (3) recovery of the Golden Fleece in the story of Phrixus, Helle, and Jason.

Hiding (E) at the surface level (pardon the oxymoron) is expressed by drowning: Phaethon, Glaucus, Ino and Melicertes, Helle, and Myrtilus. In the myth of Pelias a quasi drowning in a stew pot accompanies dismemberment. The death of Apsyrtos also combines drowning and dismemberment. Some sources say that Ino dismembered and stewed Melicertes before jumping into the sea with him. Hiding is also manifest in the theme of light versus dark: in the dawn setting of the Phaethon story and the dusk setting of the Myrtilus story. This motif also appears in the location of these stories: Ethiopia and Aea-Colchis are in the far east, and the Eridanus/Po, with the Amber Islands (the place where the Heliades wept, in one variant), appearing in both the Argonautica and in the Phaethon story, is clearly taken to be in the far west. These regions represent dawn and sunset, as we know from the meaning of the Greek geographical term Anatolia (Sunrise). This theme is echoed in color-term names such as Electra, Phaethon-Phaethousa, Nephele, Leucothea, Glaucus, Leucon, Coronus, and Pelias, and perhaps Helle and Tyro, and in the trick of dressing some children in white clothing and some in black.

Replacement is central to the structure of these myths, and the theme of replacement appears in the surface structure of the myths in a number of ways. It is often accompanied by the theme of adultery/incest (B) or the irregular transfer of a girl from one party to another (A4). Hence, in the Myrtilus story we find a contest Oenomaus rigged to avoid giving up his daughter Hippodameia by killing all her suitors; then Pelops arrives and wins the contest by promising the bride temporarily to Myrtilus. The theme of replacement is also represented by a contest, as in the stories of Glaucus (an obsessive horse racer who did not allow nature to have its way with his mares), Pelias (who gave Alcestis to Admetus only after he had yoked the boar to the lion), and Jason (who engaged in several contests, including the yoking of fire-breathing bulls). Sometimes the replacement theme is expressed in these myths as direct challenge or usurpation, as in the stories of Sisyphus and Salmoneus, and Pelias and his brothers. This mode of expression extends to stories about stepmothers who would replace their stepchildren with their own, as Ino did with Nephele's and Themisto's children. The replacement of legitimate heirs by illegitimate ones (often the sons of a god) necessarily involves adultery/incest (B), as in the stories of the several Clymenes, the bigamous marriages of Athamas to Ino (who disappeared) and Themisto, and the attempt by Sisyphus to avenge himself by seducing his niece.

Yet it is not merely the paradigmatic bundles which tie these myths together. Specific elements of content are also repeated. The result is that these myth cycles are like redundant statements in that they repeat the same patterns, varying only in details of plot and name. Genealogy is the most obvious connection whereby we may link myths into a series: we got to Jason and Medea via the stories of Jason's forebears, Sisyphus and his brothers, Salmoneus and Athamas. In fact, the genealogies seem almost freely invented as a method for linking stories that are related paradigmatically. We got to Sisyphus from Phaethon by several different routes: via the paradigm, via the theme of endless labor, which applies both to Helios and to Sisyphus, and most importantly by the identical name, Merope, of their significant female counterparts. There are other interconnections. Phaethon is a name that figures in the story of one of Sisyphus's descendants, for it is another name for Apsyrtos, and so on.

We got to Myrtilus from Phaethon and Glaucus not by paradigm alone but also by means of the sobriquet *taraxippos,* by means of genealogy (both were descendants of one of the Pleiades), and by means of a maternal name, Clymene, common to Myrtilus and Phaethon. The appearance of the name Merope in both lists of seven sisters, the Pleiades and the Heliades, and in the paradigmatic stories of the male relatives of these Meropes, Phaethon and Glaucus, enables us to claim a relationship between the Pleiades and the Heliades. More on them later.

The fund of these relationships in Greek mythology can be extended *ad libitum*. We have followed the ramifications suggested by the name Clymene, the mother of both Prometheus, who vied with Zeus (A) and saved or created mankind (G), and of Atlas, who was the father of the Pleiades. This or another Clymene was the mother of Phaethon and of the Heliades. Another Clymene was the mother of Atalanta, married off in a *contest* that Hippomenes (the Arcadians say his name was Melanion) won by rolling a golden apple (cf. Sisyphus, Helios). Yet another Clymene was the sister of Aerope, who was destined to be the wife of Atreus and who cuckolded him in strife (A) with his brother Thyestes—a struggle that involved the possession of a golden fleece (G) (or a live golden ram) as the sign of the true possessor (A4) of the kingdom. These brothers were the offspring of Pelops and Hippodameia. That same Clymene married Nauplius, whose anger was expressed by persuading Thyestes's son Aegisthus (Goatman) to *cuckold* Atreus's son Agamemnon in his absence and then to murder (A) him upon his return and to exile his only son (A), Orestes. But Orestes returned in disguise, claiming to be privy to news of Orestes's death. He joined with his sister Electra (Amber) after a recognition that involved a footprint (cf. Jason) and killed the usurper during a sacrifice. There is really no end to this pursuit, and Lévi-Strauss's metaphor taken from music (e.g., theme and variations, rounds and canons) seems apropos.

Now let us pursue a similar ramification of myth that can be built on the interconnections suggested by the name Merope. Here I will leave it to the reader to furnish the letters of the bundles from the paradigm. Cresphontes and Polyphontes were brothers (twins, to judge from the repetition of the *-phontes* element in their names). Cresphontes was married to a Merope, by whom he had three sons, but their uncle Polyphontes usurped the kingdom and Merope with it. Cresphontes and his two elder sons were killed, but the youngest, Aepytus, was sent into exile to be raised by his grandfather. Polyphontes offered a reward to anyone who could discover and murder him. When mature, Aepytus returned to his home in disguise, claiming to have knowledge of Aepytus's death. Merope was about to kill this disturbing guest as he slept, but an old man recognized him in the nick of time. Meanwhile, Polyphontes was so gladdened at the news of the supposed death of his rival that he offered sacrifice, at which the stranger was to assist. Aepytus, however, brought the sacrificial axe down on Polyphontes' head and regained his kingdom, which he ruled with justice and wisdom. He had a son named Glaucus. This myth has some connection with the myth of the house of the Theban king Laius, as we shall see, and it repeats closely the story of the return of Orestes as told by Euripides in his *Electra*.

Nycteus (Nightman) was regent of Thebes during the minority of Prince Laius (Lame?). Nycteus's daughter Antiope (an *-ope* name, like Merope), found pregnant, was forced to flee his anger despite her claim that her paramour had been Zeus. Nycteus killed himself, first appointing his (twin) brother Lycus (Wolfman, Twilightman) regent in his stead. Lycus pursued Antiope and brought her back to Thebes. Some say that Antiope was married to Lycus, who divorced her upon discovering her adultery. On the way home she gave birth to twins, Amphion and Zethus, but Lycus had them exposed. Rescued and raised in secret by herdsmen, the brothers recognized their mother just in time before killing her and then punished both her persecutor (Lycus's wife, Dirce) and the usurper Lycus. They themselves became rulers of Thebes and reigned with justice and wisdom.

Prince Laius had made his escape to the court of Pelops, where he distinguished himself as a charioteer. While teaching Pelops's bastard son Chrysippus (Goldhorse) to drive the chariot, Laius became enamored of him and kidnapped him (cf. the golden ram). Then mysteriously (because he possessed the sign of gold?) Laius was able to return to Thebes and regain his kingdom.

The childless Laius was warned by the oracle to remain so, because any son he might have would kill and replace him. Despite the warning, a son was born to him, Oedipus, whom he ordered exposed to die after piercing the infant's ankles with a pin (C-D), which some say gave rise to the child's name, Swollenfoot. Others say that the child was not exposed but was put into a chest and set afloat on the sea (E2), whence the etymology of his name (Swell or Billow). One source alleges that Oedipus was not Laius's child at all but the son of Helios.[49] This would imply an adulterous affair undertaken by Jocasta/Epikaste with Helios, making her role parallel to Clymene's, and Laius's to that of Merops, in the parentage of Phaethon.

In any case, the curse on Laius, which most sources attribute to his rape of Chrysippus and to Chrysippus's (suicidal) death in Thebes, began working itself out at the birth of Laius's unwanted son, who escaped the death Laius had planned for him. The common story is that shepherds on Mount Cithaeron handed him over to the king and queen of Corinth, who were childless. Their names were Polybos (a son of Hermes) and Periboia, or Merope, as she was also named. Another variant avers that this Merope found the chest in which Oedipus had been consigned to death. Yet another has it that Hippodameia found the chest and raised the foundling Oedipus, who at maturity returned to Thebes and killed Laius in revenge for the rape of his adoptive brother, Chrysippus.[50]

True to his heritage as a (step) child of a Merope, Oedipus's story must involve wreckage and replacement. But in this case the disastrous chariot ride belongs not to the son but to the father. At a fork in the road (A3), father and son encountered one another at a narrow pass. Laius's charioteer, whose name was Polyphontes, demanded that Oedipus step aside and make way for the king, but he would not. One of the king's horses trod on his foot (or a wheel ran over it), and either Laius or Polyphontes struck him on the head with the forked goad used to drive the team. Oedipus transfixed Polyphontes with his spear, flung Laius onto the road, wrapped him up in the reins, and drove the team onward, dragging the old man to his death. Laius and the usurper Polyphontes mentioned above are parallel in that an exiled male relative returns to murder them.

Another Merope figures in the myth of Orion. In one variant Orion was born somehow from the hide of a bull that had been sacrificed to the gods (compare the Golden Fleece and the bull that Minos refused to sacrifice). Rape, incest, or adultery are bound to occur in myths involving hides and fleeces and women named Merope, and this one is no exception. After having lost his first wife, Side, Orion went to Chios to woo Merope, daughter of King Oenopion (compare the name Oeno-maus and Oenomaus-Hippodameia). The king kept postponing the marriage, so Orion either raped Merope or seduced her. Oenopion had the hero blinded for this brazen deed (compare Oedipus). Orion was driven from the island or flung out on the beach (exposure motif). But Orion's real father, Poseidon, (as opposed to Hyrieus, his sup-posed father), had given him the power to walk on the waves (compare Oedipus and Perseus afloat in the chest and Myrtilus driving Oenomaus across the water), and he was able to make his way to Lemnos, where Hephaestus had his forge. Orion snatched away one of the god's help-ers to be his guide (compare the rape of Chrysippus) or Hephaestus willingly lent him as guide a certain Cedalion out of pity for his blind-ness. Orion hoisted Cedalion (whose name may mean phallus)[51] to his shoulders and told him to guide him to the point of the rising sun. There Helios took pity on the giant and restored his sight to him. Orion's vengeance upon Oenopion was, however, aborted because the latter had been hidden by divine intervention in an underground vault. We hear no more of Merope. Clearly, however, Orion's rise to sight and power is counterbalanced by Oenopion's eclipse, and Merope is some-how the fulcrum for these counterpoised changes of fortune. The theme of replacement is at least implicit throughout the story.

One other means of brachiation through the limbs of the *stemmata* of Greek myth would be to follow up names that have an equine ele-ment in their makeup (*-(h)ipp-* in Greek). In our several stories in-volving charioteers such as Glaucus, Salmoneus, Myrtilus, Oenomaus, Pelops, and Laius, we have already met two characters with names formed from this element—Chrysippus and Hippodameia (whose brother, incidentally, was named Leucippus [Whitehorse]). With her name, which we translate loosely as Lady Bronco Buster, we may com-pare the name Dioxippe, one of the Heliades. Most of the names given to these seven sisters have etymologies that we might expect of daugh-ters of the sun, name elements that indicate brightness, such as Helie, Aigle, Lampetie, Phoebe, and Aitherie. Only two sisters' names lack elements referring to brightness: Merope, the ramifications of whose name we have examined (though the etymology still remains to be dis-cussed), and Dioxippe. The latter name is quite similar etymologically to Hippodameia because it signifies "she who pursues horses."

One of the many children born to Pelops by Hippodameia was Pittheus, who became the king of Troezen. Pittheus had come there with his brother Troezen to share a kingdom (A2). This division of the kingdom was reflected on the divine plane, for both Athena and Poseidon wanted to hold sway there, and Zeus settled the quarrel by commanding that they share it equally. Pittheus and Troezen were interlopers, for there was a native dynasty, one of whose members, Saron, had drowned in the gulf, thus giving it his name (Saronic). When Troezen died, Pittheus took the kingdom, giving it his brother's name. Pittheus was famous for his wisdom and eloquence, living to a great age (G), surviving even his grandson Hippolytus (another horse name), about whom I will have more to say.

Pittheus's daughter was named Aethra, a name identical etymologi-cally to Aitherie, the fifth Heliad, mentioned above.[52] Her hand was not subject to being won in a *contest* in any extant variant of the myth I can find, but some elements of the story are like those from the Oenomaus-Hippodameia story. Bellerephon is said to have come her way as a suitor just after having bridled Pegasus for the first time (compare the motif of Pelops's divine team of horses) and was sent away mysteriously without winning her as his bride.[53] Furthermore, the heir that she later did bear was born in the house of her father, Pittheus, and was therefore raised as Pittheus's son, perhaps adumbrating an incestuous relationship between father and daughter. Aegeus, to whom Aethra was eventually betrothed, was childless and had sought help from the oracle, which replied that he should not untie the mouth of his bulging wineskin until he reached the highest point of Athens, lest he die one day of grief. This sounds like an oracle *prohibiting* the begetting of a child (compare Laius), and indeed, in the end Aegeus died because of his son's misdemeanor of forgetting to hoist the sail of the right color, just as Laius died by the unwittingly parricidal blow delivered by Oedipus. Furthermore, Aegeus did not willingly consort with Aethra but had to be persuaded by wine, just as Laius remained celibate until Jocasta plied him with alcohol. The etymology of Aegeus, as Goatman, given above, is in dispute among the ancient sources, some of which say that it means Seaswell (compare Oedipus).[54]

The dubious paternity of Theseus, whether he was sired by the mortal Aegeus or by the immortal Poseidon, is typical of the stories we have been examining, from that of Phaethon to that of Oedipus.[55] The implication, of course, is that the mother had consorted with a deity instead of her husband (sometimes the deity took on the guise of the husband, as Zeus did to seduce Alcmene) (B). Interesting in Aethra's case is the location of her two-man one-night stand. After lying with Aegeus, so go most variants, she received a dream from Athena, which enjoined her to wade across (the time and tide being right) to the island of Sphairia, to offer libations to the ghost of Pelops's charioteer, Sphairos (Sphereman). While wading, or while on the beach in the temple of Athena, Aithra met the avatar of Poseidon, her divine bridegroom.[56]

Theseus's divine parentage proved to be a curse to him, just as did Phaethon's, for Poseidon had granted him an unretractable wish (actually three wishes)—a wish he used unwisely, to cause the death of his own son Hippolytus. Toward the end of Theseus's career, his young wife, Phaedra (a brightness name, like that of her sister before her, Ariadne-Aridela),[57] leveled a Potiphar's-wife accusation against

Hippolytus (whose name means "he who sets loose the horses," or Stampeder). Theseus, in quick anger, first exiled him and then, recalling Poseidon's promise, called upon the god to send a dangerous beast across the boy's path. Hippolytus's fatal chariot ride upon a narrow path beset by beast(s) recalls that of Phaethon. His reins became entangled on the branches of a barren olive (F), and his chariot careened into a pile of rocks and was smashed (C/D). Hippolytus himself, entangled in the reins, was dashed against the tree trunk and then upon the rocks, and was finally dragged to death. Some sources aver that Poseidon caused an earthquake and then sent a flood to finish off the lad. The virgins of Troezen used to mourn Hippolytus (compare the Heliades and Phaethon) on the day before their marriage, offering up to him a lock of their hair. At the behest of Artemis, it is said, Asclepius used his power to call Hippolytus back to life (G). In any case, in Troezen the constellation Auriga (the Charioteer) is known as his avatar (compare Phaethon and Myrtilus).⁵⁸

Theseus's own career is paradigmatic to a T. Aegeus left his sandals (C) (compare Jason) and his sword (D) hidden under a great stone that, he suggested, only his true son could roll away in order to procure the tokens (C-D). The winning of those tokens and their presentation to Aegeus in Athens involved Theseus in many a proud adventure, most of which grew by accretion onto his legend and so are not germane to us here, save that he struggled with Aegeus's other son, Medus (by Medea), for the heirship. The later adventures of Theseus serve as a paradigmatic model in chapter 2.

There are a few final interconnections. Theseus's failure to raise the white sail is an image of solar disaster (too light and hot, too dark and cold) also symbolized by Phaethon's career in the chariot. Aegeus's suicide at this juncture parallels the death of Oedipus's father, Laius, at a moment when a vehicle came to a fatal junction. Aegeus's drowning in a sea that is then named for him is a type parallel to Myrtilus's drowning. Myrtilus, like Phaethon, was a hapless charioteer, and the story of Myrtilus involves the replacement of a father figure by a hero of a younger generation in which a girl is reluctantly exchanged. Both the Oedipus story (Laius killed, Jocasta taken as a prize) and the Theseus story (Minos killed, Ariadne taken, and his marriage later to Phaedra) are similar in this respect.

SUMMARY

The Replacement Paradigm, developed from Indo-European traditions, was applied in this chapter to the same body of South American mythic material that Lévi-Strauss used in his work *The Raw and the Cooked*. While acknowledging that some of these myths involve a dichotomy between (irregular) nature and (regularizing) culture, we found that the application of the paradigm to them yielded insights beyond those given by the Lévi-Straussian methodologies. The South American natives seem to have composed (independently, of course), myths in which the same chief elements are bundled together as in the myths of the far-flung descendants of the Indo-Europeans.

The paradigm was applied, in due course, to a body of Greek myth, commencing with the story of Phaethon for its obvious connections with replacement, with the right- and wrong-running of the sun, with disaster, and with subsequent re-creation. The Phaethon myth, it was discovered, is merely one in a constellation of paradigmatic myths in Greek mythology—myths that furthermore can be interrelated on grounds from outside the paradigm. These grounds are (1) common names: the several Phaethons, Meropes, Merops's, and Clymenes; (2) relationships between the Heliades (Phaethon's sisters) and the Pleiades, including the repetition of name types (Merope-Sterope, Dioxippe-Hippodameia-Hippolytus); and (3) significant objects such as the *taraxippos*. The wider constellation of myths includes the stories of Sisyphus, Salmoneus, Athamas, Jason, Glaucus, Oenomaus, Myrtilus, Pelops, Hippodameia, Atreus, Thyestes, Aithra, Theseus, Hippolytus, and so on.

CHAPTER V

ZEUS AND HIS OPPONENTS

At last, the reader must be thinking, we have come to the stories about Zeus, his forebears, and his antagonists. The experience has been deferred because these myths exist in a stupefying number of versions and variants, and without the practice in analysis by means of the Replacement Paradigm gained in the previous chapters, our attempt to find a coherent path through some of them would result in complete confusion. The reader with even a casual knowledge of the histories of the Titans and the Olympians would recognize within them many instances of the motifs of replacement. Even after he had established himself as the eternal king of Olympus, Zeus was the subject of myths of replacement. The sequence of the dynastic succession Ouranos–Kronos–Zeus reflects the classic three phases of the replacement myth (A3)—what Aeschylus calls the *trigeron mythos*[1]—and upon it were modeled stories of heroic dynasties of three generations such as Atreus–Agamemnon–Orestes and Laius–Oedipus–Eteocles (and Polynices) (A3). The stories of these dynasties involve a disloyal or mischievous woman in the first generation (A5); incest, adultery or suppositious offspring in the second generation (B); and sibling or cousin rivalry in the third generation (A2). Each of the myths involves a general destruction on a vast scale: Titanomachy, Troy, and a plague and destruction at Thebes (F). In two of these three myths, the world order changes: Atlas is forced to support the revolving heavens as a punishment for being a rebellious Titan, and the world reverses the direction of its revolution as the result of Atreus's crimes against Thyestes (F4). Stability or a Golden Age is a recurrent theme here as well: Zeus's reign persists, the Golden Age of Kronos follows him to retirement in Elysium, Orestes's bones become a source of solace and power for the Spartans, and Oedipus's burial site (or his place of apotheosis) is fraught with supernatural power for whatever land possesses it.

Even about Zeus there was an oracle to the effect that a son more mighty than he would replace his father; an oracle that was averted when Zeus cooled his lust for Thetis and married her to the mortal Pelius, from whom came Achilles, a son greater indeed but nevertheless mortal. In fact, the other tripartite dynasties technically do not end in the third generation (though the sons of Orestes and Eteocles are shadowy figures with no great role in myth). Nonetheless, the *trigeron mythos* (A3), with its story of three generations, is a permanent feature of these stories of replacement.

OURANOS AND KRONOS

The beginning of the dynasty of Zeus was found in the union of Gaia (Earth) with the Ouranos (Colored-Sky), whom she had made equal to herself so as to conceal herself in every direction.[2] Ouranos, with whom Gaia mates to produce the Titans, is not the god of the sky or "sky" as we know it. The name, which only later became a common noun, refers to that particular aspect of the sky in which the stars are manifested and disappear. This is not Nightsky but the sky between Aither (Brightair) and Night[3]—the colored sky of twilight in which heliacal risings and settings take place. This is Sky, the progenitor, in whom phenomena are first manifest and into whom they disappear. It is due to this role that Ouranos is considered one of the original procreators. A similar conception is found in Egyptian mythology. The female deity of the sky, Nut, was thought to bear anew each day the morning sun, Ra-Khepri (in this aspect known as Bennu). The redness of the morning sky was said to be due to the blood she lost during parturition. In some representations of Nut, she is seen to bear forth the sun from her lap in the morning (Nut's morning aspect was Hathor) and swallow it into her mouth in the evening.[4]

Earth gave birth to the twelve Titans (E8) after submitting herself in love to Ouranos. But as soon as any of them was born, Ouranos hid him away from sight in a dark place of earth (E1); he did not allow his children to come up into the light. This mythologem seems to derive directly from Ouranos's role as progenitor-and-concealer of phenomena. Celestial "children" are "born" at their heliacal rising, coming up from earth's limb, from the hidden places ("a womb") beneath and achieve visibility in the colored twilight of Ouranos, who, as it were, summons them forth. Conversely, they "die" or are hidden by Ouranos at their heliacal setting: he pushes them back into the dark places of Earth. Yet in myth, which by its nature must account for things in terms of human motives, hiding becomes a willful crime. Hiding the children is not merely concealment but a monstrous act. Ouranos is depicted as a fiend who rejoices in his crime and who is guilty not merely of shameful deeds (*aeikea erga*) but of the worst kind of moral fault (*atasthalos*) and outrageous behavior (*lôbê*).[5] Crime has its cultural consequence— punishment.

The castration of his father, undertaken eagerly by Kronos, is the enactment of the Oedipal fantasy; he replaces his father's sexual potency with his own (A1). In terms of the paradigm, castration is the perfect denouement to the career of Ouranos. The old and cast off becomes substance for regeneration in the generation of Aphrodite from the fallen members (F becomes G). The toothed sickle Kronos used for the deed is the most fundamental tool of the ancient harvest, and the verb used to describe the act is *amaô*, "to reap." Kronos threw his father's members behind him, a magical act used at sowing time (compare the sowing of stones over the shoulder of Deucalion to produce a new race of humanity). Finally, the sprouting of the Erinyes, Giants, and Ash-tree nymphs from the fallen seed is said to have taken place in the circling of the seasons. Something hidden is set free and fertility is regained in the right season; the world is running right.

The wounding of the monster-god in a vital place is a commonplace of the paradigm that finds expression in tamer traditions as laming or the breaking of bones (F5). A wound in the foot or a joint out of place reflects the idea of the world gone awry. But the notion that the wound is the source of regeneration is peculiar to the theme of castration. It can be synopsized thus: The tree of life bore good fruit when the universe ran right. When the old god went mad, the good fruits failed. The old god was wounded in the genitals, resulting in his replacement by another and better god. The seed falling from the wound fertilized the earth just as does the seed falling from the great tree itself. The universe runs well again.

The linkage of this complex of ideas is established for the peoples of Indo-European derivation by a complex of extant lexical items. The oak was the Indo-Europeans' sacred tree, an object of cult worship among several of the descendent peoples—sacred to the Greek Zeus, for example, and to the Celtic druids. These people made a fast connection between the acorn, the fruit of the oak, and the testes or the penile head; hence, in several of the daughter languages the word for acorn and the word for testicle are the same, (e.g., Lithuanian *gile,* which furthermore has a derivative, *gilendra,* meaning simultaneously "fecundity, happiness, good crops.")[6] Compare Latin *glans,* "acorn, ball, penis head," and the related *iuglans,* "Jupiter's glans," the usual denotation of which is "walnut." So, too, the Greek *balanos,* which means "acorn" or "glans." The semantic connection between oak trees, fertility, and the male sexual organs is not just a loose one based upon a similarity of shape and some vague notion linking phallic shapes with fertility. This fact is evident from a third meaning of *balanos*: "pivot point." The connection is based in the paradigm: pivot point equates with the right running of the universe.

Kronos learned from Earth and Ouranos that he was destined to be replaced by his own son (A1). This oracle gives the ostensible reason for his decision to swallow all of his children, but in fact their hiding and that of the Titans (offspring of Ouranos) is one and the same mythologem (E). Hiding is a common motif in the stories of many of the heroes of Greek mythology, where it appears as birth in a cave and paradoxically as infant exposure (the unwanted child is hidden from the sight of the father and left to die alone and unrecognized). In such stories the father's attempt to intervene in the oracle that predicts his replacement is in vain, for the son survives and grows to maturity through a twist of fate, a kindness, a stratagem, or a lie. Sons raised up in caves have wild animals or strange beings in attendance, often in the company of a twin, a sibling, or a half-sibling. Such also was the birth and nurture of Zeus, destined to replace his father, Kronos. Prodigious Earth took Zeus from Rhea into broad Crete to nourish and raise him. Broad Crete is simply Mother Earth (Gaia of the Titan story) identified as a specific locality: Earth's fosterage of Zeus is a direct substitute for that of Rhea, who is herself an earth goddess. Ouranos's Titans were kept in secret places of the earth; Zeus was concealed in a cave. In distress at her Titanic burden, prodigious Gaia kept groaning inside. Rhea, unhappy at Kronos's treatment of his children, was gripped by incurable suffering. Gaia's twelve Titans match Rhea's six Kronides. The myths of replacement involving Ouranos–Kronos and Kronos–Zeus are essentially the same vis-à-vis both the hiding motif and birth from Mother Earth.

The complex of ideas already mentioned permits the identification of the stone Rhea gave to Kronos to swallow in place of Zeus with the dismembered organ fallen from Ouranos. After his victory over the Titans, Zeus took the stone as a reminder of his birth and set it up at Delphi, where it was called "the navel of the world" (*omphalos gês*). We may compare this with the shape and function of the *balanos* pivot point, alias glans. Organ and stone are antitypes of the archetypical acorn from the sacred tree. We have seen that such stones may serve as tokens of a hero's birth—a monument left by the father which the hero must move to recover the symbols of the father's manhood. Such stones are also symbols of the turning of the universe—the millstone grinding out plenty in its right running, and the maelstrom the mill grinding salt or the fruitless labor of Sisyphus in the wrong sky.[7] These elements come together in a Germanic folktale concerning a monstrous wolf that swallowed (E) an entire set of siblings except one, who had taken refuge in a clock (I). While the wolf was sleeping, the survivor came out of his hiding place, slit open the belly of the wolf, and replaced his still-living siblings (E10) with stones (E9). Unquenchable thirst (F) drove the wolf to the well (C) for a drink, where the weight of the stones dragged him to his death by drowning (E). The wolf represents the monstrous parent whose greedy devouring of his offspring has sent the world awry (F) and rendered him unfit to rule. Right running (C-D) is invested in a chosen son (AI). The stones are the empty labor of a universe moving to no accord, useless appendages, like the genitals of an outworn father, bringing ruin. Swallowing (E, F) precedes release (G); thirst (F) leads to a well that brings not slaking (C/D) but rather drowning (E). The father hid away the child who was to replace him, but the right-running universe (symbolized by the clock) fostered the child, who returned to eclipse his father.

Like some heroes whose stories we have examined, Zeus was connected to goats. He had goatish beginnings. The cave Dicte, where he was nourished, was on Aegean Hill named after Aex (the Goat). He was nursed by, among others, Amaltheia, a goat nymph, and he shared her udder with his foster brother Aigipan (Goat Pan). After the Titanomachy Zeus repaid Amaltheia's kindness by setting her in the heavens as the Goat, Capricorn, and by taking one of her horns and rendering it a horn of plenty (Cornucopia), which is always filled with whatever food or drink its owner may desire (G). Furthermore, Zeus's victory over the Titans is said to have been dependent upon his Aegis, an emblematic shield of goatskin.

There are various accounts about the origin of the Aegis and the genealogies surrounding it. It is said (1) that it came from a pet goat named Aex that belonged to Amaltheia; (2) that this Aex was a daughter of Helios who was ugly of face (like the Aegis) but beautiful of body and who was herself the nurse of Zeus; (3) that Aex was the wife of Pan, but Zeus consorted with her to produce Aigipan; (4) that Aex or Aigipan was catasterized as the star Capra (modern Capella), chief star of the constellation Auriga, the Charioteer.[8] The relevance of these observations will become clear later.

HADES AND KRONOS

During the Titanomachy, Zeus needed assistance, and on Gaia's advice he called up his hundred-handed auxiliaries—Obriareus, Kottos, and Gyes—"into the light" from the hiding place within Earth where their

father had placed them.[9] Here we have another variant of the motif of
the hiding of the children of Earth by their father and their subsequent
liberation. Once Kronos and the other Titans had been defeated, these
same minions of Zeus hurled the hapless vanquished Titans "beneath
the wide-pathed earth." It is as if they, now liberated, needed to replace
themselves with some other captives to satisfy the demands of a regular
cycle of bringing to light and hiding. Indeed, some of the Titans (before their fall) are described in brightness terms: Phoebe, one of whose
children, Asterie, is also a heavenly light; Hyperion, whose children are
all deities of the sky: Eos (Dawn), Helios, and Selene (Moon); and
Eurybia, called bright goddess,[10] wife of the Titan Krios, to whom she
bore a son, Astraios (Starman). Likewise, and parallel to the Titans
whom they commit to hell, Obriareus, Kottos, and Gyes themselves are
given a brightness epithet: "gleaming."[11]

The place *from which* Obriareus, Kottos, and Gyes were summoned
had a proper name, Erebus. In Hesiod's account, Erebus, personified
as a god, fathered upon Nyx (Night), his wife, two children Aither
(Brightair) and Hemera (Day): light from dark. On the other hand,
the place *to which* the Titans were sent was given the proper name
Tartarus.[12] Erebus and Tartarus, however, can be seen to represent the
same place through a common middle term applied to them both—
zophos. Zeus's three minions, whom he brought to the light from
Erebus, were said to have lain in bondage under the misty *zophos.*[13]
Tartarus, too, is haven for the "misty *zophos,*" under which the Titans
are kept hidden.[14]

Another epithet, *euroeis,* links Tartarus (and with it Erebus) to
Hades, for *euroeis* is an epithet of Hades in the Homeric poems. The
usual translation of *euroeis* is "moldy" or "dank," and in later contexts it
(and its parent noun) do have this meaning—probably from the association with graves, with Hades as an intermediary idea. Originally,
however, it was a color term. It is applied to "gulf of the sea" (which
one cannot think of as moldy) and to an old man's hair. A key context
for the aboriginal meaning of the word occurs in the *Iliad,* where
Poseidon is said to have brought on an earthquake so great that Hades
(here called Aidoneus) is afraid that his abode will be made visible to
mortals and immortals alike—his abode, "hateful to the gods, horrible

to see and *euroenta*."[15] The syntax of the passage dictates that either the place is horrible to see and hateful to the gods because it is *euroenta* or it is hateful to the gods because it is horrible to see and *euroenta*.[16] In either case, *euroenta* refers to a visual stimulus, probably meaning grey (as the old man's hair) or shrouded. The latter is perhaps the better alternative, for *euroeis* is often linked with *eeroeis* "misty," *zophos*.

But is this shrouded, misty place (call it Erebus, Hades, or Tartarus) located at the center of the earth? Such a location seems to be implied in passages such as the one in the *Theogony* asserting that as far as Ouranos is from Earth, so far is Earth from Tartarus below: "a bronze anvil falling nine nights and days from the sky would land upon earth on the tenth and, in turn, one would land in Tartarus after falling nine days and nights from earth."[17] But the direction to Tartarus seems ambiguous in some passages: Zeus does not give a whit for Hera's anger even if she should pout and withdraw to Tartarus: "not even if you should arrive to the outermost boundaries of earth and sea where Iapetos and Kronos have their seats, enjoying no ray of Helios-Hyperion, and deep Tartarus is all around."[18]

The term *zophos* definitely refers to an aspect of the western sky near the horizon at twilight, especially over water but also over land,[19] a phenomenon at the limit of visibility which does not permit the horizon line to be seen; it is the region of perpetual *aer*, a Turneresque light that may be the norm all year around in England but which in Greece appears only in the evening and in winter.[20] A passage from the *Odyssey* makes the direction and time of day for observing this phenomenon quite clear: The sun has set and a speaker says, "the light has already departed under the *zophos*."[21] Another passage makes it clear that *zophos* is a condition of the twilight sky as well.[22] A third passage, from the close of the *Odyssey,* in which Hermes is said to lead the souls of the suitors to Hades, links these ideas into a more-or-less concrete geography: "Hermes the guide led the way for them along the hazy (*euroenta*) pathways. They passed the streams of Ocean and the rock Leucas (Whiterock), that is past the gates of the Sun and the realm of dreams. Then they came to the meadow of Asphodel where dwell the souls, phantoms of those who toil."[23] He is leading them along the path of the sun westward (or possibly eastward) to Erebus-Hades-Tartarus.

Passing far enough in the east-west direction leads one to the gates of the sun, beyond which lies Erebus-Hades-Tartarus, indifferently gotten to by going far enough westward or eastward. Ouranos consigned his children to this place, and here the hundred-handed ones were concealed. Disappearance or hiding under the earth, being swallowed or hidden by the monstrous father, drowning in Ocean, being produced or hidden by Ouranos, and going to Hades are all reflections of an archetype that is the phenomenon of setting on the horizon. Conversely, being vomited up, rising from Ocean's bath, and being recalled from Tartarus refer to the rising of some body from invisibility into the sky.[24] Such things as can disappear and then reappear at a later date are the Greek equivalent of some of the amphibious beings of Bororo myth.

But what of the seeming dichotomy that makes Kronos at once the denizen of Tartarus (with Iapetos and presumably the other Titans), a place where no ray of Helios-Hyperion rejoices them, nor any breeze,[25] and also sovereign over the denizens of another world, variously called Elysium and Isles of the Blessed?[26] As we have seen, all these places— the home of Zeus's monstrous minions, Tartarus, Hades, Elysium, the Isles of the Blessed—are said to be situated at the limits or ends of the earth.[27] It sounds as if in their aboriginal conception they were all one and the same place. In the *Theogony,* Tartarus is described as the *temenos* (sacred precinct) of some fallen lord, for it has a gate and is surrounded by encircling walls. It is home for at least two denizens, Night and Day, who reside there alternately, greeting one another at its threshold, one outside, passing over the earth, while the other stays inside, waiting for the time of her journey.[28] The same conception is found in Pindar's *Threnoi*: "for them the might of the sun illuminates the night below."[29] Day is resident in Tartarus-Elysium while night holds sway on earth and vice versa, because after the sun passes off the face of the earth to the far west, it gives its light to a second world. Common altars dedicated to Kronos and Helios together have been found at Olympia and in third-century A.D. Beirut.[30]

In Hesiod's description of Tartarus, Atlas stands in front of the gates of Night's house, bearing up broad Ouranos on his head and tireless hands. The world support is sometimes conceived of as pillars steadied by Atlas, but often Atlas is himself the pillar. The same conception is found in the Caryatids of Greek architecture. The pillars of Atlas and their nearby cousins, the pillars of Herakles (recall that Herakles relieved Atlas of his burden for a moment), are the gates of a temple far to the west—one and the same, we surmise, as the gates of the sun through which Hermes passed with the souls of the suitors. This is the picture that Pindar gives of the realm of Kronos, the blessed isles: "Those who have managed three times, while living on either side, to keep their soul completely free of wrong-doing complete the path of Zeus unto the high tower of Kronos where the daughter-breezes of Ocean blow about them and golden blooms blow flaming."[31] Kronos's tower at the rim of the world, bathed in a golden ambience, is the same as Atlas with his pillars bearing up the world in the west, and these must be antitypes of the archetypal *temenos* of Hades described by Hesiod.

Are not, then, Pindar's pilgrims to Kronos's tower parallel to those who journey to Tartarus? Surely it is the same journey as that guided by Hermes at the close of the *Odyssey*—past the streams of Ocean, past Whiterock, past the gates of the sun to the meadow of Asphodel.[32]

Tartarus-Hades-Erebus and the Blessed Isles–Elysium[33] seem to be one and the same in conception—a place where outworn or unwanted gods and souls are hidden from earth but itself an alter-earth illuminated by an alter-sun. It also echoes the banished Golden Age, which once held sway on earth in the time when Kronos was king[34]—that is, when the world ran right—for in Elysium there is always a fair Zephyr blowing, fruit ripens three times a year, and work is unknown.[35]

But if Hades and Elysium are parallel places, then must not Hades (the god) and Elysium's king, Kronos, be parallel too? The two underworld deities could then correspond to Zeus *chthonios theos* (Zeus of the Underworld), whose upperworld counterpart is Zeus *hypsistos theos* (Zeus on High).[36] One aspect of Hades is "the god-who-cannot-be-looked-upon"; images of this god depict him with his head facing backward. Similarly, Kronos is often depicted with a veiled head. These matters are themselves shrouded in layers of obscurity: in *Iliad* 8 (cited above), we read that Kronos and Iapetos possess seats of judgment someplace in Tartarus; in *Odyssey* 4, Rhadymanthes rules Elysium, while in other sources Kronos holds sway there as judge. In some depictions of the place Hades, King Hades himself is judge of the dead, whereas in other sources it is Minos, brother of Rhadymanthes.[37] It looks as if at one time there was a conception of a single place with two judges which later came to be thought of as two (vaguely) distinct places, each with its own judge.

In any case, Kronos and Hades were both hosts for the dead, a function recognized in Hades' alias, Polydegmon (Receiver of Many). As the host of guests who never leave (i.e., a hoarder of souls), Hades was identified with the god of wealth, Pluto. All persons, animals, and things devolve, eventually, unto him. Persephone, daughter of the deity of fertile earth, Demeter, was one of his involuntary guests. This mistress of plenty was forced to spend part of each year in the underworld as Hades' queen. In this regard Hades might well be called the god of (hidden) treasure, wealth underground.

Kronos, too, was a god connected with fertility and plenty. He is often depicted carrying a sickle or a pruning hook. In Olympia, rites of the Kronia were celebrated at the spring equinox. In Athens this occurred during the spring month of Elaphebolion, at which time sacrificial cakes were offered up to the god. And like Hades, Kronos was connected with death. Numerous tumuli in Sicily were dedicated to him, and visitors to the cave of Trophonius (a mystery trip involving death and rebirth) made first offerings to Kronos.[38] Perhaps Hades and Kronos were both thought of as winter kings, gods of fertility-locked-up, symbolizing the planted seed before it has sprouted into the green shoot, which is sent above ground.

The myth of the hero Tantalus brings into focus the parallelism of Hades and Kronos in their opposition to Zeus. Pindar refers to Tantalus's son Pelops as the "Kronian one."[39] Coins of Himera in Sicily feature Kronos on one side and Pelops on the other. The founders of Pelops's line (the parents of Tantalus) were said to be Zeus (Tmolus, Lord of Oak Mountain, Dodonian Zeus) and Pluto (cf. Hades, but here a feminine name), a daughter of Kronos and Rhea. Hades' name in feminine form, sharing with Zeus the parentage of Tantalus's forebears, illuminates a feature of the Replacement Paradigm. The unfaithful female is a rival to her husband from the outset (B = A), and she produces a line of offspring, one of whose male members will challenge the paterfamilias.

Tantalus, indeed, had a Kronian career; he was cast into Hades for his crimes. He challenged divinity and was punished. Beloved by the gods, he enjoyed their highest favors, including dining on ambrosia and drinking nectar in their company (G) (compare the Golden Age of Kronos).[40] But he betrayed their confidence and shared out the gift of deathlessness (the use of ambrosia and nectar) with ordinary mortals (compare again the Golden Age). To test the gods' wisdom (or as some say, to repay their kindness), Tantalus prepared his own feast, to which all the gods were invited. The main course was the flesh of his own son Pelops (compare Kronos's cannibalism). Demeter, alone of all the gods, distracted as she was by the detention in Hades of her daughter Persephone, was deceived into eating a portion of Pelops's flesh, the shoulder joint (C/D).[41] One of the gods restored Pelops to life, replacing his missing joint (C-D) with one of ivory.[42] Just as the swallowed children of Kronos were regurgitated to new life, so Pelops, partially swallowed, was restored to life and repaired with a gleaming new part. This is the opposite of hiding, and with it we compare that of Persephone, who was only partially hidden in Hades, for she was freed to spend part of each year above ground.[43]

Tantalus and Sisyphus were the most notorious denizens of Hades. As eternal punishment for his having distributed the foods of immortality to mortals, Tantalus was tempted by a constant and abundant supply of food and drink (G, the Golden Age), always suspended just out of reach (F). He was not able to quench his thirst or stay his hunger, eternally laboring in vain in the attempt. This is the plight of an agricultural people in the face of natural disaster, and it is comparable to Sisyphus's slavery to his boulder, with which we have compared the labor of the sun. Tantalus, too, was beset by a boulder, ever hanging over his head like the sword of Damocles. Their mutual predicament is that of humankind, ever attempting in vain to master nature, only to find surpluses wasted before the eternal vagaries of dismal economics.

It is tempting to surmise that Tantalus and Sisyphus are heroic reflections of the divine Hades-Kronos, gods banished to the underworld for having broken a taboo: letting people have plenty without work. This would be the other side of the coin to the explanation of man's fall as due to his rape of Mother Earth.

Tantalus may well have had a divine archetype in Greek mythology who was a direct opponent of Zeus. The name of Tantalus's wife was Dione, the same as that of a consort of Zeus (perhaps prior to Hera). The common name of their spouses links Tantalus to Zeus through rivalry. It also links Tantalus with the Titans through affinity. This Dione is said by Hyginus (Fab. 83) to be a Pleiad, a daughter of the Titan Atlas, who was, with his siblings, punished for siding with Kronos and the Titans against Zeus. Furthermore, a Cretan myth about Tantalus ties him to the archenemy of Zeus, Typhoeus. Tantalus and Pandareos, son of Merops, conspired to keep the wonderful golden (G) hound (a symbol of kingly or divine office) of Zeus away from its owner (A4). Then Tantalus plotted to cheat even Pandareos and keep the hound for himself (A). Zeus turned Pandareos to stone and then flung Mount Sipylos down upon Tantalus. It is as if Pandareos became the stone mountain that bore down on Tantalus in Hades. In any case, the punishment is comparable to the one that Zeus exacted upon his archenemy Typhoeus.

Furthermore, Tantalus was the ruler of a mighty city on the flanks of Mount Sipylos, which sank and disappeared.[44] Did it sink Atlantis-like into the underworld? An exile from heaven and likely denizen of a banished kingdom, Tantalus, who was confined to Hell, bears a likeness both to Kronos and to Hades.

If behind the Kronian Tantalus we infer the existence of a challenger to Zeus, Hades is parallel to that unknown antagonist. Hades and Zeus were both suitors of their own sister, Demeter. Compare this to the existence of the two Diones. This information does not come to us in a direct way from the corpus of Greek mythology; some of these facts were obfuscated because they were likely ritual secrets of the Eleusinian mysteries, yet we can infer much of what was hidden. A hunter named Iasios coupled with Demeter in the furrows of a field. Zeus saw them in the act and blasted the youth with lightning. The alias of this hunter is divulged by the name of the posthumous son born to him by Demeter: Plutus, a variation of Pluto, Hades' second name. We can conclude that Iasios and Hades are parallel. Iasios-Hades, therefore, was Zeus's rival for Demeter (A4). The story of Persephone and her rape by Hades is a version of this story. Persephone is an alter-form of her mother, Demeter. The parallelism is made complete by the existence of a story about Zeus and Persephone in which Zeus raped her after

having taken the form of a serpent.[45] Their son was Dionysus. Both
father and son were given the title Zagreus (Great Hunter), which
evokes the occupation of Iasios.

ZEUS'S ENEMIES

Stories about Zeus's other enemies can be viewed as versions of his
antagonism toward Hades-Kronos. Tartarus (Hades-Kronos?) was said
to have fathered upon Gaia a monster who was powerful enough to
have overthrown the gods and rule the universe. This was Typhon.[46]
Typhon made a direct assault on Olympus (D1), whereat all the gods
but Zeus fled to Egypt. Zeus fought back with thunderbolt and sickle.
They wrestled on Mount Casius in Syria (seat of Zeus, an eastern
Olympus). Typhon took the sickle (the weapon of Kronos) and cut out
the sinews of Zeus's hands and feet (F5). He pulled the helpless god
through the sea (E2) and hid him in the Corycian cave (E1). He hid the
sinews under a *bear*skin (C-D, 1),[47] but Hermes and Aigipan stole the
sinews and restored Zeus's strength (G4). Zeus procured some new
thunderbolts (D1) and, riding a winged chariot (C-D), flung them
against Typhon, driving him to Mount Nysa.[48] There the Fates persuaded Typhon to eat mortal food by saying that it would strengthen
him, but of course it had the opposite effect (F6). His waning strength
was still sufficient to hurl a few mountains at Zeus (F1). Typhon was
struck by thunderbolts, and his blood spurted over the mountain on
which he stood (E3), giving it its name, Mount Haemus (Blood Mountain). Typhon fled through the sea (E2) to Sicily, but Zeus followed
him there and buried him under Mount Aetna (E1), where his fulmi-
nations can still be heard and seen (F1).[49]

Zeus was challenged by still other beings, including the four sons of
Iapetos (Kronos's hellmate) and Clymene: Menoitios, Prometheus,
Atlas, and Epimetheus. Of Menoitios we don't hear much; he was
simply blasted with a lightning bolt and sent to Tartarus during the
Titanomachy. The other three can be paired in one way or another.
Prometheus can be linked with Atlas[50] owing to the fact that they are
posted at opposite ends of the world, denizens neither of Earth nor of

Hades but of the boundary between them. One stood supporting the world on his head and shoulders (or propping up the pillars that supported it) (C-D, 1). The other was pinned to a rock (C-D), with an eagle pecking at his self-renewing liver (C-D, F7) for a period of thirty thousand years (G10). Prometheus is naturally paired with Epimetheus because they both play a role in the story of Pandora and because of their similar names. The pairings suggest A1 of the Replacement Paradigm, and the figures, as we will see, are, individually and in pairs, enemies of Zeus.

Prometheus, as the subject of the famous story in which he champions mankind, comes into direct conflict with Zeus. The Titan's punishment, being nailed to a rock for thirty thousand (A3) years is the consequence of his action, but I will defer the discussion of this crime and punishment until later in the chapter. Another story about Promethean confrontations with Zeus links Prometheus to the Zeus-Kronos conflict. As creator god, Prometheus was wont to present his creatures to Zeus for inspection. But one time his creation was so glorious, excelling all others, that the god kept him back. Eros saw through the subterfuge and reported the facts to Zeus. Hermes was sent to induce the lad, named Phaenon (Gleaming One), to come over to Zeus and be made immortal. He did so, and he was translated into the sky as Zeus's star, the planet Jupiter. So goes the version of Heraclides Ponticus reported in Hyginus.[51] Cicero, however, and others state that Phaenon is the name of Kronos's planet (Saturn) and that Phaethon is that of Zeus (Jupiter).[52]

We can see here, perhaps only in silhouette, the outlines of a story of replacement. Phaenon is a *rival* to Zeus, being at least his equal in terms of immortality and glory. Although no element in the story's plot manifests this relationship, the curious mix-up in the names does. Cicero repeats the generally known identities between the mythological gods and the names of the planets: Zeus's star, Jupiter, was called Phaethon while Kronos's star, Saturn, was called Phaenon.[53] The reversal of the two names in Heracleides adumbrates a variant myth in which there was replacement or attempted replacement, the brilliance of Kronos in trial with the brilliance of Zeus. This variant of the Kronos-Zeus conflict must have fastened upon celestial facts, the relative brightness of the planets Saturn and Jupiter. In some lost version, Phaenon (the alter-

Kronos) challenged Zeus so as to retake his former glory and attach his own name to Zeus's star.

Prometheus the Titan was the natural rival of Zeus the Olympian, even though some variants of the Titanomachy story say that Prometheus foresaw the outcome and took the part of Zeus. Furthermore, Prometheus is a creator god, rivaling Zeus, creating mankind, as some say, and bringing forth from Zeus's Athena the goddess of wisdom, for which favor he was taught all of the creative arts. Furthermore, Prometheus himself possessed secret knowledge about the mother who might bear so great a son to Zeus as to rival and replace his father. All of these facts make Prometheus the likely possessor of the secret boy whose brilliance might outshine Zeus were he to become antagonistic. Of course, the story, as we have it, is resolved in Zeus's favor and the rationalization reverses the otherwise universally attested identification of the stars' names with their corresponding deities so that Phaenon can become the immortal person of which the planet Jupiter is the celestial embodiment.

The story is a version of the Ganymede myth. Ganymede (who, like Phaenon, had no mother) was taken from his father because of his peerless beauty. He became an object of admiration even on Olympus, where he was taken to draw the blushing nectar from the golden cup and distribute it to the gods. Again Hermes played the role of messenger and persuader, being sent to Ganymede's father (Tros) at the behest of Zeus to announce to him that Ganymede had been made ageless, immortal, and a peer of the gods. The parallelism is almost exact. Furthermore, the etymology of the name Ganymede parallels that of Phaenon, for it must be connected with the root *gan-* the first meaning of which is "glitter and gleam," used to describe the sheen of metals and the bright look on a joyful face. In the variant told above,[54] Ganymede was stolen and swept up from his father by a wondrous whirlwind (C-D). In most variants, however, an eagle was sent to seize him. The eagle, some say, was catasterized by Zeus into the constellation Aquila, while Ganymede, like Phaenon, took on a heavenly embodiment as the constellation Aquarius.[55]

A number of branching avenues lead from the story of Ganymede and his eagle back to Prometheus, the creator of Phaenon. Some say that Ganymede's constellation, Aquarius, is rather the catasterism of

Prometheus's son Deucalion because, before his term on earth as first man, such quantities of water poured from the sky that the great flood resulted.⁵⁶ We have seen, as well, that Deucalion's flood was supposed to have occurred as a result of the conflagration brought on by someone named Phaethon, the second figure in the Phaenon-Phaethon mix-up.

According to Aglaosthenes, Aquila was not the catasterism of the eagle that stole Ganymede but the eagle of good omen that Zeus sighted during a sacrifice commemorating his decision to attack the Titans.⁵⁷ Now we are back to square one, the Titanomachy, which involves Zeus and the brothers of Prometheus on opposing sides. Furthermore, Ganymede's eagle may be compared with the eagle that rent the liver of Prometheus. Zeus singled out Ganymede's eagle among all birds (to catasterize) because it alone strives to fly into the rays of the rising sun, and so it flies above Aquarius, who, as many imagine, is Ganymede.⁵⁸ These facts, as reported by Hyginus, were true at the time of the spring equinox during his era. An hour before sunrise, Altair, the bright star of Aquila, was poised in the southeast sky above Aquarius, which itself was hanging low over Pisces in the east, where the sun had already broken through the gloaming into dawn. In the traditional configuration of the constellations, Aquila looks as if it were flying directly for the sun in the V of Pisces, while the other bird constellation, Cygnus, seems to be veering to the north as if to avoid the sun's coming. Prometheus's station in the Caucasus Mountains was thought to be the point of sunrise. May we not then associate Aquila with the eagle of Zeus, which was sent to rend Prometheus's liver? This eagle is said variously to be a creature of the dark (a son of Typhon and Echidna, or of Earth and Tartarus) or of the light (a creation of Hephaestus animated by Zeus).⁵⁹ Prometheus's eagle was said by one source to come with the dawn (disappearing at night, during which respite the destroyed liver regenerated itself), and he was described as "shining."⁶⁰

Aquila, moreover, was identified with a certain Merops, ruler of the island of Cos. We have met this name type several times before, as one of the Pleiades and in the genealogy of Phaethon, where either Merops is the stepfather of Phaethon or Merope is his mother. The word *merops*,⁶¹ from which the name derives, is the name of a bird that the Greeks made much of, the beehawk. The beehawk was thought to produce its young from the earth directly (its nest is underground). Hence the birds are autochthonous, or born directly from earth, *gêgeneis* in Greek. Eagles, beehawks, and ants are all amphibians; they know the secrets of sky and earth or of the underworld and the earth. The merops is especially significant, because it comes from the underworld directly into the sky. Prometheus's eagle must have been thought to be like a beehawk, because in one account it was the offspring of Earth and Tartarus—a creature of the dark born to do its work in the light of the morning sky. The explanation of the "dark birth" of Aquila may well lie in another astronomical fact. At winter solstice during the time of Hyginus, Altair was a harbinger star of the solstitial sun, rising an hour before the sun almost due east on the darkest day of the year and bright enough to be seen for some time in the dawning light.

Ganymede and Phaenon are motherless as far as our sources go, and as with other motherless creatures, Earth may be posited as their mother; like the beehawk they were gêgeneis. Furthermore, each was set into the sky, one as a planet, the other as a constellation. Significantly, Ganymede's asterism was thought to be important to the morning sky, to judge from certain facts cited in his myth. His ransom was a pair of golden horses (compare Phaethon-Helios's steeds) or a golden grapevine (C-D, G), and in one variant he was said to have been stolen by Eos (Dawn) (E) before Zeus got him. We are bound to conclude that Phaenon and Ganymede are parallel. They are dim mythological vestiges of the archetypical son, foretold to be born in the fourth generation as a god who would replace Zeus as ruler of the universe. Their transmogrification into celestial bodies at once nullifies their threat and acknowledges that they were rivals of Zeus. Another story about Zeus, eagles, and beautiful boys confirms this conclusion. A boy born to Earth was given the name Aëtes (Eagle). He was a boyhood playmate of Zeus, but Hera was jealous of Zeus's love for him and so turned him into the celestial eagle.[62]

PROMETHEUS-ATLAS

The creator of man, or the father of the creator of man, Prometheus was an enemy of Zeus. Pinioned to a rock in the far east, where the sun comes up, he was devoured at his core by an eagle every day for thirty thousand years (G10) until Zeus needed him to make clear (G9) the riddle (F8) that threatened his replacement as king of the gods. In Hesiod's *Theogony*, Prometheus receives the same epithet as Kronos— "he of the crooked counsel."[63] Is the rivalry between Prometheus and Zeus yet another version of the Replacement Paradigm as it applies to Zeus, Kronos, and Ouranos?

A story was told about a certain Prometheus who was a favorite of Demeter, who had given him certain secret gifts. He was a member of the tribe of the Kabeiroi, a group of deities who, like the Prometheus of the more common story, were thought to have brought safety, good fortune, and bounty to mankind. The name of this Prometheus's son was Aitnaios,[64] man of (Mount) Aetna, with whom we must compare Typhon, Zeus's archenemy, who was buried beneath the mountain of that name. This Prometheus as a favorite of Demeter evokes the rivalry of Zeus and Hades-Iasios for Demeter.

The names Prometheus and Epimetheus have a common etymological element. This would lead one to believe that they were twins. Except in Protagoras's story of creation as told by Plato, Epimetheus is a shadowy figure in myth, appearing only in connection with the story of Pandora, of which Hesiod is likely the ultimate and only source. Prometheus, on the other hand, plays a role in several major stories, as does his other brother, Atlas. Furthermore, both Atlas and Prometheus are connected with mountains, one punished in the far east, the other in the far west. These two would seem to be like the scheming twins who would assault heaven, namely Otus and Ephialtes.

Other sporadic facts link Prometheus more closely to Atlas than they seem to be in extant myth. The name Merops is a clue. Applied to the earthborn beehawk, this name is also given to several mythological characters who are autochthonous heroes, visionaries (as a creature that lives beneath the earth, the beehawk, like the serpent, knows earth's secrets), or creators: the (step) father of Phaethon, an inhabitant of Cos by some accounts, was the creator of the race of Coans, the first race of human beings to be called *meropes,* a name that later came to be generalized to all mortals, since ultimately people, too, are gêgeneis, sprung from their Mother Earth. Prometheus is, like this Merops, a creator of mankind. Merops is also an alias of the eagle that devoured

Prometheus's liver, perhaps referring to the Aquila of the winter solstice, which leaps directly (not obliquely) from the earth to foretell the sun's rising, but in any case linking Prometheus to the name Merops.

Atlas and Prometheus are linked together by the name Clymene, their mother, which is also a name for one of Phaethon's parents, the other of whose names, Merope or Merops, is also a link back to Atlas through his daughter, Merope, the Pleiad. This name provides a link to Orion, whom his girlfriend's (Merope's) father blinded—a disability that led him to the sun god for a cure. This deed that links Orion to Phaethon both through the name Merope and through the approach-to-the-sun theme. Prometheus, too, approached the sun-god—in order to procure fire for the first time.[65]

A great king named Atlas—said by Plato in the *Critias* (114ff.) to be the son of Poseidon but by allusion also identified with the Titanic Atlas—founded the royal line and was therefore the creator, along with his twin and their four other sets of twin brothers, of the inhabitants of the fabled island of Atlantis. The location of Atlantis was in the far west beyond the pillars of Herakles, beyond the place where the Titanic Atlas was said to support the world. Atlantis was a place of inexhaustible wealth, the soil of which bore unceasing yields. In short, it was an Elysium, as its location alone would suggest. At its center was a sacred perimeter, fenced in gold, which marked the place where Poseidon begot the brothers on the lady Clito (C-D).

This Atlas is a dyshemerized[66] reflection of the Titan Atlas. Their common location in the far west is prima facie evidence for saying so. Furthermore, the disappearance of Atlantis into the sea sounds much like the disappearance of the city on Mount Sipylos, mentioned above in connection with Tantalus. From the cleft into which that city disappeared flowed a great tide of water, which may be compared with the marine location and submarine demise of Atlantis. This parallelism suggests a pre-Platonic story of an Atlantis on the flank of Mount Atlas. Tantalus, regent of the eastern city that disappeared into Mount Sipylos, is like Atlas in that they were both criminals in the eyes of the ruling gods: both fetched divine food and gave it away (Atlas brought the apples of the Hesperides to Herakles), and both were punished with mountainous threats and eternal labors. Furthermore, Tantalus as

Zeus's rival in the east is parallel to Atlas's eastern-stationed brother, a rival to Zeus and connected to another eastern mountain.

The name Atlas appears only one other place in the Greek tradition. One of the Kerkopes was named Atlas.[67] The two best-known Kerkopes were called Akmon (Anvil) and Passalos (Peg) (C, D). They were said to be sons of a certain Theia, daughter of Ocean, elsewhere a Titaness and therefore directly related to the Oceanid of various names (Clymene, Asia, Aithra, Themis), who was the mother of Prometheus and Atlas. These beings were called Kerkopes (creatures with tails, i.e., monkeys) because of their wily nature. In this they are like Prometheus and Kronos, who in Homer bear a common epithet descriptive of their guile. The Kerkopes were said to have been turned to stone for trying to deceive Zeus.[68] Such punishment resembles that of Atlas, Prometheus, Tantalus, Sisyphus, and Typhoeus—other enemies of Zeus. The Kerkopes were warned by their mother to keep on the alert for Melampygos (Black Bottom), alias Herakles. They tried to steal the visiting Herakles's weapons while he was asleep, just as Typhon tried to steal Zeus's sinews, but the hero woke up, caught them in the act, tied them by their feet to a carrying pole like two buckets, and let them dangle, staring at his black bottom as he went along. He released them when their laughter at the recognition of the warning about "Black Bottom" stimulated his own.[69] Zeus is said to have turned all the tribe of the Kerkopes into monkeys and sent them to populate Pithekusai (Monkey Island).[70]

These stories about the Kerkopes are versions of the Prometheus and Atlas stories. The names Atlas and Theia are common to both groups, as noted above. The creation of a new race of beings (G4), found in Zeus's populating of Monkey Island, is common both to the myth of Prometheus and the Atlantis myths. The transformation into stone is also common. Prometheus, deceiver of Zeus, was transfixed to a mountain, and Atlas was petrified into a range of mountains, which bear his name. The stealing of weapons by the Kerkopes is comparable to Prometheus's theft of divine fire. Suspension of the mischievous brothers on the end of a pole over Herakles's backside suits the geographical distribution of Prometheus and Atlas: one in the east and one in the west, with the center of the earth (Delphi) between them. Herodotus tells us that a geographical feature called Melampygos was the name of a prominent rock in the foothills of Anopaia Mountain in Locris and that it was located near the seats of the Kerkopes (*hedras Kerkopon*), a narrow defile.[71] Herakles's bottom was the narrow defile near which was situated the prominence of his *membrum virile*. The center of the earth at Delphi is marked by Kronos's stone, the *omphalos gês*, a prominence echoed in the heights of Parnassos overlooking a deep-cleft valley. Parnassos in the center is balanced by Mount Atlas in the west and the Caucasus in the east, and not incidentally, Parnassos is the next mountain in the range south of Mount Anopaia.

Kerkops means "tailed," to be sure, but metaphorically, "phallus." Hence the stone Melampygos is a phallus stone like the omphalos ges. Omphalos ("navel") has a female connotation as well, which finds expression in the myth as Herakles's black bottom. The ultimate etymology of *kerkops* is "tail opening." Akmon and Passalos, therefore, are perfect names for the two Kerkopes.[72] These names retain both the female (anvil) and the male (pestle) sexual connotations of the word kerkops and refer at the same time to the cosmological significance of the archetypal myth, the world upon the pivot point of Atlas's shoulder (I).[73]

PANDORA AND HER GIFTS

Demeter was said to have given the Kabeiros Prometheus a secret gift. What was this mysterious, unspeakable gift? The series of myths we have been discussing has touched on two taboo gifts, the gift of divine food, given mankind by Tantalus, and the gift of fire, given to mankind by Prometheus. The story of Pandora reveals that these gifts are ultimately parallel and reveal for us why they are taboo.

Fashioned from clay, molded like a statuette, Pandora was no ad hoc creation designed to punish evildoers, as Hesiod represents her in the *Theogony*. Nor was she created to repay mankind for their possession of divine fire or to be the source of deceit and evil for mankind on general principles, as Hesiod represents her in the *Works and Days*. But alas, Hesiod is the earliest and almost the only independent source for her story.[74]

Her generation from clay or earth is an indication of her true origin—

aboriginal woman. Many stories, from both Greece and elsewhere, give the origin of mankind in the creation of the first humans from clay. Yet most such stories envisage the creation of undifferentiated people (such as Meropes and Myrmykes) or of an aboriginal male-female pair (Deucalion-Pyrrha), not of a female alone. There is vestigial evidence for a variant in which an original primal pair had Pandora as its female member. Hesiod makes Pandora appear like a bride bedecked in all her finery and endowed with virginal charms, and indeed in some variants Epimetheus (or Prometheus himself) is the bridegroom. Pandora was worshiped in several places in Greece as the earth goddess Rhea. She was connected with Ge and Demeter by a common cult title, Anesidora (She Who Sends Up Gifts). She is often depicted as a large and comely head rising up from the ground while men (often Epimetheus is named) work upon her with hammers and picks, as though she were the cloddy earth herself. She *is* Earth or the produce of Earth, and like other Earth mothers, she needs a consort, as Persephone had Hades; Demeter, Iasios (or Zeus or Poseidon); Ge, Ouranos; and as Rhea had Kronos.

The consort must be there, Earth and farmer work in partnership to produce grain crops: no labor, no grain. Iasios must plow the field three times (even though he would rather be a hunter) before he can lie with Demeter in the furrows. And despite Hesiod's misogyny, which represents women as a worthless tribe who stay indoors all day and harvest the work of others into their bellies like drones, the presence of a primal creative pair is an acknowledgment among mythmakers of the division of labor, men and women alike sharing the burdens of the labor that civilizes.[75]

Yet despite the collaboration between the primal partners, between mankind and Mother Earth, procreation by them is marked by a taboo act and a taboo object. The taboo act is plowing itself. In Greek antiquity, plowing and intercourse are metaphors for each other. In plowing the ground, a farmer like Iasios is guilty of having intercourse with Mother Earth—of committing incest, if you will. This can be seen in the story of Ixion. A favorite of Zeus, he had been brought to dine at the table of the gods, but he repaid his hosts' hospitality by attempting to rape Hera, that is, to violate Mother Earth. So he was bound forever to an ever-revolving fiery wheel. Tityus, likewise a favorite of Zeus, made an attempt on Leto, for which crime he was bound in hell with eagles tearing out his liver and letting it grow back again in keeping with the phases of the moon. Infernal punishment links these criminals with both Tantalus, who violated the food taboo, and Prometheus, who violated the fire taboo. One obscure detail from the Prometheus story extends the association. In order to justify his harsh treatment of Prometheus, which seemed arbitrary to some of the gods, Zeus circulated the rumor that he had been enjoying a clandestine love affair with Athena.[76] Here we find the aboriginal crime (not reported by Hesiod) for which Prometheus was punished. His punishment was like that of Tityus and the others because his crime was like theirs—committing the taboo act and delivering the taboo object.

In the case of Tantalus it is easy to see that the taboo object was connected with food—the flesh of Pelops. But how does his crime of quasi cannibalism—feeding his son's flesh to the gods—jibe with the others' crime, which involved an attempt (or the act) of lying with Mother Earth? There is an agricultural analogue that involves both hiding and plowing Mother Earth. The act of sowing requires plowing as its antecedent, it involves hiding the seed in the ground, and it is quasi cannibalism. Sowing is metaphorical cannibalism because it demands that we take something near and dear to us—seed from our own larder of hard-won grain—and give it back to Mother Earth to be "swallowed." Whether this dear and kindred "flesh and blood" will be regenerated, as Pelops's shoulder was, lies on the gods' knees. Demeter (Mother Earth) alone ate (hid in her bowels) the flesh of Pelops. And the etymology of Pelops is a clue to the "cannibalism" that befell him, for he is Mr. Seed Corn, and his name means "opening in the mud."[77]

But what is the nature of the taboo object? The answer lies in the very nature of seed corn itself. Grain as food is a very ordinary object in itself, but as seed it is filled with manna. Ground grain becomes flour and bread, which become offal; planted grain becomes a green living thing that reproduces itself a hundredfold. The importance of this paradox to ancient peoples can be seen in John 12:24: "Unless the grain of wheat falls to the earth, it remains just a grain of wheat. But if it dies, it bears much fruit." A seed is ordinary foodstuff, but it is also that-which-cannot-be-touched. It is food-no-food.

The gods demand this no-food from us. People plant it; the gods take it, returning it willy-nilly as the hazards of their weather and the fertility of Mother Earth will have it. During their sacrifices to the gods, people repeat this act of *do-ut-des* ("I render a gift so that you will return it") by offering barley grains and/or first fruits to them.[78] Yet the gods do not seem to need these offerings, planted or sacrificed, for their own sustenance. The fully anthropomorphized gods of Homer enjoy the savor of burnt offering as it spirals from Earth Olympusward, and they are depicted as feasting and regaling themselves, but they do not devour sacrificial offerings. They do not, like man, possess brazen stomachs, peremptory reminders of the mortal state. They are deathless because their drink, nectar, confers deathlessness. Nectar means "that which alleviates death."[79]

Yet there may lie in the word *ambrosia* (the gods' food) the vestige of a belief that the gods needed food that was taboo for humans as food for their own sustenance. The etymology of ambrosia is "immortal," and so the Greeks understood it—"immortal food" or "food for the immortals." Yet, being the great folk etymologists that they were, the Greeks thought that the second element of the word was akin to the etymon *brô-*, "eat," so that the negative prefix *a(m)-* would make *ambrosia* mean "no-food."

To explicate this I must digress. Much of the imagery and vocabulary of books 14 and 15 of the *Odyssey* turn on this double etymology. Eumaeus used to live on an island called Syria, "where lie the turnings of the sun," a paradise "rich in cattle, sheep, wine, and grain," where poverty never comes, nor any disease. Old people there do not die in miserable old age; rather, Apollo and Artemis slay them with gentle arrows.[80] But Eumaeus fell on hard times and was forced to wander, which condition is worse than any for mortals, who own their evil cares on account of their ruinous stomachs.[81] Despite this mortal factor, people sometimes attain the condition of plenty—when the product of their labor has been increased by the blessed gods. At such times, they eat, drink, and are able to donate to those who deserve respect—that is, to strangers like Odysseus, to beggars, to suppliants, and to the gods themselves.[82] "The god grants one thing and lets another go as his heart wishes, for he is all-capable."[83] Hence Eumaeus urges his guest to eat, drink, and be merry. Who knows when the gods will take away even this worked-for plenty?

But Penelope's suitors do not work. They consume the larder of their absent host and behave high-handedly (compare Hesiod's Perses), a particularly nettling state of affairs for Eumaeus.[84] They will fall from their paradise in time, he is sure, and the tables are turned (literally), when Odysseus is again in charge.[85] The evils that Odysseus has in mind for the suitors is described in an agricultural metaphor: "he plants it for them."[86]

The culmination of the conversation between Odysseus and Eumaeus is a moral summary made by Odysseus: "Zeus has provided you with good alongside evil, since you came through your suffering to the house of a gentleman who affords you food and drink (*brôsin kai posin*) without stint. You live the good life. As for me though, I came here wandering the cities of mortals (*brotôn*)."[87] That is, despite being a slave, Eumaeus has lived the life of a god or of one who takes food with the gods, in contrast to the slavish wanderings of Odysseus among the haunts of mortals. The order, the meaning, and in part the sound of *brôsis kai posis* suggests the immortal food and drink, ambrosia and nectar.[88] This ordering of a word containing the element *brô-* coupled with some word for drink occurs many times in Greek literature. Hence, we can conclude that to the Greek mind the words for mortal (*brotos*) and for food (*brôsis*) always stand by, in implicit contrast, when mention is made of immortal nonfood (*ambrosia*).

The fall from paradise is at its worst for mankind during a state of wandering, for then nothing is planted, and during a state of beggary, in which there is only need, never any surplus. The two go hand in hand, not only from the obvious point of view but also because a lack of planting and surplus denies mankind the wherewithal to make donations to the gods and win their favor; hence the rootlessness continues.

The gods demand (and consume) their due from rich men like the lord of Ithaka. In a sense, the suitors behave like gods, eating and drinking the substance of others without work, and this is their crime. It is interesting to note that these otherwise godless suitors, who have no fear of divine retribution, are never said merely to "kill" Odysseus's animals for feasting. Rather the verb *hiereuô* (and the noun *hiereion*) appear; these words are appropriate only for properly sacrificial slaughter.[89] In a sense, *gods* are consuming Odysseus's capital.

Gods can consume human resources, but man's wretched state will not allow the converse. Even in his uttermost destitution, he may not consume the food reserved for the disposition of the gods (seed corn). This fact is brought home in myth. Look what happened to Odysseus's men because they devoured the cattle of Helios. Compare the crime of Athamas's wife, Ino, who misused the divine gift, fire (see below), to parch the seed corn, an act for which the oracle suggested human sacrifice as a remedy.

Pandora's jar, therefore, was taboo not because it contained all the evils destined for mankind but because, like other jars (*pithoi*) of the sort she carried, it contained seeds—the food-no-food garnered from Mother Earth after violence had been done her. Yet, in a larger sense, the seed-corn jar did hold some evil for mankind. Once mankind has been expelled from paradise, agriculture comes into being as a mixed blessing—it provides sustenance but only at the expense of hard labor. Seed corn might become a symbol for this ambiguity, since it is itself ambiguous. Furthermore, seed is a symbol of hope (which alone remained in the jar), for in it lies the only hope of survival into the next year. This ambiguity of food-no-food is contained in a jar filled with mixed blessings. Some evil mixed with good is converted by Hesiod's pessimism into a jar from which the evil is set loose and in which the single good is confined. Babrius preserves a more logically consistent variant in which Zeus gathers all the good and useful things in the world, puts them in a covered jar, and gives it to man. Indomitable man, however, desiring to know the contents, uncovers the jar, allowing the *goods* to escape the earth. They flew to the homes of the gods. Only hope remained, retained by the replaced lid, and so hope alone dwells among men—the hope that in time the goods that deserted mankind for the gods will be restored (that is, that seed corn planted will yield a harvest).[90]

PROMETHEUS, BRINGER OF FIRE

But fire, not grain, was the taboo object stolen by Prometheus and given to mankind in the *narthex*. On more than one level, fire concealed in the fennel stalk represents the seed corn hidden in a jar. Fire represents gold, the gold that surplus grain will bring, the gold of the Golden Age. It represents hope, and it represents the gift of special knowledge. Just as in the case of cereal produce, of which there are two kinds—one for the use of humanity and the other that must be given to the gods—so, too, in the case of fire. The Indo-European mother tongue had two words for fire, one for the sacred fire of the hearth and altar, and the other for the profane fire of the forge.[91]

Now we can understand why Pandora (all giver) deserves her name in the context of the Hesiodic poems. She is an artifact fashioned by Hephaestus, god of the mundane fire. In some sense she is the prototypical cultural implement, for she stands in a one-to-one relationship with fire—formed from clay by the god of the forge, Hephaestus, fired like a statuette, bedizened by the fires of the smith, and adorned by the subsidiary arts and crafts. Given the agricultural associations surrounding Pandora, we can understand her name as referring to the gifts that material culture (the chief branches of which are metallurgy, ceramics, and agriculture) has bestowed upon mankind. Pandora symbolizes nature (Mother Earth) made over by culture.

Just as Tantalus brought the divine foods, ambrosia and nectar, from the gods and shared them out to humans, so Prometheus brought divine fire from the gods and shared it with the creatures of a day. In each case the divine nature of the gift was lost. Mankind does not have ambrosia, which grows from ever-bearing trees; instead it has labor-produced grain, which rots and is wasted, which dies and becomes offal like its user, and which must be divided and shared back with the sometimes-ungrateful gods. Humans do not have lightning-generated fire from heaven, which is generated continuously by the gods; instead they have mundane fire, which is kept alive only at the expense of consumed fuel and vigilant watching, and which, once dead, is rekindled only with great toil. Divine fire is only on loan from the gods; it must be kept strictly apart from mundane fire, and woe to the Vestal who allows the immortal spark to die on the hearth.

Just as seed corn is set apart to become food-no-food, only to be hidden away at the pleasure of the gods in order to make new produce or not, as the gods will, fire kindled from rubbing sticks or by using the fire drill is thought to be the god-willed manifestation of something hidden. In the Indic system, divine fire is personified as the god Agni. Agni has three abodes: earth, sky, and ocean. On earth, he exists as sacrificial fire, in heaven as lightning, and from the ocean he is born again every morning. Ocean-born Agni has the special name Apam Napat (Grandson of the Waters). He rises from the waters every morning in response to a burnt offering made on earth through the offices of the earthly Agni; without the sacrifice there would be no rebirth of fire. Apam Napat prefigures the sun god Savitri. Every day Savitri rides on his solar journey, illuminating our mortal sky, traveling downstream along the celestial pathway. At night he dips into the water. At dusk a horse is offered up to earthly fire; the horse's spirit follows Savitri on his journey upstream to illuminate the unmentionable sky of the underworld and next morning is resurrected into the steed that will carry Savitri during the new day. This fire is hidden away at night in the water and is reborn every day.

Ritual fire-sticks (live wood become dead) are used to kindle sacrificial fire. They have within their wooden womb latent fire,[92] brought down to earth by celestial waters. In them lie hidden the heavenly fire that manifests itself as lightning.[93] Compare seed corn, which is a latent plant and which paradoxically can be productive only when it "dies" and is "buried." This sexually charged symbolism,[94] which surrounds the use of fire, pervades the Indo-European vocabulary and practice. The circular enclosure into which the Hindu household fire is laid is called *yoni,* "vagina, womb." There are separate kinds of fire in the male and female of the species, *perusah,* whence comes the sperm, and *yosa,* whence the embryo. Similarly, the Roman hearth (*focus*) and the temple to the public fire-goddess, Vesta (*aedes*), were circular in shape, as was the Athenian prince's building (*prytaneum*), in which was kept burning the perpetual flame. The Vestal virgins, who were assigned the duty of guarding Vesta's eternal flame, also were charged with the protection of the Ordained Pledge of Supremacy (*fatale pignus imperii*), which was hidden in the inner sanctum of the temple. The nature of this sacred relic was kept so secret that no notion of what it was has survived to us. Suffice it to say that it was probably kept in a covered earthenware jar, which stood near to an identical but empty facsimile.[95]

Fire and seed corn are therefore parallel. Prometheus broke the taboo of distributing fire-no-fire for mundane use just as Epimetheus did in taking the lid off the jar (to use it) that contained food-no-food. Prometheus's stealing the gods' fire in a pithy chamber and transferring it to mankind is parallel to the secret gift by Demeter to Prometheus (Kabeiros),[96] to the gift of Pandora with her *pithos*,[97] and to the unmentionably sacred jar kept in the *aedes* of Vesta.[98] Each, in its own way, is bound up with sacrifice as well. Unlike seed corn, fire is not itself committed to the gods in the hope that it will be returned many times over, but the fat of sacrificial victims is consumed by the divine fire, and its smoke rises heavenward to the gods for their consideration.

Zeus's portion of the sacrifice, allotted him (deceitfully, according to Hesiod) by Prometheus at Mekone, was the fat wrapped around the bones. This is, in fact, the choicest portion, for fat and marrow are the most calorie-rich parts of the animal, necessarily and eagerly consumed by those confined within an economy of subsistence. Hesiod's account, therefore, can be viewed as a story of etiology: why the tribes burn white bones (and fat) to the gods upon fragrant altars.[99] An expression of the high value people put on the fat portion is found in the text that describes mankind's portion of flesh and innards as "rich with fat."[100] Fat is the basis for burnt offerings; flesh and innards, after all, will not burn. The sacrifice of the choicest part was a quandary whereby hangs a tale of explanation. So, too, was the setting aside of a portion of the harvest that could not be eaten.

But fire does more than to consume the sacrifice and send it transformed to the sky. Savitri's sacrificial horse is reanimated on the far side. Like seed corn, fire brings on new life from the death of the old. The green plant dies, but its genetic archetype remains to be transformed into new, green life by being hidden in the ground. The animal is ritually killed, and its spiritual archetype is transformed by being obliterated in the fire to become a new being. Myth confirms this function of fire as the transformer that brings the dead (sacrificial) animal back to the light and life. In Indic eschatology, immortal beings reside in a third sky, distinct from the two skies of Savitri (the sky of this world and the sky of the underworld). In the third sky resides the highest form of fire.[101] There, too, resides the primordial mortal Yama, king of the fathers (ancestors). Yama was the first man to die, to follow the sun Savitri downstream across the dreadful sky of night, and to be re-born with the sun. He became immortal in the third sky.[102]

According to the abstract model, primary fire from the third sky came down to earth: from lightning to the rain cloud, from rain to growing things, and from dead sticks through friction back to fire. There is a mythological model as well. A messenger named Matarisvan brought fire down. The name is significant, for it means "womb" (literally "swelling in the mother").[103] Matarisvan is the messenger of Vivasvat,[104] who is at once the ancestor of humankind and the founder of the institution of sacrifice to the gods. Vivasvat was the father of Yama. To this pair we must compare the Avestan pair, father and son, Vivahvant, instituter of the sacrificial rites using Haoma,[105] and his son, Yima, prince of Var-kam-gard, a place of immortality. In later Hindu litera-ture, Vivasvat had an alter ego named Manu: ideal sacrificer and ances-tor of the human race. He established a new code of laws, and his foundation of the sacrifice brought him prosperity and progeny (G).[106]

If we consider mythological themes, Prometheus is the Greek parallel to Vivasvat (and to his messenger): he brought fire to mankind in the womb of the *narthex,* and he is the father of the first man, progenitor of all the human races, Deucalion; and he is parallel to Yama/Manu as the originator of sacrifice. Atlantis is parallel to Var-kam-gard of Yima, though in Greek myth it was not the firebringer's son but his brother, Atlas, who ruled this land of the Golden Age. But the etymology of the name Prometheus is not transparent like those of Vivasvat (Shining One) and of Matarisvan. It is perplexing. Greek authors took the name to be related to the verb stem *math-,* "to learn, to know." Hence the name in full could be interpreted as "he who has foreknowledge."[107] The name of his brother, Epimetheus, would therefore mean "Mr. Afterthought." All other etymologies of the name are "fantastic," as the author of the article in the *Oxford Classical Dictionary* says, referring by innuendo to that given by Adalbert Kuhn a century ago, who re-lated the name to the Indian place-name Mount Mandara (also spelled Manthara) and to the word for fire drill in Sanskrit, *pramantha.*[108]

Certainly the author of the article on Prometheus in Pauly-Wissowa, *Realenkyklopaedie der classischen Alterthumswissenschaft,* agrees with the *Oxford Classical Dictionary,* citing several works that he agrees consign

Kuhn to oblivion.[109] But there is a real difficulty with the accepted etymology, for *math-* has a short vowel, but the name Promêtheus has a long one. Comparative historical linguists will not commit themselves on the issue: Pokorny does not even discuss the name Prometheus; Chantraine says that one could propose an *e* vowel in the base to account for the opposition of *math-* with another base, *menth-*, appearing in a word cited by Hesychius (*menthere = phrontis*). Noting that the parallels cited by others have an *o* vowel and meanings that are seemingly distant from *math-*, he cites two Indic parallels, Sanskrit *medha*, "wisdom," and Avestan *mazda*, which might be assimilated to the *math-* of Prometheus by proposing an aboriginal **madh-*. He continues by proposing that an affinity with Greek *menos* (I.E. **men-*[3]) is also possible.[110]

Some interesting facts come to light from these considerations. The name of Prometheus's brother, Menoitios, does indeed derive from the root *men-*[3].[111] The same root gives rise to the Hindu name Manu.[112] Prometheus and Epimetheus are linked by etymologically similar names, typical of twins; just so the etymology of the first man in the Indic tongues, Yima (Avestan)/Yama (Vedic) is "twin."[113] Zeus and Prometheus are associated in myth in many ways, as we have seen. We possess a cult name for Zeus, which, despite asseveration to the contrary,[114] must have something to do with the Titan Prometheus: Zeus Promantheus.[115] A title of Jupiter among the lower Italian Sallentines is similar, and has been taken to be a translocation of the Zeus cult: Jupiter Menzana. To the latter, our sources tell us, the Sallentines sacrificed young horses.[116] Are Jupiter Menzana and Zeus Promantheus (and Prometheus himself?) parallel to Savitri, for whose continuing labor in the sky of bringing up new fire every day the Hindus sacrificed a horse?

The Hindu fire bringer, Matarisvan-Vivasvat, to whom Prometheus can be correlated on the grounds of mythological function and genealogical relationships, created fire for the sacrifice by using the fire drill pramantha. The sum of these relationships is too overwhelming to reject Kuhn's etymology in favor of what appears to be a folk etymology of Greek origin based on the Hesiodic telling of the Pandora story, in which Prometheus "knows beforehand" what the gods have in mind and so warns his brother, and in which Epimetheus (his supposititious brother?) takes thought of the warning only as an "afterthought," being charmed to the point of stupidity by Zeus's gift. Ultimately, perhaps, comparative linguists will be able to link the etymon *menth/meth-* "to drill," with *men-*³,[117] just as they have linked the latter with an etymon *mne-*²,[118] and find a way to include Greek *math-* in the lot. Until then we are limited to the asseveration that Prometheus Firebringer, originator of sacrifice, (twin) brother to the world mover, who lies pinioned at the eastern edge of the world during an eon of time because of his opposition to Zeus, has strong Indo-European ties, and that he fulfills, in stories told of him, the Indo-European paradigm of the Indo-European Myth of Replacement.

SUMMARY

In this chapter the paradigm was applied to the myths of dynastic replacement about Zeus and his forebears. I argue that the motif of castration and the motif of swallowing were both paradigmatic instances of hiding. Castration is at once the stripping of the fruit from the great tree (wrong-running) and sowing that fruit to make a new creation as suggested by the Indo-European semantic complex *acorn-genital*. Hiding is equivalent to sowing as well: sowing seed equals hiding it in Mother Earth, a theme that will be expanded in a subsequent volume. The myths of Zeus's birth are fraught with omens of replacement—a pattern to be found in many hero-myths. Zeus's birth, moreover, is laden with goatish characters and names, a curiosity noticed in hero myths as well (Aegeus and Aegisthus, for example), the significance of which is explained in chapter 6.

In examining this complex of myths, our attention was directed to the similarities among Tartarus, Hades, Erebus, *zophos*, and Elysium. Tartarus and Elysium both seem to be *temenoi* with pillared entryways that can be reached by traveling to the far west. This suggests that Hades and Kronos are parallel, and indeed we found this to be the case on both conceptual and genealogical grounds. In keeping with this parallelism, Hades, like Kronos, should be an antagonist of Zeus, and variants of the Demeter and Persephone stories bear out this inference.

The Typhon-Zeus conflict is similar to the Kronos-Zeus antagonism in certain respects as well, but it is in the Prometheus-Zeus conflict that we find the most significant parallels. Kronos's hellmate, Iapetos, was the father of Prometheus. In one story Prometheus presented to Zeus a boy named Phaenon (an alter-name for the star of Kronos). The lad was made immortal and placed in the heavens. This story is a version of the Ganymede myth, which provides other links to Prometheus-Zeus, the most important of which hinge on the name given to mortal man in the Homeric poems—Meropes—and on the involvement of predatory eagles, which are catasterized as the same eagle in the sky, Aquila.

Prometheus and his brother, Atlas, bound by Zeus to mountains at the opposite extremes of the earth, were shown to have geographical connections with Kronos-Hades and to share with them the idea of paradise lost (or removal to a nonearthly location). A minor character named Atlas was said to have deceived Zeus and so been turned to stone; the Atlas in question was one of the Kerkopes. A consideration of this word and associated proper names reveals that the stories of the Kerkopes have both mythic and geographic correspondence to the Prometheus-Atlas conflict with Zeus.

Prometheus led us to Pandora, and I have tried to show that Hesiod's misogyny fails to do justice to her aboriginal importance. She is Mother Earth, giver of all, whose partnership with farmers in the production of food is the prototype of the agricultural and sexually based division of labor. Pandora is one of the primal pair of procreative partners about whom are erected two taboos: an act and an object.

The taboo act is plowing itself, for this is metaphorical intercourse with Mother Earth and so an act of incest.

One taboo object is divine food, the seed corn that must not be eaten by mankind but rather must be committed to Mother Earth, who swallows it. Hope alone sustains people during the growing period, the hope that Earth will return their gift many-fold. And this act of sowing and hoping is the prototype of sacrificial offering, based on the notion that surrendering something to the gods will dispose them to return it with dividends. Agriculture is a mixed blessing, for while it usually supplies a surplus over the labor and capital invested, sometimes the expected dividends from the gods are not forthcoming and the labor is in vain. The myth preserves this ambivalence, involving as it does the breaking of the taboo whereby Eden is lost and the constant fear that the atonement for the original crime of plowing Mother Earth, of stealing divine food, will find the gods intractably angry.

A parallel taboo object is fire. In Indic (Vedic and Avestan) sources we found a full explication of beliefs about fire: heavenly fire came from lightning and was transferred by the falling rain to green sticks, where it lay latent until the tree was dead and dry. Then the fire sticks must be toiled over to bring forth this gift for man's use in his sacrificial oblations. Examining the Hindu counterparts of Prometheus, the Greek fire bringer, led me to suggest that the etymology of his name is as Kuhn suggested it: from *pramantha* (cf. *amritamanthana*), the fire drill.

During the discussion of this tangled nexus of myth based upon ideas from outside the paradigm, the paradigm, as developed earlier, has been kept in mind throughout and even refined in the process.

CHAPTER VI

PRECESSION

We have established that paradigmatic myths have a component of cosmic right running essential to the fertility of nature and that both myth and ritual recapitulate the intervention of culture in the extraction of a steady food supply from nature. Yet this is not enough; so far, theology is lacking from this model. Early anthropologist-mythographers like Frazer proposed a "primitive" theology for many myths based on the dying-and-rising god, the succession of the seasons being impersonated in the *Eniautos Daimon,* or Year Spirit. But Frazer's model covers only a minor portion of the extant material and fails to account for its most dramatic elements: these myths speak more strikingly of utter catastrophe than of reliable seasonal succession. The sun reversed its course at Atreus's crimes; the Milky Way is the burned-out track that the sun used to follow before the ride of Phaethon.[1] Here we see something closer to man's loss of Eden, not the mythical equivalent of an occasional drought or of predictable seasonal change.

The difficulty of achieving a clear interpretation of myth is often attributed to its origin in the allegedly nebulous thought of primitives, whose awe of the universe was born of ignorance shrouded in mystery. To allay this allegation, I shall be concrete: The names, actions, and objects of myth and ritual have as their antecedents specific celestial phenomena as conceived in a coherent pattern by the ancients.

Oenomaus's chariot wheel, first running on the axle and then falling off, stands as a concrete model of the running of the universe. The universe of sky phenomena appears to the viewer to rotate wheel-like about his fixed station, with a nonrotating central axis somewhere overhead. Beyond this basic analogy, however, the model of the wheel is inadequate to describe carefully observed phenomena. Why, then, was the model of the wheel so frequently used in Indo-European myth and ritual, and why the even less likely models of the churn and mill? And what phenomenon of nature do the mythical references to disaster evoke—the wheel falling off its axle, the mill shattered or grinding salt? To answer the first question, we must turn to a cultural complex of great antiquity, a basic nexus of Indo-European thought and language. To answer the second, we must study the facts of nature and reexamine our appraisal of the ancients as observers of nature.

NAVE AND AXLE

The Brahman sang his Saman hymn to a cartwheel set up on a post reaching to his navel. The singing of the hymn is a ritual act paralleled in mythology by the running of a chariot race, but the rewards for these performances were not parallel. Winning the race results in winning the terrestrial world; proper singing of the hymn results in winning the world of air, and finally, by the power gained by erecting the post and wheel the Brahman achieves the world of the gods.[2] To these three realms of victory we may compare the three kinds of fire (Agni) in Indic tradition—earthly fire, heavenly fire, and the fire of the third sky.

Indeed, the Brahman's prayer beseeches the sun-god Savitri that his impulsion (*sava*) may be true enough to carry the Brahman to the highest heaven of Brihaspati.[3] The ritual action, therefore, is designed to abet the action of Savitri in his setting forth from Agni of the waters in the morning through the first sky of day. But it may have efficacy as well in the third sky. Sayana, a commentator on the text, compared the turning wheel with the disk-shaped thunderbolt *vajra*, which is the source, in the third sky, of the highest form of fire.[4]

In this ritual we find implicit features that are recapitulated in myths derived from the same considerations. The wheel with its pivot point (nave) and the navel-high upright upon which it runs are reiterated in the person of the Brahman himself—a vertical member whose center of gravity is marked by the navel. This same comprehension of male and female elements in one entity is to be seen in the oak tree, which springs from a hole in the ground and which produces fruits that are at once male and female, the acorn (*glans*) and its cup. The lotus blossom that grows atop the root is another parallel, and so is the world tree Yggdrasil, sprung from the three roots (compare the three skies), one extending into the sky among the gods (Aesir) from the spring of destiny, Urd, one across Ginnungagap to the spring of Mimir, where understanding lies latent, and one over Niflheim's bubbling cauldron Hvergelmir. About the base of Yggdrasil twine countless serpents.

The world axletree image, fundamental to the cosmology of the Norsemen, is also to be found in the Vedas. The fundament of the universe, conceived as Maya (matrix) or *garbha* (womb), is the center for the support of the world. It is called Hiranyagarbha (the golden germ) and is given a masculine title Prajapati (Lord of Creatures),[5] and it too was conceived of as a phallic post centered in a matrix. This world pillar is elsewhere given the name *skambha*.[6] The world foundation (*dharma*) was thought to rest upon the supporting coils of a world serpent (Ananta-Sesha). It is interesting to note in this regard that one of Shiva's names was Nabhoyoni (Sky Vagina), from *nabh-*, "cloud, sky," and *yoni*, "vagina, womb." The world as sky was therefore thought to possess a central point: *garbha, yoni,* or *nâbha* (nave, navel, with assonance to *nabh-*, "cloud, sky"). With this we must compare *niflheim*, "home of the sky, cloud" (*nifl-* probably being cognate with *nabh-*).[7]

These facts show how the denotations of the words *rita* and *ritu*, source of our *rite* and *ritual*, are to be derived from their etymological underpinning: the verb *ri-*, "to fit, join." The fitting or joining of the male into the female element on the mundane plane begets creation (or agricultural plenty when the procreators are Iasion and Demeter), while the fitting of an imaginary sky axle into a sky nave produces a right-running universe, orderly and regular in its seasons (*ritu*) and imitated by correct ritual behavior (*rita*) and natural law. The opposite terms show similar semantic content, *nirriti* reflecting the decay, destruction, and death implied in a universe gone awry, and *anrita* the deceit and falsehood of moral disorder.

The ambrosial product amrita from the Churning of Ocean (Amri-tamanthana, literally "Immortality Drilling") adheres to this model perfectly. The god Indra and his three worlds (compare the three skies) began to degenerate: *nirriti* was at hand. Vishnu agreed to produce a plan whereby the natural order might be restored. Mount Mandara served as the churn stick (*skambha*), while the ocean, or rather a denizen of Ocean, the tortoise Akupara, served as the pivot point (*yoni, nâbha-*). The choice of a tall mountain as an axle suggests that the sky was the ultimate theater in which the churning was done.[8] Cosmic fire was generated from the churning, and so was the drink of immortality, amrita (cognate with *ambrosia*). Immortal fire and immortal food are parallel. Amrita is the jewel in the lotus, the golden germ, and the spring of destiny. It is the spark of intelligence produced at a center named Niflheim in one tradition and Nabhoyoni in another. Amrita, incidentally, like Nabhoyoni, is an alternate name for Shiva.

HAMMERS, MILLS, AND LIGHTNING

The production of fire during this cosmological churning is the focus that links several other facts into a complex. The turning of the Brahman's wheel during the Saman was compared to the thunderbolt *vajra*, which is Agni of the third sky. Celestial churning produces fire; earthly fire is produced by the churning motion of the fire drill, *pramantha*. When, in the *Astika*, Garuda stole amrita, it was guarded by Indra's whirling discus set with scimitars, which wheel-like weapon is an aspect of his thunderbolt, *vajra*. The conclusion is inescapable: the ancients (let us restrict this term for now to the Hindu tradition) believed that lightning was the product of the churning of the heavens on their axis, just as earthly fire is the product of the fire drill.

It is interesting that these conceptions jibe closely with some of those examined from the body of South American myth: the goatsucker purloined fire in its beak, the beak being metonymic for the vagina in the story of the old woman who produced fire for mankind from her vagina (cf. Nabhoyoni). In another story, fire was the possession of vulture deities (since they spend their time circling the heavens); they brought embers to cook the culture hero who was shamming death. The hero and his son stole the embers and put them inside two pieces of wood that would thenceforth be used by mankind to produce fire by a process of rotation, the archetype of which is the vultures' circular motion.[9]

The most sacred of the Hindu sacrificial fires was called Garhapatya, meaning "Fire of the Lord of the Household," a common epithet for Agni in the *Rig Veda*. If extinguished, this fire had to be rekindled from fire sticks alone through rotary motion (*manth-*).[10] This fact links it to the myth of the fire bringer Matarisvan (Swelling in the Mother), and this etymology demonstrates another common feature: Garhapatya was laid in a special enclosure called *yoni* (womb).[11] A circular enclosure surrounding the hearth fire *yoni* was thought to symbolize the earth on its inside and the surrounding ocean on the outside. Drilling for fire within this enclosure, with the fire drill centered in the *yoni,* would therefore imitate the motions of the universe about the *skambha,* which is centered in the *yoni* of the sky. The fire of the hearth used on earth originates both in material and in process from fire drilled from the sky.

Garhapatya used in the home was just one form of fire. Another, Ahavaniya, was set up in a quadrilateral fireplace enclosure designed to represent *dyaus,* "sky." Ahavaniya must represent a second type of celestial fire. A lotus leaf was placed inside the four-sided enclosure to represent the waters, thus making the ritual act of kindling this fire parallel to the rising of celestial fire every morning from the father of the waters, Apam Napat.[12] The third kind of sacrificial fire is built in a fireplace facing south. Its name is Dakshina (the right-hand one; compare *pradakshina*). Dakshina symbolizes atmosphere (*antariksa*), just as the other fires symbolize earth and sky, and since the other fires represented earth-born Agni (born from fire sticks) and water-born Agni respectively, it follows that Dakshina represents the sky-born Agni of lightning.[13]

Thus the sky-born Agni of lightning is to be equated with right-hand motion on the basis of its ritual counterpart, named Dakshina. And their common realm, *antariksa,* is the sky theater in which Indragni (later tradition fused these gods into one) uses his weapon, the thunderbolt,[14] against the demon Vritra. This fire thunderbolt had been given to Indra by Agni.[15] Garhapatya is to Dakshina as earth-born Agni is to sky-born Agni. Earth-born Agni is sky-born Agni transmitted through rainwater to growing greenwood and then to dry twigs, from which are made fire sticks.

In addition to *vajra*, or *ojas*, (another name for *vajra*), we hear of Indra's other weapons as well. The *chakra* (discus) really belonged to Krishna, having been awarded to him by Agni for his assistance in defeating Indra (A). Its by-name was *vajra-nâbha*, "navel lightning." Even more important is Indra's weapon called *asman*, a fiery stone not often referred to in the literature. Since lightning can assume the form of a ball or even break up into a discrete "hail" of charges, one wonders whether this was just another form of *vajra*. In any case, *asman* also has the denotation "sky" in Sanskrit.

The reflex *asman* has many cognates in the sister languages, which have led to the reconstruction of Proto-Indo-European **Haek-mon*, **ak-mon*.[16] But attaching a meaning to the proto form is difficult because of the startling polysemy exhibited by the reflexes: Vedic *asman*, "Indra's stone missile, sky"; Avestan *asman*, "sky, heaven"; Lithuanian *akmuo*, "stone"; Slavic *kamen*, "stone"; Gothic *himins*, "sky, heaven"; Icelandic *himinn*, "sky, heaven"; Icelandic *hamarr*, "Thor's hammer (from which word English borrowed *hammer*), cliff"; Greek *akmon*, "anvil" (in Homer and Hesiod, "anvils" fall from, or are suspended from, heaven).

This polysemy is most puzzling. Scholars have attempted to account for it purely on the grounds of semantic shift,[17] but their attempts are not wholly convincing. A hypothesis concerning the meaning of both etyma and their relationships emerges, however, when we examine a similarly curious polysemy surrounding the Indo-European etymon **mel*—the central meaning of which is "to crush, grind," whence English *meal* and Latin *mola* (which yield English *mill, molar* and *maelstrom*) but also Latin *malleus*, "hammer."

From **mel* comes the Greek *amblys*, "dull" (with a negative prefix); Icelandic Mjollnir, the name of Thor's hammer; and Icelandic *mylln*, Russian *molnija*, Welsh *mellt*, and Old Prussian *mealde*—all meaning "lightning." Therefore, the reflexes of both **Haekmon* and **mel* refer to divine weapons, to lightning (which may be a divine weapon), and to more mundane weapons and tools, the axe, hammer, and mill. Both refer to the sky or to sky phenomena. But what do hammers, stones, mills, lightning, and sharpness all have in common?

The answer is circular motion. The model found in Indo-European ritual and myth above, wherein lightning is conceived of as the product of the grinding of the heavens, explains the link between *Haekmon* in its meaning of "lightning" and *mel,* meaning both "lightning" and "grinding." The cosmic whirlpool produces lightning, weapon of the sky god. Then other weapons derive their names from this chief weapon.

But yet to be explained are the connections between hammers/axes, stones, and circular motion. A general meaning for the etymon *Haekmon* can be offered only if such an explanation is forthcoming. Archaeologists have linked the speakers of Indo-European-based languages, whom we cannot identify per se until some text they wrote is found, with many different cultural groups identifiable by, for example, the tools they used, the way they buried their dead, their pottery, and their methods of sustenance. Great controversy surrounds the whole subject of where the Indo-European language began, how it spread, and how and whether the language can be attached to the various peoples of early Europe identifiable by their cultural remains.[18] Of these, a culture called the Kurgan from its ubiquitous burial mounds has been identified by many scholars with one group of Indo-European speakers. Perhaps the most characteristic artifacts of the Kurgan peoples (other than their burial mounds) were their stone axes, heavy artifacts hafted by wooden handles mounted through centrally drilled holes. These axes were so much a part of the culture that their form was reproduced in bronze when that technology was learned, even though metallurgy makes possible a more streamlined axe, cast in one piece.[19] Great labor goes into the fashioning of a stone axe, and the most labor-intensive feature of the axe is, of course, the drilling of the central hole for the haft, which must have been ground into the solid stone by means of a bow drill using a succession of quickly dulled stone bits.

The conclusion one must draw is that *Haekmon* referred to the bearing or pivot point of a bow drill or fire drill. The Greek reflex *akmon,* "anvil," is a simple extension of this meaning to "a surface on which useful work was done." But, of course, the word had a celestial denotation too, which Greeks did not forget utterly in the denotation of *akmon*; Homeric anvils fall from heaven or are suspended there. In the Hindu tradition, the pivot point of the heavenly axle—called Nabho-yoni or simply Yoni—is a Vedic reminder that the structure and operation of fire drills has a male and a corresponding female element. This fact is retained in Greek as well, for the word *akmon* also refers to pestles, and to the heads of battering rams. The paired names Akmon-Pessalos of the paired Kerkopes suggests that the working surface (mortar) and the instrument used (pestle) were paired in thought as well as in use. The meaning "stone" found in the several languages would have come about because the fabric of the axe and of the drill point were stone. The notion "missile" comes from the use of the axe as a throwing weapon, as with Thor's use of Mjollnir. (The homonymy of anvil-stone-weapon is well attested in the myth of King Arthur, who succeeded in drawing forth the sword Excalibur variously from an anvil or a stone.) The axe acquired its name from the drilling necessary to make its haft hole. The idea that lightning was a celestial weapon came about through a blending of these ideas. Lightning produced from the heavenly fire drill is like the throwing weapon produced from the earthly bow drill, on the basis of both their means of production and their destructive effects.

The root **Haekmon* was compounded in one culture with the word for oak: the Lithuanian name for lightning is *perkuno akmuo*. The word *perkuno* means oak and is of such antiquity as to antedate the operation of Verner's law (whereby *p* Germanic *f,* e.g., **pəter‹father*), which was one linguistic feature separating the Germanic from other subgroups of Indo-European. Proto-German **perkunaz,* "oak," yields the modern English *fir*. In its pre-Germanic form, this same root, **perkwu-* led to Latin *quercus,* "oak." The oak, being tall and straight, attracts more than its fair share of lightning. Furthermore, oak trunks were used for mill shafts. For the making of a fire drill, too, a hardwood such as oak would be preferable to a softwood. Yggdrasil, the pole tree of heaven, was thought to be an ash or oak. Compare the polysemy of the word for acorn: penis head, testicle, pivot point, ball, fertility.

The cult of Perkunas still persists in the Baltic lands beneath a thin veneer of Christian elements. It is patently inspired by celestial antecedents. Perkunas is thought to traverse the sky in a fiery chariot. When thunder is heard, one says, "God is coming—the wheels are striking fire." Perkunas lives in a castle mounted on a hilltop. Furthermore, Perkunas is the god of the awakening spring (the equinox), and farmers will not plant before they hear the thunder of his arrival.[20]

The universe was therefore envisioned as a macrocosmic fire drill, and later, after the invention of a new technology, as a turning mill, grinding out its plenty in season. It is not surprising, then, that the two Kerkopes, whom we have correlated with Atlas at one end of the universe and Prometheus at the other, have the names Akmon (pivot point, anvil) and Passalos (peg). But the universe did not maintain its right running. The mill wheel broke, as in the catastrophic event of "The Mill Song." In some variants it was submerged in the maelstrom, where instead of plenty it grinds out salt. Amrita is lost, as in the "Amritamanthana" or *Astika,* and plans must be made for its retrieval. In Greek myth the wheel falls off Oenomaus's chariot, and he is replaced by a newcomer. The universe has run backward ever since the concatenation of crime and countercrime committed by Atreus and Thyestes over the golden ram culminated in internecine slaughter and cannibalism. Phaethon's misguided attempt at chariot driving resulted in conflagration and flood, the sun following a new course ever afterward, while the Milky Way marks the burned-out path of the boy's runaway steeds. Ragnarok will ensue upon three devastating winters, and the world will end in great upheaval despite the efforts of Thor and the other Aesir.

PRECESSION

Occasional disturbance of the regular succession of the seasons on the plane of celestial phenomena does not seem drastic enough to account for the stories of upheaval, ruin, and a lost world order which we find on the plane of myth. Nor is there any analog in seasonal phenomena to account for the mythic idea of the breaking up of the mill, the coming apart of the wheel (c/d). Only one phenomenon of the cosmos can accommodate all these features of the myth. Eclipses and occultations might forebode general upheaval. Comets and meteors might do the same or even create tangible disasters. But only precession can account for the idea of regularly recurring replacement coinciding with a universe out of order. Precession is a feature of the motion of every spinning body whose center of gravity does not coincide exactly with its center of rotation, like the wobble of a top that is not spinning exactly upright. Since the earth bulges at the equator, and since the plane of its rotation (the equator) does not coincide with the plane of its revolution about the sun (the ecliptic), the pull exerted on the earth by the sun and the moon creates a moment of inertia between the center of gravity and the center of revolution. This force produces a slow wobble in the earth's spin that has a period of twenty-six thousand years, while the displacement of the equator from the equinox varies between 22° and 24° (currently about 23.5°). If you set a gyroscope to spinning and push up or down on its outer rim, you will find that its pole begins a conical motion—*voilá* precession.

Though it is true that precession of the equinoxes is a continuous, not a stepwise, process, the shifting of the equinoctial points and their associated poles can be perceived only in relationship to their recurrence near a proximate star. Figure 6.1 shows that precession shifts the axis of the earth's rotation continuously and at a nearly uniform rate so that the north celestial pole (the earth's north pole projected into the sky) describes a circle in the heavens. The pole is now near Polaris (at 9 o'clock in the diagram). The pole was once near Thuban (fig. 6.2), and in the future it will pass near gamma Cephei (fig. 6.3), delta Cygni (fig. 6.4), and Vega (fig. 6.5). In about the year 15,000, as in 11,000 B.C., the pole will reside at tau Herculei (fig. 6.1). During the intervals between these widely spaced points, the pole lacks a "home" (or its home star is dim and insignificant). We can certainly speak of epochs in this regard. The Polaris epoch, now about at its culmination, began in the sense of its becoming a noticeable pole star about 1300 and will cease to be when Polaris no longer serves the pole, by 2700 or so. Thuban enjoyed its epoch as a pole star between 3600 and 2200 B.C. Between 2200 B.C. and A.D. 1300 the pole was not within 10° of a star visible to the unaided eye.

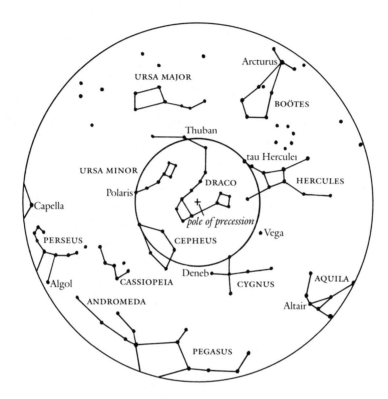

FIGURE 6.1

This figure is centered on that point in the constellation Draco which is never moved by precession, the so-called pole of precession. The circle drawn with this point at its center shows the path of the north celestial pole among the stars as it completes its circuit about every 26,000 years. Note that the circle passes near several stars. Currently Polaris, which is less than one degree from the north celestial pole, is the polestar. Eons ago the polestar was Thuban in Draco. In the future, gamma Cephei will become the polestar, and later delta Cygni and Vega (see figures 6.3–6.5). The outer circle in this figure encompasses the expanse of sky that is, was, or will be circumpolar to a viewer placed at latitude 44° N; that is, a circle with Polaris at its center and a rim at the edge of the outer circle will encompass all those stars that currently never set as viewed from the area generally accepted as the Indo-European homeland.

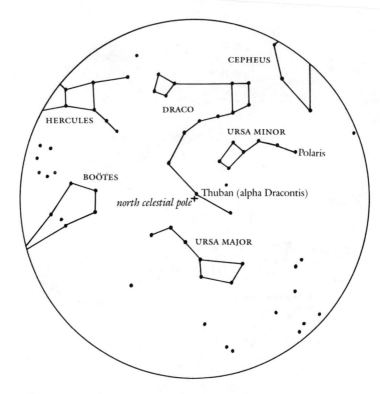

FIGURE 6.2

The northern sky as viewed from latitude 44° N in 2900 B.C. Thuban (alpha Dracontis) is the polestar, as it is less than one degree from the north celestial pole. Polaris has not yet gained its place as polestar.

The stars trace out arcs of circles as they rise, pass through the sky, and set. These arcs shift their orientation with changes in the position of the pole. Hence our perception of the stars' places in the sky depends on the position of the pole. When the pole shifts, all the stars change in the aspect they present. For example, if you travel northward, Polaris will rise higher in the sky, while some southern stars will completely disappear from view. Stars that you used to see in your previous location will cease to be seen, while others that rode across the mid-sky will now travel a shorter, more southerly path. The same general effect oc-curs because of the precessional shift of the pole, but without the ob-

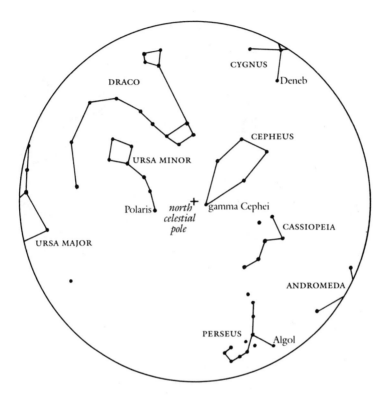

FIGURE 6.3

The northern sky as viewed from latitude 44° N in A.D. 3830. Gamma
Cephei is the polestar, as it is two degrees from the north celestial pole.
Polaris has lost its place as polestar, and hence our descendants will either
have changed its name or will be employing an anachronistic one.

server moving on the earth's surface. Yet the effects owing to precession
are slight and can be noticed only with instrumented scrutiny or by
comparing the star charts of one's ancestors with the current appearance of the stars. The latter is what Hipparchus did about 130 B.C. in
order to measure the rate at which precession takes place.

As the framework of our perception of the stars shifts at the pole, so
it shifts everywhere. Other noticeable but imaginary points in the sky
are no less affected by precession than the poles. So the equinoxes and
the solstices also seem to move among the stars. If the sun currently
seems to stop its seasonal north-south motion near a particular star, in

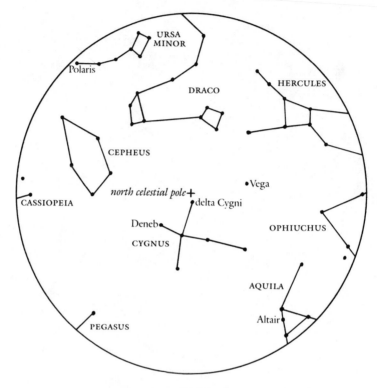

FIGURE 6.4

The northern sky as viewed from latitude 44° N in A.D. 11,600. Delta
Cygni is the polestar. Polaris is so far from the polestar of that era that it
is just barely circumpolar; at its lowest point in the sky it grazes the
horizon.

seven hundred years or so that star will be useless as a solstice marker.
If today the equinox occurs when the sun rises just after the rising of a
certain bright star, that star will no longer be a harbinger of the equinox
in 2700.

This fact is illustrated in a series of diagrams (figs. 6.6–6.10). In
5800 B.C., Pollux rose just enough before the sun on the date of the
equinox that it shone noticeably for a few moments before the light of
dawn encroached on its shining (fig. 6.6). By 4700 B.C. the equinoctial
sun rose before Pollux. Then Elnath was spring's harbinger (fig. 6.7).

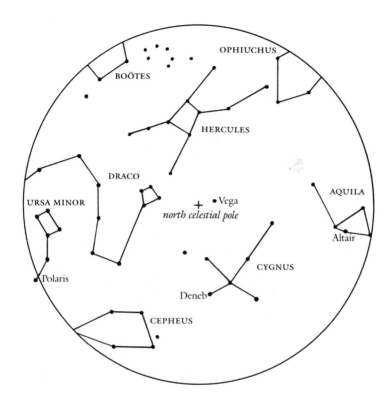

FIGURE 6.5

The northern sky as viewed from latitude 44° N in A.D. 13,810. Vega, five degrees from the north celestial pole, is the polestar. Polaris is just outside this circle and thus, far from being a polestar, would in fact set for a brief period each day.

By 4501 B.C. there was a further shift. Elnath was now too close to the sun to shine out on the first day of spring (fig. 6.8). In 3102 B.C. the equinoctial sun was in the center of Taurus, and the Pleiades would have shone for some moments before being dimmed by the rising sun (fig. 6.9). By 2300 B.C. the Pleiades were too close to the sun so to serve (fig. 6.10). Hamal or Algol may have been the markers in 1500 B.C., but the rising of Capella may have been significant (fig. 6.11).

As a given phenomenon (e.g., the spring equinox) recedes from the vicinity of one star and approaches the vicinity of another, one star

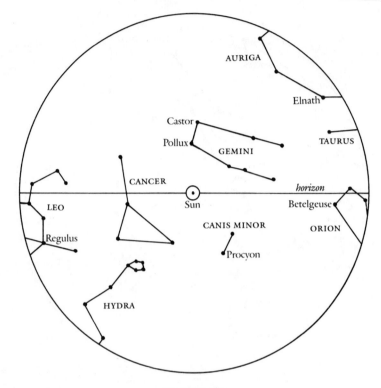

FIGURE 6.6
The eastern sky seen just before sunrise at the spring equinox in 5800 B.C.
At this time Punarvasu (Castor and Pollux) were, at their heliacal rising,
harbingers of the equinox. This is the date farthest in antiquity for which
there may be any record of the position of the equinox.

could be said to replace the other. During periods when the phenomenon takes place outside the vicinity of *any* star, the universe could be
said to be in a condition of chaos, the equinox lacking any "home," the
pole displaced from its center.

Myth seems to agree with Chicken Licken that the sky is falling. But
what Henny Penny and Chicken Licken's five other companions fail to
realize is that the king whom they want to inform of the disaster is the
subject of it: *he* has been replaced. Frodi is no longer king of the mill;
Indra is replaced by Shiva and Shiva by Buddha as the Mahachakravarti
(Turner of the Great Wheel). A new age has been ushered in. The very

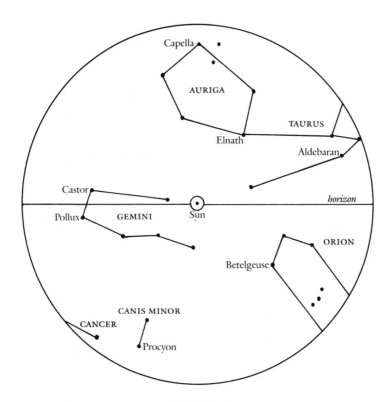

FIGURE 6.7
The eastern sky seen just before sunrise at the spring equinox in 4700 B.C.
The equinoctial point lies at the foot of Punarvasu (Gemini). Elnath is the
only ready star to serve as an equinoctial marker.

word *world* is indicative of a succession of eons, one of which will replace another: **wer-*, "man, mankind," and **-aldh* "age."[21]

On the face of it, this proposition seems hardly tenable; the very
idea seems fantastic. According to the written traditions of astronomical knowledge, precession of the equinoxes was "discovered" by
Hipparchus in about 130 B.C., much later than the origins of the myths
under consideration. But a gulf separates technical knowledge about the
rate of the precessional effect, which Hipparchus was the first to ascer-
tain, and formal knowledge that a continuous, nondirunal, nonseasonal
motion alters the stars' positions relative to the equator. And these both

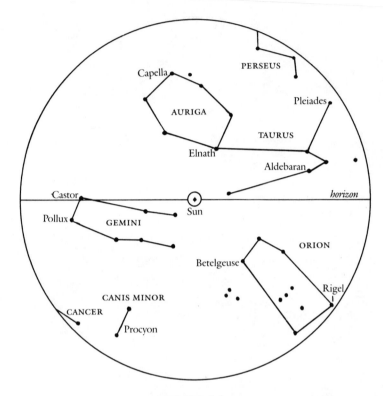

FIGURE 6.8

The eastern sky seen at the spring equinox in 4501 B.C. Here there is no star whose heliacal rising is a harbinger of the equinox. The Pleiades are too far from the sun to be harbingers, and the other stars in the neighborhood are too close to the sun to be visible. Under such circumstances, the Nakshatra system works much better than one that depends on a heliacal rising to predict the time of the equinox. Compare figure 6.15.

differ from the informal knowledge that cherished equinox markers and pole stars no longer function as such. What we are at pains to prove, therefore, is that the ancients used equinox markers eons before Hipparchus, for if they used them, they surely noticed, although not in a single lifetime, that these "landmarks" of cosmic recurrence ceased to function after a time and that new ones needed to be chosen. Furthermore, we are under the onus of demonstrating that certain equinox markers are indelibly linked with a given myth. Evidence for these difficult propositions will be presented in as coherent a fashion as possible.

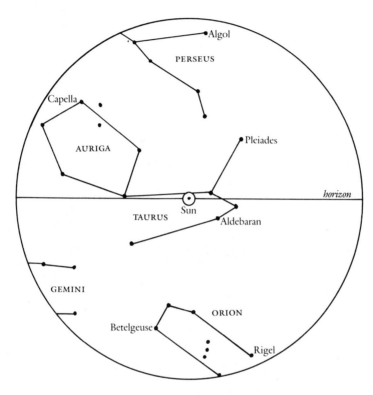

FIGURE 6.9

The eastern sky at sunrise on the day of the spring equinox in 3102 B.C.
The heliacal rising of the Pleiades is the sign of the equinox. The Pleiades
rose an hour before the sun and have become visible, since their separation
from the sun is just beyond the minimum distance of 16° that a star may
be from the sun and still be visible.

One seasonal name has reflexes in almost all of the daughter languages: spring. The reflexes of it (Latin *ver*, Greek *er*, Old Bulgarian
vesna, and Sanskrit *vasanta*) enable the reconstruction of a root, **wesr*.[22]
One cannot definitely posit an etymological meaning (that is, a verbal
idea) behind the meaning "spring," but we may say with confidence
that this seasonal name was the subject of a verbal notion. In the *Odyssey*
we find a verbal phrase that implies as much: *earos neon histamenoio*,
"spring newly standing."[23]

This idea is important in discovering how early peoples might deter-

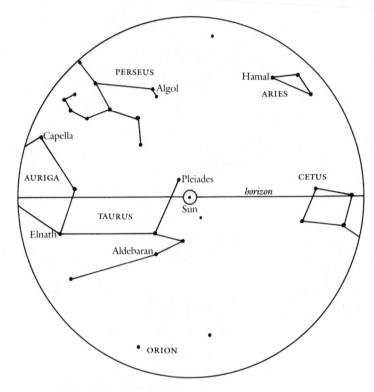

FIGURE 6.10

The eastern sky at sunrise on the day of the spring equinox in 2300 B.C.
The heliacal rising of the Pleiades can no longer serve as the sign of the
equinox because they have "verged" into the glow of dawn. But the second-
magnitude star in Aries, Hamal, is now positioned to serve as a harbinger.
It was 19° above the horizon by sunrise and would have become visible
during the glow of dawn just long enough to be a marker of the season of
the equinox.

mine the onset of the seasons. In historical times we know that the
solstices were determined by the use of the shadow cast by a gnomon—
a vertically placed rod or stick. Its shortest shadow is cast at noon on
midsummer's day. The direction of the shortest shadow's line will be
north–south. Once this line is marked out, the longest shadow along
it will be that cast at noon on midwinter's day. Determining the equinoxes, however, would be more difficult. One would need an accurately

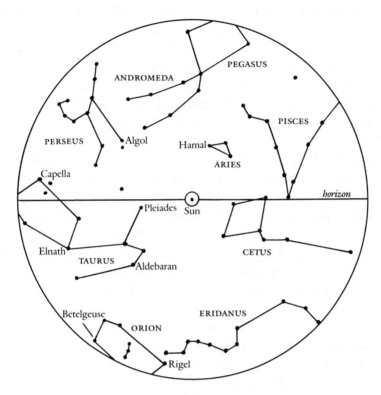

FIGURE 6.11

The eastern sky at sunrise on the day of the spring equinox in 1500 B.C. Here we find that precession has rendered useless all of the previous harbingers of the equinox in Taurus, including the Pleiades. Aries—whose brightest star, Hamal, may have served as a harbinger some centuries earlier—has by now been washed out in the dawnglow. But Capella, in the constellation of the Charioteer (Auriga), rises at about the same time as Aries and is bright enough to be seen even when it is close to the horizon as dawn is breaking. Capella (Little Goat) first corroborated and then replaced Aries as the harbinger of the equinox during this era.

and finely divided ruler to bisect the line between the two extremes on the north–south line mentioned above or a square to find true east–west from the north–south line. Either method requires a quite sophisticated technology and painstaking work. But recurrences of the equinoxes could have been estimated by a more practicable method: the observation of celestial phenomena.

Phrases from the Homeric language permit us to infer that at the time of the poem's composition one method used was direct empirical observation of the heavens. A series of verbal compounds with the prefix *peri-,* "around," were used to describe the recurrence of the seasons. The repeated phrases "in the circling of the seasons," and "in the circling of the year(s)," imply that by the eighth century B.C. the Greeks knew that the annual course of the sun describes an arc along the zodiac that ends where it began. The inference is corroborated by several considerations. One verb with which *peri-* is compounded, *tellomai,* is compounded with another prefix, *ana-,* yielding *anatellomai*[24] and *anatolê* (cf. Anatolia), the normal words in Greek for "sunrise" and "sunrise direction." Another compound verb, *peritropeô,* is used of driving or moving animals in a circle, and of Hermes "perplexing" mankind.[25] The latter use is ambiguous[26] but may refer simply to the complexities of timekeeping. The noun from which the verb derives, *tropê,* refers to "turning" in a special sense, the solstices of the sun's course.

In one passage, the idea of a circular course completed at a recognized point is stated explicitly: *aps peritellomenou eteos* "the year finishing its circle backward from the beginning," *aps* precisely because the apparent course of the sun along the ecliptic from west to east is "backward," retrograde to its diurnal turning from east to west. If spring be taken as the beginning of the year (March was once the first month), then the above statement is equivalent to "spring newly standing," where the verb "to stand (up)" (*histamai*) is equivalent to *ana-tellomai,* used of sunrise. Such language was used not because sunrise is any different at the equinox than at any other time of year (although it is, for at that time the sun rises most vertically, directly, and suddenly from the horizon) but because some guide star or sign star rises up in the dawn (its first heliacal rising) to signal the advent of the equinox. The use of such a sign star is the most practicable method for determining the equinox directly from celestial phenomena, and it is this star, appearing heliacally each year at the same time, which finishes its circular course backward from the beginning.

All this is implicit in the very English word *spring* used of the season. As a noun it means "the place where something leaps up from the ground," as in the case of a water source. This usage is clearly attested for celestial phenomena in the term "moon spring," equal to (and replaced by) moonrise. The *Oxford English Dictionary* reports no *sun-spring,* but there is *dawnspring* and *dayspring,* and the springing up of a seasonal sign from the horizon is not limited to the vernal equinox, for Shakespeare uses "Summers spring."[27]

Once the time of the equinox had been established by the difficult process of using noontime shadows, another practicable method for determining its recurrence would be through the use of azimuth markers, points on the horizon known to be the rising point of the equinoctial sun as determined by the shadow method. These would continue to serve as markers of the equinox year after year without redetermination. A mountain peak, a low point, or better yet a pole or pair of poles embracing the sun's limb at its equinoctial rising would serve well, as at Stonehenge and many other astronometric sites discovered and described recently by archaeoastronomers.[28]

But which stars would have served the ancients as guides for determining the date of the equinoxes and solstices? The answer, of course, depends on the eon one is considering, for precession inexorably renders one such star useless and enables another. Further, the use of azimuth markers would make it clear to the priestly astronomers that the stars had failed them.

THE PUZZLE OF THE PLEIADES

No sign star for solstices or equinoxes is mentioned in the almanac section of Hesiod's *Works and Days.* Yet the farmer must have known the time of their occurrence: plowing at winter solstice is plowing too late (479ff.); Arcturus rises sixty days after the winter solstice (565–567); and the spring equinox is signaled by the appearance of the swallow into the light (568–569).[29] One thing is clear: the rising and setting of stars was used to mark the seasons. But in Hesiod's time the beginnings of the four astronomical seasons were simply not marked by the rising or setting of any of the bright stars of the zodiac.

For some reason, however, in this text of Hesiod the important dates of the farmer's year are made to coincide with the phenomena of the Pleiades. Harvest is said to begin with their rising, and plowing with their setting.[30] There is something illogical in Hesiod's presentation. The almanac portion of his work begins with the heliacal rising of the Pleiades, a phenomenon then unimportant for the astronomical seasons. Hesiod says that their rising corresponds to the time of the harvest (of the grain). But harvest should not be the *beginning* of the farmer's year. Plowing and sowing are the commencement of that affair with the soil that *ends* in the harvest. Why did Hesiod violate this naturally imposed sequence by assigning to the rising of the Pleiades the role of marking the end of the year?

One suspects it was not the demands of the farmer's almanac that presupposed the choice of a celestial sign convenient to mark its beginning but the demands of a celestial event that was important per se: the rising of the Pleiades, which forced its way into the farmer's calendar even though no calendric, modern or ancient, could precisely mark a purely agricultural season, which was in fact determined by local conditions of readiness and ripeness. Hesiod may have preserved the ancient importance of the rather dim Pleiades for determining the equinox by mentioning their heliacal rising, their cosmic setting, and their forty days of invisibility even though by his time, because of precession, they had ceased to mark any phenomenal season at all.

At one time, indeed, the heliacal rising of the Pleiades was all-important, for their up-springing was the sign of the year's having circled back upon itself: the vernal equinox. The era when they were seasonal was far beyond Hesiod's recollection or even Greek recollection. If, as I argue, Hesiod's use of the phenomena of the Pleiades as important signs is a vestige of their long-lost importance, he must have fallen back on lore derived from his Indo-European forebears. We can calculate the date at which the Pleiades rose 16° in advance of the sun so as to be visible in the dawn on March 21 of the Julian year at 40° N to be roughly 3500 B.C. This is just prior to the period in which, according to most scholars, the Indo-European tribes were beginning to migrate from their homelands.[31]

One would not expect tribal memories to extend across 2800 years without evidence that the facts of which the lore was but a dim recollection were of considerable importance to the aboriginal culture.[32] There is, indeed, linguistic evidence that the Pleiades enjoyed such deep-seated importance. With the possible exception of a designation for Ursa Major, Pleiades is the only name for an asterism to be represented in several Indo-European daughter languages: beside the Greek Pleiades one places modern Persian *parvin*, Pashto *perune* "Pleiades," and Avestan *paoiryaeinyas*, the name of an unspecified constellation. The Avestan and Persian forms could well have been derived from the Avestan word *paoirya*, "first." Both the Greek and the Pashto forms have undergone deformation, probably owing to folk etymologizing.[33] The ultimate root would then be **pel-*, "to fill," with its extended form **pelu-* indicating "surfeit, primacy."[34]

The Pleiades were the "first" constellation, and their heliacal appearance fulfilled the year in the era 3102 B.C. (see fig. 6.9). Their function would have been to mark the "center" of the sky, the spring equinoctial point. The equinox is central in a number of ways: it brings the onset of the most important season; it marks the time of year when day is equal to night; its occurrence on the north–south line of noonday shadows cast by a gnomon is at the midpoint between the extremes; and it occurs at the juncture of the ecliptic and the equator (x marks the spot, if you will) as imaginary lines in the sky. In this regard it is fascinating to learn that in an early Persian work to be examined shortly in more detail, the *Tir Yasht* 12, there is a compound word, *purviyôni*, that probably refers to the Pleiades.[35] It is composed of two etyma we have just discussed: *purvi*, "first," and *yoni*, "vagina, womb" (compare Nabhoyoni, "Sky Vagina").

But with the passing of centuries, precession acted so as to bring about changes: whereas at one time their appearance in the predawn darkness was a sign that the sun had found the equinox, later the apparition of the Pleiades slipped eastward at the equinox so as to appear in an ever lightening sky until they disappeared into the sun's glow (see fig. 6.10). Their heliacal rising occurred ever later—well after the equinox in the late spring—as was the case by Hesiod's time.[36]

Slipping ever farther into the light so as to be barely visible, they would seem like someone drowning in the vast gulf of the sea. This recalls the myth of Phaethon, who drowned after making too close an approach between the sun and the earth. It recalls Phaethon's seven sisters, whom we associated with the Pleiades on the grounds of similarities between their numbers, names, and myths. These Heliades-Pleiades sat on the edge of the gulf, endlessly weeping for their lost brother until they were changed into poplar trees. They continued to weep amber tears, their golden color reminiscent of the tinge of dawn. It recalls the story told by Apollonius Rhodius that when the Argonauts visited the lake into which Phaethon had fallen, the noxious odor created by his corpse was enough to kill the birds that flew overhead. Given that the Pleiades were thought to be doves, we can say that the double death of Phaethon by drowning and by cremation was a precursor of the uselessness of the Pleiades owing to their having "drowned" in the sun. They "died" and dropped from the sky.[37]

The Latin name for the Pleiades was Vergiliae, and indeed, as seemed to be the case with Hesiod, the Romans connected them with spring long after they ceased to be in the heavens. *Vergiliae* looks as if it may have *ver,* "spring," as its first syllable, hence an etymology: *Eas stellas nostri appellaverunt quod post ver exoriuntur,* "Our writers named these stars [Vergiliae] because they rise *after* spring."[38] Hyginus continues with a notice seemingly designed to save some respect for the failed Pleiades: "They have still greater honor than the other (stars), too, because their rising is a sign of summer, their setting of winter—a thing which is not true of other constellations."[39] This folk etymology involving the etymon "spring" had absolutely no application in Hyginus's day, since by his time (the age of the Antonine emperors) the rising of the Pleiades was more a sign of the onset of summer than of spring.

The true etymology of the name Vergiliae is not certainly established; semantic difficulties counter the obvious choice. Despite these misgivings, the editors of the *Oxford Latin Dictionary* accede that the etymology is still most likely to be connected to the verb root *vergo.* Under the entry *vergo* they list several meanings: "to move on a downward slope, to sink towards something." The semantic difficulty disappears under the thesis we are considering here, for this etymology fits the declining Pleiades sinking inexorably into the sun and invisibility at the equinox. The definitions continue: "of elevated positions," "to look out to, point towards." Observations of heliacal risings would naturally be taken from an elevated position with a pointer (an azimuth marker) to mark the expected apparition. The definitions continue: "of states of affairs," "to incline, tend to a (worse) condition." This can certainly be attributed to the Pleiades after 2800 B.C. (compare figs. 6.10 and 6.11) Finally: "of color," "to shade into," which again befits the change of conditions by which the visible Pleiades in a dark sky became less visible in a rosy sky. It looks as if the proto-Romans chose a basic verb root, "to turn, bend," to make a proper name for the declining Pleiades and then by similitude ascribed other meanings to the verb from the conditions surrounding the observation of the Pleiades from a height looking out into the reddening sky.

Yet there is some evidence that the hypothetical Indo-European root *wer-,[40] from which the verb *vergo* derives, had importance for celestial phenomena before the breakup of the Indo-European association into far-flung tribes. Its reflexes include English *weird,* the original (verbal) meaning of which was "to preordain by a decree of fate," as in the proverb "A man may woo where he will, but he is wed where he is weard."[41] The idea of "fatefulness" as a denotation of a verbal notion meaning intrinsically "to turn" seems to be of no consequence in discovering an early celestial denotation for the word. It barely hints at an astrological connection. But the existence of the Greek cognate *rhombus* makes a celestial denotation all but certain. The verb *rhembô* is neutral in meaning—simply "to turn around." But the noun refers to several religiously charged articles of Greek culture: (1) the bull-roarer, a whistle on a string, slung about rapidly in a circle, intoning its music during the mysteries; (2) a magic wheel, spun alternately in each direction by the torque applied by two cords wrapped in opposite directions about its axle, used to enchant a resistant lover; (3) a tambourine or drum used in the worship of Rhea and of Dionysus; (4) the phallus; (5) circular motions: an eagle's flight, the motion of the heavens, the sun's course; and (6) an epithet for a demon of fate (*alastôr*) in the phrase *Nemesis kai rhombos alastôr.*[42] The semantics of this word recapitulate ritual circular motion involving sexuality and sexual symbolism (the phallus [D] and the drum [C]). Could the bull-roarer be distant kin to the *mani-chhos-khor* of the Tibetan monks?

In the Indic branch, the Indo-European family name for the Pleiades seems to have been lost. In its place we find the Sanskrit name Krittikas. These six sisters of Hindu mythology are not mere asterisms but figure in a myth that, like the myth of the Pleiades and Orion, seems to have astronomical antecedents. The Krittikas were said to be the six[43] nurses of Skanda, usually known by his matronymic Karttikeya (Nursling of the Krittikas), the god of war and avatar of the planet Mars. This god was the son of Shiva (or of Rudra), who was produced without the intervention of woman, hence his need for female foster-parentage. In this role each one of the Krittikas tended one of the god's six heads. In other variants, Karttikeya is the son of the firegod Agni and Ganga, the heavenly river (Ganges) that flowed out from Vishnu's big toe and fell to earth in seven streams, buffered by the mound of hair on Shiva's head. The name of Karttikeya's mother is also given as Parvati; this is the by-name of the great goddess Maha-Devi, wife of Shiva and daughter of Himavat (the Himalaya). It is one of several by-names of Maha-Devi referring to her origin in the mountain.[44]

The etymology of the name Krittikas is uncertain. It may have been derived from *krttih,* "skin, hide," or from *krtt,* "wickerwork." Contextual information allows us to attach other connotations to the name as well: (1) flame, (2) cart (wheel), and (3) shears (as if from *krntati*).[45] Folk etymology played a role in the interpretation (and perhaps the spelling) of the name. Some Hindus pictured the constellation as a razor, a configuration determined by the folk-etymological belief that the name derives from the root *kart-,* "to cut."[46]

We would like an etymology that favors the meaning "being first" or "slipping," as in the cases just examined from Greek, Iranian, and Latin. Lacking that, one that had to do with fertility would suit the position of the Pleiades as onetime harbingers of spring. The connotation "cart (wheel)" for the name Krittikas certainly fits in with the idea of the heavens as a celestial wheel and with the notion of plenty borne by a farmer's cart. Of the other connotations, "flame" fits in with the celestial production of lightning, and "shears" or "cut" with the idea of sheaves of grain. There are two Sanskrit roots that, given the deformative effects of folk etymology or taboo alteration, might be proposed as an aboriginal etymology for Krittikas: (1) *kr-,* "to strew, scatter," which would fit the idea of sowing grain; and (2) *krs-,* "to plow," which is the better choice because it has the advantage of having a cognate in Avestan, *karesh,* "to drag, to draw, to sow grain," and the Afghan *kisht,* "sown field."[47] Though none of these can be seriously proposed as the ety-mology for Krittikas without more direct evidence, we will keep them in mind for the sequel, which will be an examination of Vedic and Avestan mythology having to do with the Pleiades and with celestially based stories about seasonal phenomena.

Myths involving the war god Skanda, whose matronymic, Kartti-keya, derives from Krittikas, are important to understanding the im-portance of the Pleiades. The god was an ad hoc creation, made to rid the world of Taraka, a powerful Daitya. The Daityas were a race of demons and giants who warred against the gods (A) and interrupted sacrifices (F). We may compare them with the Asuras, who challenged the gods at the Churning of Ocean for amrita, and with the Greek Titans. But Taraka's name means "star." Skanda, the planet Mars, named after the Pleiades, was created to oust an evil star.[48]

In another story about Karttikeya, Indra and he had a dispute about their respective powers (A). The issue was to be decided by contest: running a race around (one of) the Himalayas (C-D). Yet they failed to agree as to who had won and so appealed to the mountain for judgment. Indra was favored. In his fury at the mountain, Karttikeya hurled his lance (D) at it, pierced it (C-D), and created the pass called Krauncha. The name Krauncha is also attached to a demon who was the confederate of the Daitya Taraka. Krauncha is also the name of one of the seven Dvipas of Hindu cosmology. The Dvipas are usually con-ceived of as insular continents having Mount Meru as their common center, stretching out from it like the leaves of a lotus, each separated from the others by a surrounding ocean.

A hole rent by Karttikeya in the fabric of the world, a feature of geography in the Hindu conception, a demon connected with an evil star—these are seemingly totally disparate entities. Why, then, do they have a common name? The Dvipas are seven in number; so, too, the Pleiades (though usually the number of Krittikas is given as six). Is there any association between the celestial seven and the seven of geography?

The best argument for the existence of an association between the two is made not from Vedic but from Iranian sources. Throughout Iranian literature we find mention of the seven Karshvares. Scholars have associated them with the Dvipas, not on any etymological grounds but because they seem to be geographical regions, six surrounding a central seventh,[49] each surrounded by a circumambient sea and with a great mountain in their midst. The Pleiades are so configured in the sky; Alcyone, roughly in the center, has an apparent magnitude at least twice as great as any of her sisters. One is west of her, one is east, one southeast, and two north. Not incidentally to the function of the Pleiades as harbingers of spring, the name Karshvares derives from the Avestan verb *karesh* discussed above, meaning "to sow grain." Of interest, too, is the fact that one of the earliest references to the Karshvares occurs in *Gah Ushahin,* the Mazdaean matins spoken at dawn during sacrificial offices to the goddess Dawn: "And we sacrifice to the lights of dawn which are radiant with their light and fleetest horses which sweep over the Karshvares."[50] Are the Karshvares heavenly or earthly divisions?

PRIMORDIAL BATTLE

One of the Vedic Dvipas, Krauncha, has two namesakes, one connected in myth with a hole in a mountain and the other with an evil star. The Avestan Karshvares were created on the day upon which the benevolent star par excellence, Tishtar, brought rain into a thirsty world.[51]

Tishtar's role in bringing rain is told in detail by the *Tir Yasht,*[52] a collection of prayers to be uttered during the month of the summer solstice as drought gives way to the rainy season. The alternation of seasons is viewed as a battle between Tishtrya and the Daeva of drought, Apaosha. Tishtrya (an earlier form of Tishtar) has been identified with Sirius on the somewhat shaky grounds of a single citation from Plutarch;[53] a more positive argument for the identification lies in the phenomenology of Sirius, dog star of summer, because in the Persian calendar Tishtar presides over the first month of summer. The epochal battle is said to have taken place when Tishtrya was "in" the sign Cancer.[54] Now, Sirius cannot be *in* the constellation Cancer, but in about 2000 B.C. Sirius was a *paranatellonton* with Cancer, i.e., it rose at the same time. Since Sirius is so bright as to be visible even when the dawn's light is quite advanced and since Cancer is a rather dim constel-

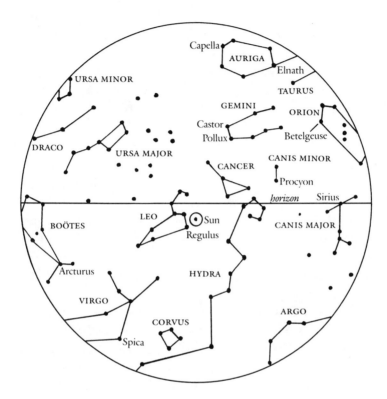

FIGURE 6.12

The eastern sky seen just before sunrise at the summer solstice in 2000 B.C. from latitude 30° N, the latitude of Persepolis, the Persian capital. Cancer is not quite high enough in the sky at its heliacal rising to serve as a marker for the solstice. Its stars are dim, and it would be difficult to detect in the dawnglow. To the south, however, at about the same time as the last star of Cancer, rises Sirius. It is the sky's brightest star, so bright that its heliacal rising over a flat horizon can be seen just before sunrise, as here. Sirius, then, though not on the zodiacal circle, could serve as a surrogate marker for the solstice, which occurs in Leo and which the heliacal rising of the dim Cancer should mark.

lation, the heliacal rising of Sirius was a sign of the summer solstice, which was located in Leo in about 2000 B.C., a phenomenon also marked by the heliacal rising of Cancer (see fig. 6.12). The celestial connection, therefore, suggests that Tishtar's battle was epochal, not merely seasonal.

The battle between Tishtrya and Apaosha (A) takes place in two acts. During the last phase of his apparition (the last third of the month Tir?), Tishtrya appears as a white horse in gold caparison (G), at which time he descends to the salt sea Vouru-Kasha (E). There the evil demon (Daeva) Apaosha appears as a black horse with a black tail.[55] They fight for three days and three nights (A3), and Apaosha wins.[56] The loss is owing to a lack of proper sacrifice (F) to the celestial god; Ahura reorders the sacrifice (G6), and Tishtrya returns to the fray. The battle lasts until noon (C-D5), at which point Tishtrya vanquishes the demon and prepares to send the waters down upon the thirsty fields (G).[57]

The battle fits the paradigm, a fact that encourages our interpretation of it as an epochal struggle. It occasions the creation of the world divisions and the sea. The involvement of opponents clothed in white and black harks back to tales of momentous struggle in Greek myth. These are hints of the story's epochal nature.

There is more: Tishtrya's battle with Apaosha recapitulates the epochal battle recounted in the *Bundahesh* (or *Bundahish*) between Auharmazd and Aharman. The inclusion of Tishtrya's battle in the cosmology section of the *Bundahesh* is one clue as to its importance: the rain sent by Tishtar marks the beginning of the world order. And in the *Zad-Sparam*, a paraphrase of the *Bundahesh*,[58] Tishtar's opponent is not Apaosha but Aharman himself.[59]

The *Zad-Sparam* is merely a précis of the *Bundahesh*, but as an account of the epochal and celestial primal battle it is even more detailed. Auharmazd continually occupies himself with the struggle to keep Aharman away from his territory (A). He does so by uttering pure words (G9) and confounding spells (F9). He appointed spirits of sky, water, earth, plants, animals, mankind, and fire (all of creation) as protectors against the feared *drug*. They were able to maintain that protection for three thousand years (A3).[60] In order to render it impossible for Aharman to seduce his creation to the dark side, Auharmazd set a maximum period as a limit to their struggle: three periods of three thousand years each. By this means it was possible to keep Aharman in check. But it was not possible to keep him from doing harm, for whenever he returns to his "requisite" darkness, Aharman (in his serpentine avatar) spreads abroad much poison, causing endless strife (E3).[61]

For 3,000 years the appointed spirits possessed bodies. They did not "walk on their navels." The sun, moon, and stars stood still. At the end of this period there was a "mischievous incursion." [62] The meaning of these seemingly cryptic statements is made clear by the arguments developed above, to wit, the equinoctial point does not move out of a zodiacal sign during a precessional epoch. (This period is actually closer to 2,000 than to 3,000 years, because a complete cycle through the twelve signs takes 26,000 years. But we must remember that an accurate determination of the rate of precession had to await Hipparchus's work in about 130 B.C.) The immobility of the navels (recall Nabhoyoni) is a symbol for the stability of the location of the equinox near an appointed star and its associated pole during an epoch.

At this point Auharmazd became dissatisfied with his stable creation and brought forth Time (i.e., Eon),[63] and Time made creatures able to move. Motion allows Aharman visible expression, but this motion is limited and temporal. We read: "At the same time Aharman came from accompanying Time out to the front, out to the star station; the connection of the sky with the star station was open, which showed, since it hung down into empty space, the strong communication of the lights and glooms, the place of strife in which is the pursuit of both." [64] The translator was obviously baffled by these words, and the references of such phrases as "star station" and "connection" are not as lucid as they might be. A possible interpretation is that "star station" refers to zodiacal signs—likely the group of three zodiacal signs that make up a season (in summer the sun passes through Gemini, Cancer, and Leo). From the phrase "the connection of the sky with the star station was open" we can infer that "sky" does not have any ordinary sense. It must mean something equivalent to Nabhoyoni or Niflheim, that is, the equinoctial point. The "connection" between the equinoctial point and the star station was fixed during the past eon of apparent stability, but now it is broken owing to the appearance of Aharman, that is, the "mischievous incursion." The connection is open; the nearest star and the true equinoctial point are divided, and their separation extends as much as one-third (of 9,000 years) over the star station.[65] This would be one zodiacal sign representing a precessional eon of 3,000 years. Hence the "connection" would be reestablished every eon in a new zodiacal sign, bringing back the stability that characterized the beginning of creation.

We must compare Aharman and his incursion with the Vedic star of evil, Taraka. In this Vedic story a rupture in the fabric of a sacred mountain is caused by demon Krauncha, Taraka's henchman. This relates the good star of the Avestan Tishtrya with the Vedic benign star Skanda, created to renew a destroyed order. This way of interpreting the texts is all but assured by the text of *Zad-Sparam* at 2.1:

> On the coming in of Aharman to the creatures it is thus declared in revelation, that in the month of Fravardin and the day Auharmazd, [i.e., at the vernal equinox⁶⁶] at noon, he came forth to the frontier of the sky. 2. The sky sees him and, on account of his nature, fears as much as a sheep trembles at a wolf; and Aharman came on, scorching and burning into it. 3. Then he came to the water which was arranged below the earth, and darkness without an eyelid was brought on by him; and he came on, through the middle of the earth, as a snake all-leaping comes on out of a hole; and he stayed within the whole earth. 4. The passage where he came on is his own, the way to hell, through which the demons make the wicked run. 5. Afterwards, he came to a tree, such as was of a single root, the height of which was several feet, and it was without branches and without bark, juicy and sweet; and to keep the strength of all kinds of trees in its race, it was in the vicinity of the middle of the earth; and at the self-same time it became withered.⁶⁷

The lost equinox is attended by the appearance of the monster of Time, seen here as a wolf or serpent issuing from the underworld through a hole (which is the place where the equinotial point used to be) into this world, creating the havoc of a world-out-of-order, symbolized by a withered world tree.

An expression of such ideas fitting the paradigm also occurs in early Iranian texts. Indeed all is implicit in the *Tir Yasht*:

> 50. I, O Spitama Zarathustra! have created that star Tishtrya as worthy of sacrifice, as worthy of prayer, as worthy of propitiation, as worthy of glorification as myself, Ahura Mazda,
> 51. In order to withstand, to break asunder, to afflict, to drive back the malice of the Pairika Duzyairya, whom evil-speaking people call Huyairya.

The etymology of Duzyairya and Huyairya are transparent. *Duz-* and *Hu-* correspond to Greek (now English) *dys-* and *eu-*, and *yairya* comes from I.E. **yero-* (English *year*). The Pairika demon is the beast of the eon of confusion. The dispute between evil-speaking people and their good-speaking counterparts would refer to a disagreement among the priesthood, some of whom might be called "evil-speaking" by traditionalists since they were ready to acknowledge a change in the home sign of the equinoctial point. At such times the equinoctial point is thought to reside outside a home sign:

> 54. Then all day long, all night long, that Pairika Duzyairya would wage war against this material world of mine, wanting to extinguish its life, and she goes on rushing upon and around it.

Hence we may say that Tishtrya's battle with Apaosha is epochal, being reminiscent of the dynastic battles waged by rivals for possession of the equinox. In Avestan literature it finds expression in a primordial dualism in which the theology of Zoroastrianism is rooted. A similar battle is fought by Indra against the drought demon Vritra. It reminds us also of the Churning of Ocean. Light and dark horses prefigure these primordial battles. The world has gone awry and is beset by demons whose venom and stench mingle with the earth and spatter the sky. In the one account, Tishtar dived to the bottom of the sea to carry away the poison, and it was that poison mixed up in the water which caused the sea to become salt.[68] The latter mythologem reminds us of the destruction of Frodi's mill. The poison also reminds us of Phaethon and of his weeping sisters, because the sea, into which he fell and they wept, retained their pollution so as to kill birds that flew by.

THE DESCENT OF THE GANGES

Tishtrya's creation of rain is reminiscent not only of the battle between Indra and Vritra but also of the descent of the Ganges. Ocean, impounded in a Rishi's stomach, was released at the coming of the monsoon as the river Ganges. The Ganges descended from heaven through Shiva's hair to bring water to a drought-stricken world.[69] This story bears recounting. It can be divided into two parts, the origin of the drought and its ending.

The drought had its inception with a Rishi named Agastya. Agastya was given the by-name Samudra-chuluka (Ocean Drinker) from his having drunk the ocean dry to help the gods discover their enemies, the Daityas, who were concealing and renewing themselves in the ocean.[70] For this feat he was made the regent of the southern (good) star Canopus, which bears his name. It is not surprising, therefore, that Agastya is a holy man of the south, who kept the region out of the control of the demons called Rakshasas.

The significance of the descent of the Ganges can be fully understood only after an examination of the nature of the being who caused the drought in the first place. Agastya figures in many stories that involve both the theme of replacement and celestial elements. The most grand of these is the *Ramayana,* to which we will digress momentarily. Visvamitra, born into the caste of the Kshatriya but raised through his own devotions to transcend his caste (A), was one of the seven great Rishis.[71] Visvamitra was beset by Rakshasas, demons[72] thought to have sprung from Brahma's foot and created by Brahma to guard the waters he had just formed.[73] Rama-chandra, prince of the solar race (i.e., descended from Vaivasvata) and the seventh incarnation of Vishnu, born into the world at the end of the eon Treta[74] (I), was the only possible source of succor for Visvamitra. Here is where Agastya comes in. A Rakshasas had been created by Agastya from a Daitya (Titan-demon) named Taraka ([evil] Starlady). (Compare Auharmazd creating Time as the visible expression of Aharman.) Her confederate was Krauncha.[75] They lived in a forest near the confluence of the Ganges and Sarju. Visvamitra asked Rama-chandra to kill Taraka. Reluctant to kill a woman, the hero instead cut off both her arms (F). She retaliated with a fearful shower of stones. Rama shot her with an arrow. As a boon for his help, Rama was given celestial weapons (D) and eventually taken to king Janaka's court, where he met his betrothed, Sita (Furrow) (C). In order to win her, Rama was required to string Shiva's bow (C-D), which he not only strung but broke (C/D). This had consequences. Parasu-rama, sixth incarnation of Vishnu, was still living. A Brahman (priestly caste), he had tried to exterminate the Kshatriyas (warrior caste) (A). As a follower of Shiva, he took offense at the breaking of his bow and challenged Rama-chandra to a trial (A). Rama won but spared his opponent's life since he was a Brahman (A). Preparations were made for Rama to succeed his father, but his stepmother Kaikeyi's spiteful humpbacked (D) servant Manthara (cf. *manth-*, "to churn") made trouble by influencing Kaikeyi (favorite wife of Rama's father) to be jealous and use her influence to favor her own son Bharata. She persuaded Rama's father to exile Rama for fourteen years (A). This set up a feud between the half-brothers (A2). This goes on and on, to epic length.

As regards our character Agastya, he was himself created in a curious way. Urvasi[76] was the most beautiful of the Apsarases, celestial nymphs who "move on the water" (i.e., on the dawn sky?), as their name implies.[77] These goddesses were created at the Amritamanthana.[78] The (twin) brothers Mitra and Varuna were so moved by her (unattainable) beauty that they spontaneously ejaculated their seed; some fell on the ground to produce Vasishtha. The rest fell into a jar of water to produce Vasishtha's brother Agastya,[79] a fish of great luster.[80] This tiny fish, destined for greatness, outgrew his bowl. He drank the ocean, as we have seen (E). His name supposedly derives from an incident in which he commanded the Vindhya mountains (D) to prostrate themselves before him. In so doing they lost their height (A).

One of the Rakshasas who opposed Agastya was Vatapi, who assumed the form of a ram. Offered in sacrifice by a devotee, the ram was cooked and eaten. Vatapi, hidden in the devout Brahman's stomach (E), was then summoned forth by his brother Ilwala. The monster would break forth (F2) from the victim's stomach, destroying him (A).[81] But when the fish Agastya performed these rites and ate this ram,[82] Vatapi was completely digested by Agastya's superior digestive power. When Ilwala summoned his brother forth, nothing was left to escape but a little gas.

Of even more importance in the story of the Descent of the Ganges than Agastya is his brother Vasishtha, whose name means "most wealthy."[83] Vasishtha possessed a cow of plenty (G, C) named Nandini, offspring of Surabhi, the cow produced at Amritamanthana. According to a story recounted in the *Ramayana*, Visvamitra coveted this cow and attempted to take her away by force (A4). A great battle ensued. Vasishtha won the first round by reducing a hundred of his opponent's sons to ashes with a blast from his mouth. It was at this point that

Visvamitra determined to acquire the power and status of a Brahman. By means of his priestly power he cursed (F9) Vasishtha's hundred sons to be reduced to ashes and then to be reborn as outcasts for seven hundred births. In a variant of this battle, told in the *Markandeya Purana,* Vasishtha was serving as priest to King Haris-chandra. Visvamitra so insulted the king that Vasishtha cursed him. Visvamitra was transformed into a crane. He then retorted with a curse of his own, dooming Vasishtha to become a bird as well. The two monstrous birds fought their battle so furiously that the course of the universe was disturbed (F4). Many creatures perished. In a variant, Visvamitra interceded evilly in a contest between Vasishtha and a certain king by causing a man-eating Rakshasas to enter the king (compare Agastya and Vatapi). This royal demon then devoured Vasishtha's hundred sons.[84] In grief, Vasishtha either (1) cast himself from Mount Meru (C/D); (2) threw himself into the sea with a stone about his neck (E, C/D); or (3) plunged into a river in flood with his arms bound (E, F5). In any case, he was saved (G) unharmed and unbound. In yet another variant, Visvamitra commanded the river Sarasvati to bring Vasishtha to him so that he could kill him. The river obeyed his command only upon Vasishtha's insistence. Upon bringing Vasishtha into Visvamitra's vicinity, however, the river promptly swerved its path and carried Vasishtha away from his armed and ready opponent.

With mention of the theme of hiding-reappearance and of these rivers of salvation, we may return to the discussion of the Descent of the Ganges. In India drought is followed by monsoon. So the ocean impounded inside Agastya released in the Descent of the Ganges on one plane symbolizes a seasonal event. But as we have seen in the case of our incursion into Greek myth beginning with Phaethon, anywhere we enter the fabric of Hindu myth concerning Agastya and Vasishtha we find that the myths are celestially referenced and paradigmatic. They are also linked by theme, genealogy, and name typology. So the waters of the Ganges are not merely seasonal; they are epochal, just as are those of Tishtrya. They symbolize several things. They are the obscuring "waters" of the dawnlight, which over the centuries come to blank out the Pleiades (and all sign stars) as precession makes the equinoctial point move westward along the ecliptic. But the equinoctial point itself "floats" until a new sign is found to be its harbinger; hence the hero is said to float on the water into which he has tried to immolate himself, only to be cast ashore unbound or unharmed. The waters are said to "remove" him from the armed opponent (the previous sign) and transport him to safety. Vasishtha's attempted suicide on Mount Meru is also doubly symbolic. The mountain represents the pivot point of the cosmos in its wrong-running; hence it is a symbol of doom. Yet certain mountains, observed from a fixed station, were used to mark the recurrence of seasonal phenomena—a mountain due east of a point would mark the equinox when the sun rose over it. Such a mountain is a place of salvation.

This whole mythic complex is summarized in a single story told in the *Satapatha-Brahmana* about the deluge that came during the tenure of Vaivasvata, the seventh (and current) Manu.[85] In the water brought for his morning ablutions Manu discovered a fish. It admonished him to care for it, for it would preserve him from a great deluge. Meantime, it told him, "House me in ever larger vessels as I grow, removing me eventually to the ocean" (compare Agastya). Manu was to build a ship in which to preserve himself when the time came. He did so, and when the flood came as predicted, he went to sea in order to find the fish and do it homage. The ship's line was fastened to the fish's fin, and it pulled Manu over the northern mountain.[86] The fish then ordered Manu to fasten the ship to a tree and wait for the waters to subside.[87] All living creatures had been destroyed save Manu alone. But woman was created for him after much devotion, and he was able to repopulate the earth. The symbolism is clear. Manu was saved by finding the point of stability. In order for this to happen, his bark (the equinoctial point) must weigh anchor and be taken by the fish (the new equinoctial sign) in the right direction. Fertility is restored when it finds its haven at the pole-fast world tree.

The heavenly Ganges (Viyadganga), identified by the Hindus with the Milky Way, flows from the toe of Vishnu and descends thence to earth. Similarly, Brahma created the waters from his foot, stationing the Rakshasas to guard them. It is clear from the connection with the toe of Buddha (Mahachakravarti), discussed in the first chapter, that the toe of the god, marked by a swastika, from which flows the Milky

Way represents the equinoctial point—or better, perhaps, the north pole associated with it. God's waters—whether they are a destructive flood (F) or a fertilizing dew (G), a place of drowning or a source of salvation—are paradigmatic.

The pious prayers of Bhagiratha induced Shiva to allow the Ganges to descend. Bhagiratha was the scion of a lineage of kings descended from Manu Vaisvata—that is, he was of the solar dynasty reigning in Ayodhya, whose most famous issue was Rama. His more immediate forebear was Sagara (Poison Bearer), born posthumously in exile (A) after a jealous second wife had prevented his mother's giving birth for seven years.[88] Sagara determined to recover his rightful kingdom (A), and after obtaining fire-weapons (D) from Aurva, he succeeded. Yet he pursued vengeance unnaturally and would have continued his death-dealing except for the intervention of his family's priest, Vasishtha. Later he found himself childless (F) and sought assistance from Aurva. One wife, Su-mati (daughter of Kashyapa), had 60,000 sons. They were all intemperate (F), the subject of complaints to the gods. As a consequence, a sacrificial offering of a horse, supervised by Sagara, was perverted by the sage Kapila. Although the horse was guarded by the 60,000 sons, it was spirited away to Patala, one of the seven infernal regions. The sons tunneled into the underworld[89] and found the animal there, alive and grazing contentedly, with Kapila nearby deep in meditation. Believing him to be the thief, they challenged him, and he, roused from his meditation, reduced them to ashes at a glance. Their step-brother's son found their ashes and beseeched Kapila that he might raise them to heaven. Kapila promised salvation with the advent of Bhagiratha. Sagara (Ocean) was the name given in memory of Sagara to the passage dug to the underworld.

Ultimately Bhagiratha's devotions at Go-karna (Cow's Ear) (C) brought down the Ganges. Its waters cleansed the sons of Sagara from all impurity by washing their ashes. For this reason the Ganges is given the by-names Sagara and Bhagiratha. Its descent rendered the spirits of Sagara's sons fit for admission to the heaven of Indra, Swarga, with its six by-names,[90] situated on Mount Meru, which also has six by-names.[91] The Ganges descends from Shiva's brow (or from Vishnu's toe) in seven streams, the Sapta-Sindhava. Three go east, three west, and one south.

Thus did the heavenly river become an earthly one and its seven streams become identified with seven earthly rivers. Seven precincts are in the heavens and seven Dvipas on the earth, and they seem to be connected by the seven streams of the Ganges flowing from on high into their earthly courses. The number seven seems to be of paramount importance in this connection.

The notion that there were seven earthly rivers is well ensconced in the Indo-Iranian tradition, for there is an Avestan term, Hapta-heando, which means "Seven Rivers." Arab travelers translated the term as Saba Sin.[92] It seems clear that the earthly-heavenly river, divided into seven streams, cleansed the seven-part underworld, thus enabling spirits to pass to the upperworld of seven names.[93] All this implies a corresponding earthly geography of seven regions, Dvipas in Vedic, Karshvares in Avestan. Each has a celestial (and an underworldly) counterpart, and each is surrounded by its own ocean.

Indo-European traditions confirm that the heavenly river, the Milky Way, was thought to be both entryway to and exit from the underworld. Al Biruni reports that it was called Akash Ganga (Bed of the Ganges); other sources call it Swarga Duari (the Dove of Swarga; one of the seven names of Indra's heaven). It was the path of Aryaman, that is, the way to the home of the Pitris, the other way to which place was along the path of the sun through the unmentionable sky. It was also called Nagavithi (Path of the Snake). The Norse sagas refer to it as the path of the deceased on their journey to Valhalla. It was also the way to Asgard, and in this function it was the nighttime antitype of the Rainbow, for both are called Asgard Bridge. In the Christianized tradition, the Milky Way is the Pilgrim's Pathway, variously called, for example, El Camino de Santiago,[94] Strada di Roma, Watling Street, and Iringes Wec.[95] The idea of making a pilgrimage on these routes looks as if it had pagan roots: the heavenly road through Purgatory to Paradise (once the Milky Way) will be made easier for one who has walked the way's earthly avatar as a pilgrim to a saint's shrine.[96]

The Milky Way is therefore the analog, visible by night, of the path of the sun's journey. Both are conceived of as the rivers that connect the two oceans, one bright and shining which the sun illuminates,[97] and the other, Vritra's, enveloped in darkness.[98] One of the these oceans is on "this side," the other is on the "other side."[99] As these rivers pass near dusk and dawn they disappear—the sun over the horizon, and the Milky Way into the light sky. Hence, the seven rivers, antitypes of these heavenly pathways (the ecliptic and galactic circles), are said to "run into the jaws of Varuna (Colored Sky) as into a surging chasm."[100]

THE NUMBER SEVEN

The rivers are said to "follow the path of the gods."[101] The sun is one of the gods. He has three aspects: Pushan (Nourisher), Savitri (Generator), and Surya, one of the three great deities of the Vedas. The "path of the gods" that the waters follow is the path of the sun, the ecliptic; the other gods following upon this pathway are six in number, five planets and the moon. This is why there are said to be seven pathways or seven rivers. When they "run into the jaws of Varuna," the seven planetary ways (six roughly parallel to the seventh, the ecliptic, but none of them identical) disappear into the gloaming, which is by way of saying that each planet has a separate course on which it rises and sets heliacally. By association, the nighttime river is conceived as having seven streams as well, hence the seven streams of the Ganges and hence, too, the proliferation of the number seven throughout the myths surrounding the myth of the Descent of the Ganges.

At the important times of the year, during the equinoctial passage of the sun, Varuna's jaws, whereinto and wherefrom the seven streams flow, are located at prime junctures, directly east and directly west. During a certain eon, that prime juncture was heralded by (or located at) six faint stars set on the ecliptic. The Pleiades are six in number, a fact preserved only in the tales about Karttikeya. Somehow (probably owing to that disposition to make a great deal out of superficial similarities, discussed above), the Pleiades became seven. Six distinctly visible stars in the cluster, when they are at the prime juncture, show the "pathway" to the seven planets and the seven rivers. Six, therefore, must be renumbered seven, on the principle of identity. But only six stars are visible. Therefore etiological myths were told about how one vanished. The story of Electra, the Pleiad, is a case in point.

The beautiful Pleiad Electra incited the lust of Zeus himself. He carried her off to Olympus, where for refuge she clung in terror to the sacred Palladium. In his urgency Zeus flung the protective image down from Olympus.[102] It landed in front of the tent of Ilus at the moment he was petitioning for a sign from heaven to favor his founding of a new city (Troy, Ilium). After her encounter with Zeus, Electra fled from heaven and returned to Samothrace, where she bore two sons, Dardanus and Iasion. Of the latter we have heard: he was consort of Demeter in a sown field. Dardanus came to live in Troy as son-in-law of king Teucer. Some say that his arrival in Troy was occasioned by the death of his brother and that he then set sail in inconsolable grief from Samothrace to a new place, using for his raft an inflated goatskin ballasted by four stones. But Troy did not last many generations, for it was destroyed by the Greeks. In grief for the fate of her descendants, Electra deserted her sister Pleiades (who "led the dance of the circling stars") and took up residence in the arctic circle. Sometimes she appears with unbound hair in the dark sky as a comet.[103]

Hyginus preserves here for us a very ancient tradition: the Pleiades are thought to "lead the circling dance of the stars." If the story about Electra's having deserted the Pleiades to take up residence on the arctic circle is contemporary with the utility of the Pleiades as markers of the equinox, we can say that there is an indelible relationship between the equinox, its marker stars, and the far north, Electra's place of refuge.[104]

Corroboration of this point can be adduced from the *Tir Yasht* 12. Here we find an invocation to the heavenly bodies for whom sacrifices have been ordained: Tishtrya, Haptoiringa, Vanant, and Verethragna. Tishtrya has been identified as Sirius, star of the east; Haptoiringa (Sevenstar) is the star of the north and clearly has to do with one or the other of the seven-starred constellations of the north, Ursa Major and Ursa Minor; Vanant is the star of the south, whose office is (1) to keep the passes and gates of Mount Alborz, around which the sun, moon, and stars revolve, and (2) to prevent the Pairikas and Daevas from cutting off and breaking the road of the sun.[105] Verethragna is the Bahram of Persian literature, identified with the planet Mars.[106]

Clearly Tishtrya, as we have argued above, and now Vanant, who serves to protect the pivot-point mountain and to keep the demons from breaking the path of the sun, are thought to be guardians of the stability of the equinoctial alignment, and so are the Haptoiringa, for in *Tir Yasht* 12, and again in *Sirozah,* 2.13, they are said to be an object of prayer spoken in order to oppose the Yatus and Pairikas. The latter is identified as the demon of the Duzyairya in *Tir Yasht* 51. The seven stars are therefore maintainers of order and stability—of Huyairya.

Verethragna-Bahram is so worshiped too. Verethragna is mentioned in the same prayer (spoken to maintain good order) with the seven stars of the north. Verethragna has an antitype, Satavaesa, who is to be identified with the star Antares,[107] just as in the Greek tradition Antares is the antitype of Ares (Mars, the planetary god). Mars's Vedic counterpart, Skanda (whose deific avatar is Karttikeya), was the nursling of the six (or seven) Krittikas, that is, the Pleiades.[108] In the Avestan literature, Satavaesa lets loose waters gathered from the rains brought by the god Tishtrya, water that falls to earth to irrigate the seven Karshvares. Therefore Satavaesa, Verethragna's counterpart, maintains the order of the seasons by sending waters to the seven Karshvares every year during the rainy season.[109] The seven stars of the north, Haptoiringa, and the seven Pleiades are to be interrelated through their common association with the god of war. He is the slayer of the dragon, the god whose counterpart assists Tishtar with the production of the rains to spite the Yatus and Pairikas.[110]

The number seven, therefore, was the lucky number signifying Huyairya, because the Haptoiringa, keepers of the poles, functioned as symbols of stability.[111] Seven was the number of the planetary bodies. Seven were the stars of two constellations near the pole. By analogy, the six stars of the seasonally important Pleiades were made seven.

But as the equinoctial point moves among the asterisms along the ecliptic, so the pole moves among the stars of the north (see figs. 6.1–6.5). Given that Polaris has functioned as the polestar for only half a millennium or so, why were the Persian Haptoiringa, the Roman Septentriones, and the Hindu Saptarshi[112] noted as keepers of the pole? This implies a pan-Indo-European notion originating before the Indo-Europeans had dispersed by 3500(?) B.C. The answer is that these names refer not to Ursa Major alone but to Ursa Major and Ursa Minor together. Each asterism is shaped like the other, and each has seven stars contributing to its outline, variously seen as bears with tails, wagons with tongues, or latterly dippers with handles. Between the time when Thuban in Draco was a polestar (ca. 2900 B.C.) and the era of Polaris (see figs. 6.1 and 6.2), the pole has been located *between* the two Ursae, encompassed between the two similar asterisms of seven stars each.[113]

The position of the pole has always been much closer to Ursa Minor. Hence the brighter Ursa Major helped locate the smaller but more important Ursa Minor, a fact that Aratus acknowledges: "less in size but valued more by sailors."[114] The fact that in antiquity the pole was located between the two constellations likely gave rise to their being defined similarly and called by similar names: Ursa, Wagon.[115]

The Arabic name for Ursa Minor derives from the conception of the sky and its operation as resembling a wheel. It is called al Fass, "the Hole" in which the world axle turns. In another conception, the earth's pole is conceived of as a pivot reaching up toward this hole; hence Mount Meru, the Hindu seat of the gods, is described in the astronomical treatise *Surya Siddhanta*: "A collection of manifold jewels, a mountain of gold is Meru, passing through the middle of the earthglobe, and protruding on either side."[116] Compare the Norse Himinborg (Hill of Heaven), whose denizen is Heimdall, guardian of Bifröst,[117] the bridge connecting earth to heaven.

Columbus and his contemporary explorers believed in a mythical mountain lying under the pole that was so large as to distort the sphericity of the earth. Above it was a star named Tramontane. Various names were given to the mountain itself, among which was Mons Coelius.[118] The name Tramontane derives from a Latin prototype, but Coelius, though it bears a similarity to the Latin word *caelum, coelum,* "heaven," and may have been retained owing to this similarity, is surely a name of Greek origin.

There is an Ephesian tale about the Seven Sleepers of Ephesus, who slumbered for nearly two hundred years in the grotto under Mount Coelian (supposedly under the persecution of Decius in the third century). In Greek, *koil-* means "hollow," that is, the socket into which a pole fits. Here we have the elements of replacement (A) in the persecution, hiding (E) in the sequestered sleep, an eon of time (I) in the two-hundred-year period (three hundred would have fit the paradigmatic number better), and the number seven, which clearly refers here to the seven stars of the Little Dipper. The Finns, incidentally, refer to Polaris as Taehti (Star at the Top of the Heavenly Mountain).

DRACO: GUARDIAN AND DEMON

The guardian Ursae notwithstanding, precession moves the pole in keeping with the sliding of the equinoctial point. Only one point in the sky is free from displacement: the pole of the ecliptic. This pole lies in the constellation Draco (see fig. 6.1). Did the ancients know of this precession-free point? I refer to the myth of the catasterism of Ladon, the serpent that guarded the apples of the Hesperides. After Herakles killed him, he was placed among the stars as Draco. At the marriage of Zeus and Hera (C-D), Earth came with a present for the bride, branches bearing golden (G) apples (C). Hera asked Ge to plant them in her gardens (C) near distant Mount Atlas (D). But Atlas's daughters kept picking (F) Hera's (A) apples from the tree (C/D). That is why Hera sent Ladon to be the garden's guardian, for the dragon was thought never to be overcome by sleep or even to close its eyes. Herakles is placed above Draco in the sky, reenacting his slaying of Ladon, stepping on its heavenly head with his left foot and raising in his right hand his starry club.[119]

A version of this myth says that the Giants threw the serpent Ladon at Athena (C-D?) when they went to war with her (A). The goddess, however, intercepted its writhing form and cast it among the stars, fixing it to the very pole of heaven (C-D).[120] But the coils of the celestial Draco entwine the ecliptic pole, not the ever-moving celestial pole. The ancients seem to have known that the one area of the sky wherein the stars do not shift is located in Draco. The constellation and its mythological antitype are quite parallel: the coils of Draco enwrap the ecliptic pole just as Ladon guards the (world) tree of the Hesperides by entwining itself about its trunk—wheel, nave, and axle.

Near the precinct of Ladon and the garden he guarded lay the universal mountain, Atlas, upon which (or upon whom, if Atlas be considered as the mythological deity) the world was thought to rest. The

myth of Ladon-Draco symbolizes the fixity of the ecliptic pole preserved by an unwearying, unblinking guardian.

The eleventh labor of Herakles (the quest for the apples of the Hesperides) ties the astronomical elements found in the guardianship of
Ladon to myths of replacement we have already examined. Herakles
did not know which path to take to the Hesperides (daughters of sunset), so he visited certain daughters of Zeus and Themis (the goddess
of order), nymphs who lived on the banks of the river Eridanus (where
the Heliades wept for Phaethon). These nymphs told Herakles to visit
the sea-god Nereus, who, after a wrestling match (A), would give him
directions. On his way back from the Eridanus, Herakles went by the
Caucasus Mountains, where he shot and killed the eagle that was tearing at Prometheus and freed that Titan from his bonds (G). In remem-
brance of the bonds, Herakles thereafter wore a wreath on his head
(C-D). Herakles arranged for Prometheus to be immortal (G) by ex-
changing the Titan's mortality for the immortality of Cheiron (A), who
was suffering unending pain (as Prometheus had been prior to his release). Next he killed King Busiris, who was sacrificing (F) an unwitting
passerby (A) each year in order to end a famine (F) that had struck his
land. Herakles had been prepared as the next victim and had been
dragged to the altar (C-D), but there he broke his bonds (G) and killed
the king.[121] Herakles vanquished the giant Antaeus in a forced wrestling
match (A) by lifting him away from Earth (C/D), his mother and source
of his power. To get the apples, he had to play a trick on Atlas (D4).
Herakles offered to take on the burden of supporting the earth (A, I)
while Atlas went for the apples. Upon his return, however, Atlas earned
his name, for he refused (*a*-) to resume the suffering (*tla*-) of bearing
the earth.[122] Herakles was unwilling to upset nature by putting down
the earth to assert his freedom, a morality which symbolizes the stability of the pole. But warily he asked Atlas to assume (A) the duty for
just a moment while he put a cushion on his neck (C-D). Herakles
then said goodbye, abandoning to Atlas his age-old task of serving-by-
standing-and-waiting.[123] On his way back to Tiryns, Herakles crossed
Libya, where he stubbed his foot on a rock (C-D), causing a life-
giving spring to flow up (G) (compare the origin of the Ganges in
Vishnu's toe).[124]

The name for Draco in Persian astronomy is Azhdeha, the man-eating serpent, a later form of the Avestan name Azhi Dahaka. This three-headed serpent-demon figures in a version of the epochal battle, the other versions of which involve Tishtrya-Apaosha, Ahura Mazda (Spenta Mainyu), Angra Mainyu, Ormazd-Ahriman, and others. The seemingly evil Azhi-Dahaka does battle with opponents as numerous as are the variants of the story. In its earliest extant variant, the story is told in *Zamyad Yasht*.[125] Here there is a primordial battle between the three-headed, six-eyed, fiendish dragon and Atar (Fire).[126] The object of the battle is the possession of Hvareno, the "Heavenly Glory that cannot be forcibly seized" (A4). The scene of the battle is Vouru-Kasha (A6), the sea from which all the waters on the earth fall down, that is, the sea above, the sky.[127] After Atar frightens away the demon, Hvareno flees to the waters and is housed with the swift-horsed Son of the Waters, Apam Napat.[128]

In a variant recounted in *Yasna* 9,[129] the evil dragon is given his proper name, Azhi Dahaka. The dragon's "good guy" opponent is Thraetaona Athwya. Thraetaona[130] was the second in the generations of men—primordial men who knew the recipe for the preparation of the sacred food-drink, Haoma. The first such man was Vivanghvant,[131] whose son Yima is said to have "made from his authority both herds and men free from dying. . . . and men could eat imperishable food. . . . there was neither cold nor heat, there was neither age nor death."[132] This is a description of the Golden Age. Indeed, in the *Zamyad Yasht*, Yima was the possessor of the Hvareno, the third in sequence to have so owned this divine possession; he is said be the "ruler over the seven Karshvares of the earth, over the Daevas and men, the Yatus and Pairikas, in whose reign both food in abundance was never failing . . . and men undying . . . but when he began to find delight in words of falsehood and untruth, the Glory was seen to flee away from him in the shape of a bird."[133]

Hvareno departed from Yima in three phases, during the second of which it was seized by Thraetaona.[134] Clearly, we are dealing with a myth of replacement in which the snake or dragon is seen as possessing the desired object, Hvareno, while alternately semidivine heroes seek to repossess it from this mighty monster (Avestan *drug*), which had been created by Atar's (later Mazda's and Auharmazd's) opponent Angra Mainyu to destroy the world of good principle and thereby to forestall "the restoration of the world . . . that thenceforth will never grow old and never die."[135]

This interpretation of the text is confirmed by an epitome of a Sassanid epitome of an Avestan text, the so-called *Bahman Yasht*.[136] In this book of prophecy, Auharmazd tells Zaratust what will happen to the Iranian nation and religion. Iran will be overrun by hordes of demons and idolaters until religion becomes all but extinct (F). The manner in which religion might be restored and the demons destroyed (G) is the subject of Zaratust's reply:

> There will be a succession of three saving apostles, each of whom will have authority for a thousand years. Hushedar will be first and his sign will be that the sun will stand still for ten days [G5]. He will bring creatures back to their proper state [G]. In the millennium of the second apostle, men will become so skilled in medicine that they will not readily die, but their toleration of heretics will bring about a recrudescence of the evil spirit who will release Azhi-Dahaka from his confinement in Mt. Damavand to work his evil. At last Auharmazd will send the hero Keresasp, aroused from a long trance, to kill Azhi-Dahaka with his club.[137]

The Indo-European concept of the guardian of stability seems to be ambivalent. A monstrous serpent, this guardian issued from a hole at creation[138] and then wound itself around the world tree to guard it. Yet, because he does not guard it well enough,[139] the perfect and stable world goes awry—the golden apples are plucked—and evil comes into the world. By transference, the serpent, originally a guardian of good order, becomes a symbol or an agent of instability, one who must be vanquished by the gods or heroes of the world if right running is to be restored. The three-headedness of the snake (compare the three roots of Yggdrasil) likely reflects the tripartite battle and the succession through three ages, each of which (in the Avestan sources) is three thousand years long.[140]

The interchangeability of hero, keeper of stability (when the world is running right), and demon, world destroyer (when the world is out of order or verging upon it) is clearly illustrated in the Vedic myth of the hero Trita Aptya. This name, which has in it the etymon "three," is also given as Traitana, a form directly cognate with Avestan Thraetaona. The surname Aptya is related to Apam (Son of the Waters). He is said to have killed the three-headed, six-eyed fiend and let loose the cows.[141] These and other allusions to the story in the *Rig Veda* become the subject of a later commentary in which a legend about Trita is given in full. It runs as follows: Agni threw some ashes from a burnt offering into the water. From them, as if from seed, sprang the three brothers, Ekata (First), Dvita (Second), and Trita (Third). From having been born of the waters they were called Aptyas. Trita went to a well (C) one day to draw water and fell into it (C-D, E). The evil Asuras heaped a mound over the hole to prevent his getting out (A), but he did so with ease (G). Is not this Trita parallel to the three-headed snake exiting from his hole, which is the north (or ecliptic) pole? On the other hand, it was Trita himself who went to draw the water, which is the office of the snake's opponent (Tishtrya). Is Trita a good guy or a bad? The ambiguity is underlined by the presence of the Asuras in the story. Asura, in the earliest of the Vedas, is the supreme benign deity (compare Avestan Ahura). Under this interpretation, Trita, as the opponent, must be a demon. But in other places Trita is a helper of Indra, against whose rule the Asuras are malignant devils.[142]

A dyshemerized variant of the Trita story, preserved in the *Niti-Manjari,* is instructive in bringing resolution to the ambiguity. In this legend, Trita and his brothers are men. The three brothers were in a desert suffering from thirst (F). Trita drew water for his brothers from a well they found (G), but the brothers, in order to expropriate his property (A), threw Trita in the hole and covered it with a cartwheel (C-D), abandoning him to die. But through earnest prayer Trita was able to escape with the gods' blessing.

HESPERIDES

Stories about the Pleiades are legion, and they are interconnected at many points with stories having to do with primordial battles between the forces of the Good Year and those of the Evil Year, the annual and epochal descent of waters, and guardian dragons. The one key to the interconnection is the number seven, which clearly fits the pole, the scene of stability and of the seven heavenly lights. Its application to the Pleiades is, however, more doubtful—there are only six. This fact has given rise to etiological myths about how one of them disappeared, and even to speculation among astronomers and archaeoastronomers that perhaps at some point since the time when the heliacal rising of the Pleiades was a harbinger of the vernal sun, one of the seven stars exploded and disappeared. A more likely explanation is leveling and attraction. The six Pleiades were made seven in number to make parity (which is all important to pre-logical mythmakers) with the two aster-isms to the north—the Big and Little Dippers, as we call them—between which lies the celestial pole. Stability is ringed by the number seven, and although the celestial pole, located between two groups of seven stars, is itself lapsarian, the one point in the sky with eternal sta-bility is fixed in the north, too, in the Dippers' neighbor Draco, the guardian dragon.

Once the Pleiades had begun to slip back into the yellowing dawn, one of their number was given the name Electra (Yellowgold). Their functions as harbingers of the equinoctial point began to fail when their functionally most important member, Maia (midwife, i.e., of the equi-noctial point), failed to produce the expected live birth. Now becoming useless as harbingers of the equinox, as they resided in the sun during the time of the equinox; hence they were given the name Heliades, the seven daughters of Helios (at least one of the names of the Heliades and the Pleiades repeats: Merope). The role of the Heliades in the myth of Phaethon, their weeping amber tears, represents human weeping for the lost equinox marker, the amber representing the daylight glow into which they had sunk. For at least a millennium the Pleiades were of no value at all as equinox locaters, being hidden in the glow of the sun all through the spring. Much later, however, beginning in about 1250 B.C. and continuing for four centuries, the equinoctial point, having moved to the other side of the sun, was indicated by the heliacal *setting*[143] of the Pleiades (in the west at dusk; see fig. 6.13).

This fact gave rise to a new myth and a new set of seven sisters. The Pleiades, still known by that name at other times of the year, were given a special name to underline their newfound significance in the evening

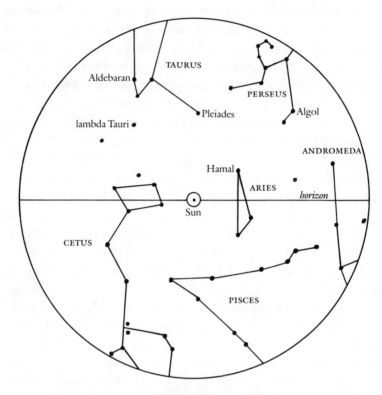

FIGURE 6.13

This figure illustrates that by 1250 B.C. precession has restored the utility of the Pleiades as a sign of the spring equinox. In 3102 B.C. the Pleiades, at their *heliacal rising,* were signs of the equinox. Here we see the evening sky in 1250 B.C. at sunset on the day of the equinox. As it becomes darker and before they set (their *heliacal setting*), the Pleiades (being separated from the sun by 16°) will shine out of the gloom as the Hesperides, evening harbingers of the equinox. When turned upside down, this figure shows (roughly) the orientation of the constellations in the morning before dawn. Aries is in the sun, while the equinox's new harbinger is the heliacal rising of Pisces.

sky. They were transmogrified into the seven (by most accounts) Hesperides (Daughters of Evening). The Hesperides of mythology are said to be the daughters of Atlas. The Pleiades, too (though by a different mother in some accounts), were daughters of Atlas. The Hesperides were stationed near their father in the far west, a location that conforms to the phenomenon of their important heliacal setting. Furthermore, like the Heliades (with whom we have already compared the Pleiades), the Hesperides are said to weep. As the Argonauts, in search of a spring, approached the gardens of the Hesperides, they found the girls weeping over the Ladon's corpse. Orpheus (one of the Argonauts, by most accounts) offered a song of prayer. Orpheus, whose music had the power of transformation, thereby changed the Hesperides into trees. One of the sisters, Hespere, become a poplar (compare the fate of the Heliades).[144]

In a story already mentioned, the Hesperides were suspected of stealing apples (F) from the world tree named after them. This mythologem symbolizes the loss of stability occasioned by the failure of the Pleiades and of their constellation Taurus as morning harbingers of the equinoctial point.[145]

Now we may return to the puzzling way in which Hesiod deals with the Pleiades and their apparitions, a problem that began this section of the chapter. In his *Works and Days* Hesiod does mention three significant apparitions of the Pleiades: heliacal rising in May corresponding (roughly) to the time to harvest winter grain; the cosmic setting, corresponding to the time of plowing for the fall planting in late October; and the forty days of invisibility between the heliacal setting (near the time of the spring equinox, as mentioned in connection with the Hesperides) and the heliacal rising in May. Other than the latter oblique reference, Hesiod makes no mention of the spring equinox.

Yet his manner of mentioning the invisibility may be significant (385–387): "These [Pleiades] in fact (as you know) are hidden away through forty nights and days but again appear, *the year moving around,* at the time of the first sharpening of the iron [sickle]." First we will notice that the order in which he mentions the facts of their invisibility— nights and days—may well indicate, as was reasoned above, that it was the evening apparition of the Pleiades that marked the equinox—that is, the Pleiades as Hesperides. Furthermore, the expression in italics in the passage is generally used for things that have a definite beginning point—a pregnancy (*Od.* 11, 248), a decision made by the gods in council (*Od.* 1, 16), and the term of a person's life when viewed from birth (*Hymn to Demeter,* 265). The definite point of time in this case would be the spring equinox.

The discussion above suggested that the Pleiades-Hesperides were, at their heliacal setting, markers of the spring equinox in Hesiod's time. That view needs some correction. The period of their utility as such was coming to a close by the time of Hesiod, a period that began in the Bronze Age (1250 B.C.; see fig. 6.13) and had its greatest utility in about 1000 B.C. In Hesiod's time the heliacal setting would occur some eight days after the equinox.

Curiously enough, however, other phenomena Hesiod mentions are also more appropriate to a date of 1250 than to Hesiod's date of 700 B.C. There is a rather technical temporal formula given at *Works and Days* 564–566: "When Zeus, after the turn of the [winter] solstice, has completed sixty wintry days, that's when the sign-star Arcturus leaves the cold streams of Ocean and first rises acronychally in splendor." The occurrence of the solstice was not determinable by any exact stellar apparition but was to be found roughly by the use of a gnomon. The apparition of Arcturus confirms that the solstice was sixty days past. Its rising is one of the few sure signposts of the year. Arcturus is the fifth brightest star (zero magnitude) visible in the northern latitudes. If it is not obscured by haze or a high horizon, it will become visible within a half-hour after sunset. Hence Hesiod's conditions are precise: At what date did the circumstances of precession make Arcturus rise in the east sixty days after winter solstice so as to be seven degrees above the horizon within a half-hour after sunset? The answer is surprising, and it has implications for Hesiodic studies beyond the scope of this book.

Sixty days after the winter solstice corresponds by astronomical definition to February 20. On that date in 1250 B.C. Arcturus rose before sunset, was two and one-half degrees above the horizon at sunset, and seven degrees above the horizon by thirty-three minutes after sunset, when it could shine through the fading glow of day. On the same date in 700 B.C., Arcturus did not rise until after sunset and did not attain a seven-degree elevation above the horizon until one hour and twelve minutes after sunset. By then it was totally dark; the facts of 700 B.C. simply do not seem to fit the circumstances of acronychal rising as defined in the passage by Hesiod. His word (its earliest extant use in Greek) is *akronephaios,* a word used by other authors to refer specifically to the rising of a body during evening twilight. One might dispute my

stipulation that Arcturus be seven degrees above the horizon for visibility, but the dispute would have to be in the direction of a greater
elevation. I have chosen the minimum. A greater elevation would serve
to push the date of the applicability of the phenomena even earlier than
I have suggested. So we may restate the case: The facts do not suit a
date near 700 B.C. at all but are appropriate for the dates 1500–1100 B.C.

Hence the dates of the two phenomena from Hesiod that we can
date with any certainty (the acronychal rising of Arcturus and the disappearance of the Pleiades after the spring equinox) jibe with one another. The heliacally setting Pleiades, an asterism we claim came to be
known as the Hesperides, gain no mention per se in Hesiod at all. The
Hesperides are mentioned several times in the *Theogony*, whereas they
go unremarked in other epic literature (with the exception of a supple-
ment generated to the *Titanomachy* from the Epic Cycle, where the
author says "[. . .] guarded the apples" [frag. 8]). In the Theogony,
the Hesperides are daughters of Night whose care are the golden apples
and the tree bearing them, which lie beyond glorious Ocean (215–216).
They are associated by juxtaposition with Atlas, who "through harsh
necessity bears up broad Ouranos at the limits of earth in front of the
clear-voiced Hesperides (517–518)." This place lies toward Night, home
of the Gorgons (275). The imagined place of their location in the far
west at the limits of earth corresponds to the place of the gates of the
sun discussed earlier, the entryway into Hades-Erebus-Zophos. The
apples and Ocean are invested with brightness-color terms suggestive
of sunset, and the epithet of the Hesperides fits their function. "Clear-
voiced" (*liguphonos*, 275, 518) is a modification of the more usual epic
formula *liguphthongos*, the standard epithet for Homeric heralds. And
the Hesperides, as I have argued, were indeed heralds, the Pleiades as
evening harbingers of the spring equinox.

MITHRA AND MITHRAISM

At this point it seems appropriate to bring up the subject of the Mithraic mysteries, which have recently been the subject of thorough re-
examination by David Ulansey and others.[146] One of the cruxes of Mith-

raism, as the Belgian historian of ancient religions Franz Cumont pointed out at the turn of the century, is the seemingly compelling connection between the name Mithras (first a Greek and then a Latinized Greek name) with the ancient Iranian god Mithra. Cumont wanted to see Mithraism as a metamorphosed and imported form of the original cult of Mithra, who in Persian belief was a god of light (Hvareno) and truth. In *Zamyad Yasht* 19.30–39 (mentioned above), we learn that Mithra seized upon the Hvareno after it was held for some time by Yima. This puts the myth of the pair into the paradigm of replacement, and in fact, in one variant of the story Yima was killed and dismembered by the serpent Azhi Dahaka, as discussed above. Now, Yima was the first man, and his sacrifice was the occasion and his body the material from which the world, including other men, was created. Yima was the first to die, and his twin brother, Spityura (Yima means "twin"), was in one version the sacrificer. In the other, just mentioned, the slayer was the serpent Azhi Dahaka. A variant myth is told of creation: the evil Ahriman (the inventor of Time) sacrificed a bull from whose blood and body sprang all the living creatures of the earth.

Cumont's irresolvable problem was to find a myth in which the slayer of the bull was Mithra, for in the Mithraic mysteries of later times, the central "eucharist" of the cult was the slaying of a bull by Mithras and the sharing out of its flesh among the worshipers. No such myth has ever been discovered. Hence, the reinterpretation of the cult and iconography of Mithras by David Ulansey and others has centered on the astrological signs and symbols that almost universally accompany full depictions of the god in the act of slaying the bull. Their interpretation coincides in some measure with that offered in this book. The bull slaying (tauroctony) "symbolizes the end of the reign of Taurus as the constellation of the spring equinox and the beginning of the most recent era. The other figures in the tauroctony all represent constellations whose special position in the sky was also ended by the force of the precession. By killing the bull—causing the precession of the equinoxes—Mithras was in effect moving the entire universe."[147] That some such interpretation is demanded by the evidence is clear; some scenes show Mithras bearing, like Atlas, the sphere of the universe on his shoulders or holding the cosmic sphere in one hand while his other spins the zodiacal belt.

Perhaps, however, this view requires some minor corrections. Ulansey is well aware that the heliacal rise of Taurus as harbinger of the spring equinox gave way, owing to precession, in about 2000 B.C. Why, then, is Mithraism a phenomenon of *late* antiquity, at the turn of the eras? One must ask why Aries, the Ram, was not chosen as the sacrificial beast, since in the hey-day of Mithraism the equinoctial point, long since having left Taurus behind, was shifting from Aries into Pisces. Ulansey glozes over this difficulty; "the beginning of the most recent era," he does not emphasize, took place 1,900 years before the rise of Mithraism. Ulansey tries too briefly to associate the newly founded belief in a deity "larger than the cosmos itself" with the then recent "discovery" of precession by Hipparchus.

The puzzle has a solution which, as in the case of the Hesperides, is to be found in the evening sky. Just as the Pleiades outlived their utility as harbingers of the equinox at their heliacal *rising* only to be renamed Hesperides 2,000 years later when their heliacal *setting* marked the time of the equinox, Taurus, outmoded as a morning sign of the equinox in about 2000 B.C., returned to importance at its heliacal setting as an indicator of the equinox during the era of the rise of Mithraism. The Bull, as it sank down to become visible as the first star (Aldebaran) in the ruddy sky of evening (symbol of its own shed blood) first in about 1500 B.C., was accompanied by a constellation that may well have represented Mithras, the bullslayer, for on its right and in close proximity was the constellation Perseus, depicted in iconography, like Mithras, wearing the Phrygian cap. In Cilicia, the first known location for the Mithraic cult, Perseus was worshiped not as a hero but as a god. By the time of the recrudescence of Mithraism in the Roman world (in 67 B.C.; see fig. 6.14), the Bull was about to be slain again, for precession was about to replace Taurus as the marker of the equinox in the evening sky with Aries, thus ending the 4,500-year association of Taurus and the vernal equinox (see figs. 6.7–6.11, 6.14).

THE SUCCESSION OF REGENTS

In Greek mythology, Zeus became a new ruler (G), coming into power after deposing Kronos, his father (A). In all its retellings, the story was

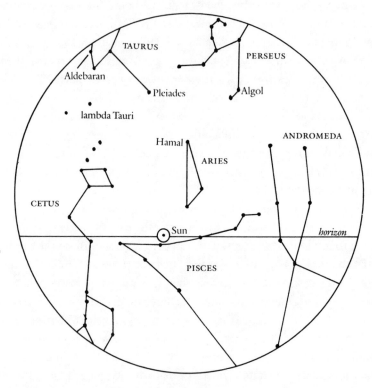

FIGURE 6.14
In this figure we see conditions as they were at sunset on the day of the
spring equinox in 67 B.C., which Plutarch recorded as the beginning of
the cult of Mithras as practiced in its aboriginal locale, Cilicia. At sunset
the brightest star of Taurus, Aldebaran, is 37° above the horizon, and the
sky would be dark enough for the star to shine forth before its setting.
Aldebaran's first visible heliacal setting at the equinox occurred several
centuries before 67 B.C. By 67 B.C. the dimmer stars of Perseus, such as
Mirfak, had also become visible before their setting.

associated with the latest shift in the equinoctial station, the last of
which was its entry into Aries from Taurus. Hence in most extant variants of the tale, Zeus is related to the Goat (Zeus was raised and pro-
tected by goats; compare Aigipan and others) and to the Cornucopia
(the magic goat's horn), which symbolizes the prosperity attendant
upon the newfound stability in the universe. Other stories that tell

about the impending fall of Aries as sign star in favor of Pisces (which must, therefore, date from later antiquity) are of disasters, and many are referenced not to Aries but to its guide star, Capella. Hence the many variant stories of fallen charioteers, Phaethon in particular, who are identified with the constellation Auriga, the chief star of which is Capella. Capella (Little Goat) also supplies the bridge between Aries (the Ram) and stories fraught with goats.

When the heliacal rising of the Pleiades was no longer the harbinger of the equinoctial point, due to the advance of precession, that function was taken on by Aries, the Ram. The apparition of this savior, of course, was in the blushing sky of dawn, whence comes the idea of the Golden Fleece. The constellation Aries, however, is a dim constellation, the least spectacular in the zodiac. It consists of four stars of between second and fifth magnitude. Therefore the apparition of Aries in the dawn sky was difficult to perceive, especially as time went by and the equinoctial point moved westward, drowning it in daylight. Yet there was a very bright star (zero magnitude) which, during this era (1500 B.C.), rose together with Aries; it was Capella. Here lies the explanation for the name of the star "Little Goat." Goats are often used by shepherds to induce the less easily trained (and more stupid) sheep to follow a certain path—for example, the Judas goat that leads the lambs to slaughter. Thus Capella (Little Goat) leads (or makes known the presence of) the Ram, which brings with it the equinoctial point (see fig. 6.11). As a finding star for the equinoctial point, Capella, the heavenly goat, tends to replace the heavenly ram (but not to exclusion; note, for example, the Ram of the Golden Fleece).[148]

Other stories that must have had antecedents dating as far back as 2000 B.C. preserve the theme of the phasing out of Taurus, the Bull, as equinoctial locus in favor of Aries, the Ram—for example, Theseus, son of Aigeus (Goatman), who destroys the kingdom of Minos, lord of the Minotaur (the Bull). Prior to this era, as early as 3500 B.C., the Pleiades were harbingers of the equinox (see fig. 6.9), and their predecessors were Aldebaran and the other zodiacal stars of Taurus; still earlier, they were predecessors of some stars in Orion and Gemini. Are there any mythical records for these "dynastic" changes? So far as I can determine, not in Greek myth, but perhaps in the Vedas.

In Hindu legend there was a mother goddess called Aditi, who had seven offspring. She is called "Mother of the Gods." Aditi, whose name means "free, unbounded, infinity" was assigned in the ancient lists of constellations as the regent of the asterism Punarvasu.[149] Punarvasu is dual in form and means "The Doublegood Pair." The singular form of this noun is used to refer to the star Pollux.[150] It is not difficult to surmise that the other member of the Doublegood Pair was Castor. Then the constellation Punarvasu is quite equivalent to our Gemini, the Twins. In far antiquity (5800 B.C.) the spring equinoctial point was predicted by the heliacal rising of the Twins (see fig. 6.6). By 4700 B.C. the equinox lay squarely *in* Gemini (fig. 6.7).

Punarvasu is one of the twenty-seven (or twenty-eight) zodiacal constellations in the Indian system of Nakshatras. In each of the Nakshatras there is a "yoga," a key star that marks a station taken by the moon in its monthly (twenty-seven- or twenty-eight-day) course through the stars. (The sidereal period of the moon, twenty-seven days and a fraction, should be distinguished from the synodic, or phase-shift period of 29.5 days, which is the ultimate antecedent of our month.)

In ancient times the priest-astronomers (Brahmans) determined the recurrence of the solstices and equinoxes by the use of the gnomon. Later they developed the Nakshatra system of star reference to determine the recurrence of the seasons, much as the Greeks used the heliacal rising of some star for the same purpose.

An example of the operation of the Nakshatra system in antiquity can be seen in figure 6.9. Here we see that the spring equinox occurred when the sun was at its closest approach to the star Aldebaran (called Rohini by the Hindus) in our constellation Taurus. But, of course, the phenomenon would not have been visible because the star is too close to the sun for observation. The astronomers would have known, however, that the equinoctial point was *at* Aldebaran by observing the full moon falling near the expected date at or near a point in the sky exactly opposite Aldebaran (since the full moon is 180° from the sun), that is, near the star Antares; see fig. 6.15.

The system of Nakshatras, then, is quite distinct from systems that use the appearance of heliacally rising or setting stars as the equinoctial marker. Furthermore, the Indian system is all but unique in that two

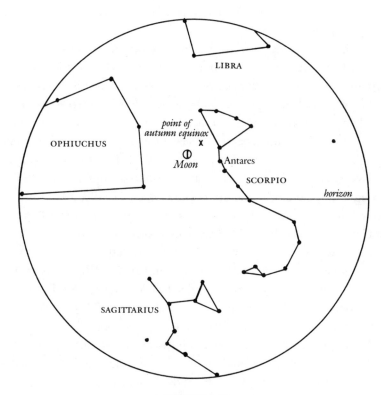

FIGURE 6.15
The eastern sky seen just after moonrise near the star Antares two days
before the spring equinox in 3102 B.C.

calendar systems competed with each other—a civil system, in which
the year's beginning was at the winter solstice, and a sacrificial year,
which began at the spring equinox. The beginning of the former was
determined by the Nakshatra method, observing the winter full moon's
apparition near the point of the summer solstice in the sky (as explained
above).[151] The arrival of the beginning of the sacrificial year might be
determined by the Nakshatra method—observation of the spring full
moon near to the autumn Nakshatra in Virgo. More commonly, however, it was determined as in the Greek system, by direct observation of
the heliacal rising of a sign star. In the current calendar, for example—
one unchanged since the fifth century A.D.—the yoga star of the

Nakshatra Ashvini (beta Arietis) ushers in the spring equinox at its heliacal rising.[152]

Yet there is evidence that the system using beta Arietis was not always in use. There are historical accounts of changes worked on the calendric system. One early text reveals a time of confusion when the calculation of the winter solstice was done ambiguously, now being reckoned from the Phalguni Nakshatra (a star in Libra) and now from the Chitrâ Nakshatra.[153] Bal Ganghadar Tilak sees this evidence, which is present in ritual, history, and myth, as proof that Vedic literature preserves in its layered antiquity signs of accommodation to the shift in the calendar brought on by the precession of the equinoxes. The oldest layer is preserved in the record that the winter solstice began with the full moon in Chitrâ (Spica in Virgo).[154] This would correspond, in the sacrificial calendar, to the spring equinox's occurrence in Punarvasu.[155]

The regent deity of the Punarvasu Nakshatra is Aditi. This means that the vernal equinox was determined by looking for Aditi near the full moon that fell nearest in time to the equinox. This would place Aditi somewhere in the constellation Scorpio. More on this later.

A ritual statement made about Aditi is that all sacrifice must begin and end in her. A corresponding myth is also told: Sacrifice (personified) deserted the company of the gods. Unable to perform any ceremonies, the gods were bewildered. But Aditi came to their help and reinstituted the proper initiation of sacrifice.[156] Hence, we may conclude that Aditi marked the beginning of the sacrificial year when the equinox was in Punarvasu.[157] The confusion of the gods refers to the confusion of mankind before the institution of this first Nakshatra. This is why "eternal" Aditi was made regent of this part of the sky, and why in myth she was made the mother of the gods, which were thought to have been in perfect alignment when "time began." No wonder, too, that Aditi was said to be the wife of Rita (World Order) and is referred to as "What-was-and-will-be."[158]

Myth tells us that Daksha (Right-handed, Competent) was born from Aditi. It is also said both that Aditi was born from Daksha and that Daksha was born of Aditi, as though the two were confused or different names for the same thing.[159] Certain legends indicate, furthermore, that Daksha was once a cardinal point among the Nakshatras. He was the ruling deity of a Nakshatra whose yoga star is called Abhijit, our Vega. In the strictest sense of the word Nakshatra, Vega could never have acted in the role of yoga star, since that star has never been near the ecliptic. In fact, at some era in the distant past, Vega was a pole star. Vega-Abhijit is, however, a very bright star—the fourth brightest in the sky—and is therefore a noticeable object soon after sunset or before sunrise. Currently, in the northern summertime it and Arcturus (in the absence of Venus or Jupiter) are the first stars to appear in the evening sky. Therefore it could, when rising at the same time as some other, fainter star on the ecliptic, act in the role of the harbinger of that star, especially if the light of such a star were obscured by the full moon. In the era about 4500 B.C., Vega rose within minutes of the rising of Antares in Scorpio. In 4501 B.C. the full moon near Antares marked the occurrence of the spring equinox, and Vega's rising confirmed these facts, as is demonstrated in figure 6.16.

Is it too facile to say that the known connection Daksha-Vega implies the connection Aditi-Antares? Daksha and Aditi are born together or from each other as these two stars were in close association at that period. If we examine the region of the sky near Scorpio during this era at the time of the spring equinox (the beginning of the sacrificial year), we find that the sun is at the foot of Punarvasu (fig. 6.7). But, of course, Punarvasu could not be seen in the sun's glare. The determination of these conditions was made by looking for the full moon in the opposite side of the sky, near Antares (Aditi?) in Scorpio, whose rising was seconded, as we saw, by the rising of Abhijit. Indeed, in the Hindu sacrificial calendar there is a certain day called Abhijit, after the star.

In the *Laws of Manu* (9.129) Manu is said to have given twenty-seven of his daughters to King Moon (i.e., the twenty-seven Nakshatras, or yoga stars?). He is said, too, to have been responsible for a curse on the moon declaring that thereafter it must wax and wane (i.e., that at the beginning of time the moon was full near the first Nakshatra, Daksha, but thereafter it had to run its waning and waxing course among the other, subsidiary Nakshatras). We learn, furthermore, of a kind of sacrifice called the Dakshayana offered at the new and full moons. This sacrifice was named when the god Prajapati took on the form of Daksha, instituted the sacrifice, and called it after Daksha. It was also

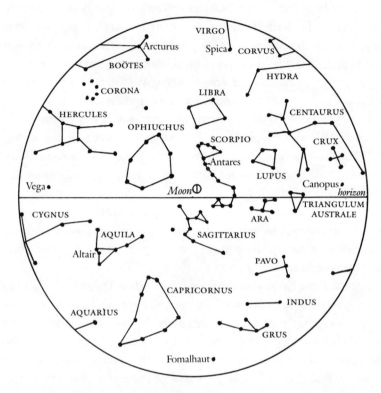

FIGURE 6.16

The eastern sky seen at the spring equinox in 4501 B.C. Here the occurrence of the full moon very near the yoga star Antares lets the observer know that it is the moment of the spring equinox. This is an example of the Nakshatra system in use. The rising of Vega (Abhijit) confirms the observation's validity.

known as the Vasishtha sacrifice.[160] But according to legend, these rites of Daksha were broken when Shiva, a son-in-law of Daksha, was refused an invitation to a banquet given to the other sons-in-law. Shiva then broke up the party during the sacrificial offering by shooting an arrow into the offering. The Suras and Asuras became alarmed, and the whole universe quaked (A, F). Thereafter, Shiva was called Daksha-yajñaprabhajñana (Daksha-Sacrifice Destroyer). As a result of this insult, Shiva's wife abandoned her body (E) and was reborn as the daughter of a mountain, "as the moon's digit springs from the sea."[161]

This story has both a celestial and a scientific explanation. Precession drove Aditi and Daksha from their stations as pointers of the equinox, and Shiva's new order took over. In fact, at some point the Nakshatra system was altered, reducing the number of lunar stations from twenty-eight to twenty-seven; Daksha and his star Abhijit were those eliminated. The daughters of Daksha except the one who married Shiva (Parvati, Gauri, Durga, and Uma are her several names), their offspring, the Asuras, Danavas, and Daityas are thereafter represented as the enemies of the gods in all literature influenced by the cult of Shiva.

The status of Shiva as prince of the equinox is best indicated by the name(s) of his consort, Parvati. The usual etymology of her name has to do with her transformation into a mountain. *Parvat-* in Sanskrit means "mountain," and Parvati was also said to be the daughter of Himalaya. Yet there are other associations that may be etymological as well as assonantal. *Parva-/parvan-* means "node" or "knot" and is used to refer to the full or new moon, especially at the node of its orbit. The second name for Parvati confirms these observations. *Gaura* means "yellow-white" and is used as a noun meaning "moon." Parvati's second name, Gauri, is a feminine form of this word. This same word is used in compound form to indicate certain festivals of the moon, and *gaurikalpa* is the name given to one of the various Hindu eons. Even today, Shiva has lunar associations: a great lunar festival is celebrated in his honor when the moon is full in the Nakshatra Phalguni. The Nakshatra originally associated with Shiva when he ousted Daksha and Abhijit disappeared has long since ceased to mark the equinox. But the prevalence of the Shiva cult has enforced a conservatism that kept the *person* of Shiva as king of the equinox while only his *station* has changed. It now resides in Phalguni. This conservatism compares with the Western practice of calling the equinoctial point Aries even though the equinox has long since moved out of that zodiacal constellation.

But what was that yoga star that Shiva took over at the ousting of the no-longer-useful Abhijit? Shiva is a euphemistic title (meaning "auspicious") given to the old Vedic god Rudra. In the Vedas, Rudra is a storm god allied with Indra and is the father of the storm gods, the Rudras and Maruts. Judging from the etymologies proposed for it, the name Rudra itself may at one time have been a mere epithet to some other name now lost. The etymology of Rudra seems to have been confused by the ancients, some insisting that it means "ruddy," others that it means "roarer" or "praised with clamor." In any case, Rudra was closely associated with Agni (Fire) and with Kâla (Time). The color of the deity is emphasized in the *Rig Veda,* where he is called the "red boar of the sky" and the "tawny bull."[162] He is also said to have a blazing form and to shine like the bright sun, like gold.[163] He is referred to as "universal ruler who looks after what is born in heaven."[164] It is no surprise, then, to find that the astronomers made out Rudra as the lord of a Nakshatra the yoga star of which was the red-colored Ardra (Betelgeuse). Ardra means "moist, tender," an appropriate name for a star whose appearance at one time signaled spring.[165]

After Shiva-as-Rudra, the next deity in the precessional succession was Manu. He was called Prajapati (Lord of Created Beings). He was the son of the sun, Aditya Vivasvat, or alternatively the offspring of Svayambhu (The Self-Existent). As Prajapati he was closely associated with Agni, even identified with him. He was also the year and the moon: "Verily, Prajapati, the year, is Agni and King Soma, the Moon. He himself, indeed, proclaimed his own self to Yajñavakas Rajastambayana, saying, 'As many lights as there are of mine, so many are my bricks.'"[166] In this quotation, Prajapati refers to the creation of his own Agni by building an elaborate fire altar to house him. It had 360 bricks, one for each day. Certain features of it were given astronomical titles: "hour holders," "half-moon holders," "month holders," and "season holders." Prajapati's work was threatened by his old age and approaching death, but by practicing austerities he was able to extend their effectiveness and his lifetime for a thousand years: "Whilst he was practicing austerities, lights went upwards from his hair follicles; and those lights are the stars: as many stars as there are, so many hair follicles there are; and as many follicles as there are so many mahurtas [sacrificial performances] there are in a thousand years."[167]

Manu is the earthly avatar of this Prajapati, and like Daksha before him, Manu is said to have instituted new laws and rites. The *Laws of Manu,* however, are extant in a great corpus, which Manu was supposed to have narrated in person to Bhrigu. The new order will protect and preserve its stability in written and codified form. This is the pur-

pose of the austerities that Manu underwent, and the result was a pros-
perous new regime, preserved for a thousand years and characterized
by its own set of laws and customs (G6). The same truth is told by the
son of Manu, a hymnist whose work is represented in the *Rig Veda*:
"Blest be the hamlet's chief, most liberal Manu, and may his bounty
rival that of Surya. May the Gods let Savarni's [Manu's] life be length-
ened with whom, unwearied, we have lived and prospered."[168] The
name of this hymnist son of Manu is Nabhanedistha, which can be
derived from *nabh-*, "navel," and *nedistha*, "nearest": the point nearest
the navel of the sky, that is, the equinoctial point. Nabhoyoni, the title
of Shiva mentioned above (notes 7 and text) is congruent in meaning
and conception.

The yoga star to be identified with Prajapati-Manu is Rohini, the red
cow of plenty, favorite wife of the Moon—our star Aldebaran. It coin-
cided with the equinoctial point in about 3200 B.C.[169] The hymn of
Nabhanedistha quoted from above has been explained as an elaborate
allusion to the establishment of Rohini as the star of the equinox, which
act began the historical period of the Vedas (still in effect) called the
Kali Yuga. The traditional date given for this event corresponds to the
equinox in our Julian year 3102 B.C. (see fig. 6.9).[170]

Several of the Brahmanas recount a Vedic myth about a Prajapati and
Rohini with enough clarity that we know that the myth was astronomical in character; hence we can relate allusions in the *Rig Veda*,
10.62, to certain features of the myth. The following version is given in
one of the sources. Prajapati, lusting after his own daughter, Dawn,
who had taken the shape of a doe (*rohit*), approached her in the guise
of a buck. The gods decided to punish his incest by creating a special
being, Bhutavat, identifiable as Rudra. The arrow of Bhutavat transfixed Prajapati, who was then bound in the sky as the constellation
Mriga (or Mrigashirsha). His daughter was placed near him as the star
Rohini, and the arrow of Bhutavat was asterized as well.[171]

Mriga is also a Nakshatra (its yoga star is lambda Orionis), a constellation pictured in the shape of an antelope's head. It lies between
Rohini (Aldebaran) and Ardra (Betelgeuse).[172] The myth probably relates the establishment of a new Nakshatra to interpolate between
two already established but too widely separated Nakshatras (Rohini

and Ardra).[173] The writers of the *Satapatha-Brahmana* seem to debate whether Mriga is a legitimate Nakshatra under which one ought to set up an altar to Agni.[174]

Because Rohini was Dawn in the guise of a doe, she is to be associated with Nabhoyoni, the equinoctial point itself. The title could apply as well to Prajapati-Mriga. In the myth a certain part of Prajapati-Mriga's body was extracted on the tip of Rudra's arrow, and semen had fallen to the ground during the incestuous act.[175] The wounding, then, was a castration (F)—a hole in the sky—and the flesh-tipped arrow is a phallic symbol (D), antitype of the pole. The result of the wounding (A) is renewed fertility (G), and as in the case of the castration of Ouranos (A), a new race of beings sprang from Prajapati's seed (G).

In Hindu astronomical works, the equinoctial point was called variously *ritasya yoni,* "vagina of the World Order," *ritasya sadanam,* "house of the World Order," and *sukritasya yoni,* "vagina of good deeds." The guardian of this place was called *ritasya gopam,* "guardian of the World Order." A special officer whose task was to reckon the season was called *ritvik,* "caretaker of rita."[176] Here is a final indication that the Paradigm of Replacement, instituted into ritual and proliferated in its various types through so many myths, was focused upon the hearthstone of the seasons, to which a special metaphorical vocabulary was assigned.

SUMMARY MYTH

What follows is a summary myth taken, in epitome, from a late compendium of myths about Dionysus (Nonnos's *Dionysiaca*),[177] which preserves such myths from many sources early and late. All of these myths as retold here are fraught with paradigmatic meaning. Dionysus, newly returned to the Mediterranean from travels in the east, must pass through Tyre on his way home. During his sightseeing tour of the city, he stops off in the temple to Melkart/Herakles, whose by-name is Astrochiton (Star Shirt). While standing before the image of the god, Dionysus breaks out into a hymn. He addresses the deity as Helios. At the hymn's conclusion the image comes to life. Herakles-Helios lightens, his fiery eyes shoot forth a rosy light, and, clad in a robe patterned like the sky, the god is revealed as an image of the universe. After mutual respectful greetings and a feast of welcome, Dionysus asks his host about the origin and foundation of the city of Tyre:

> Inform me, Astrochiton, what god built this city in the form of a continent and the image of an island? What heavenly hand designed it? Who lifted these rocks and rooted them in the sea? Who made all these works of art? Whence came the name of the fountains? Who mingled island with mainland and bound them together with mother sea?
>
> He spoke, and Herakles satisfied him with friendly words:
>
> Hear the story, Bacchos, I will tell you all. People dwelt here once whom Time, bred along with them, saw as the only agemates of the eternal universe, holy offspring of the virgin earth, whose bodies came forth of themselves from the unplowed, unsown mud. These by indigenous art built upon foundations of rock a city unshakable on ground also of rock. Once on their watery beds among the fountains, while the fiery sun was beating the earth with steam, they were resting together and plucking at the Lethean wing of mind-rejoicing sleep. Now I cherished a passion of love for that city; so I took the shadowed form of a human face, and stayed my step overhanging the head of these earthborn folk, and spoke to them my oracle in words of inspiration:
>
> "Shake off idle sleep, sons of the soil! Make me a new kind of vehicle to travel on the brine. Clear me this ridge of pinewoods with your sharp axes and make me a clever work. Set a long row of thickset standing ribs and rivet planks to them, then join them firmly together with a well fitting bond—the chariot of the sea, the first craft that ever sailed, which can heave you over the deep! But first let it have a long curved beam running from end to end to support the whole, and fasten the planks to the ribs fitted about it like a close wall of wood. Let there be a tall spar upright in the middle held fast with stays. Fasten a wide linen cloth to the middle of the pole with twisted ropes on each side. Keep the sail extended by these ropes, and let it belly out to the wind of heaven, pregnant by the breeze which carries the ship along. Where the newfitted timbers gape, plug them with thin pegs. Cover the sides with hurdles of wickerwork to keep them together, lest the water leak through unnoticed by a hole in the hollow vessel. Have a tiller as guide for your craft, to steer a course and drive you on the watery path with many a turn—twist it about everywhere as your mind draws you, and cleave the back of the sea in your wooden hull, until you come to the fated place, where driven wandering over the brine are two floating rocks, which Nature has named the Ambrosial Rocks.
>
> "On one of them grows a spire of olive, their agemate, selfrooted and joined to the rock, in the very midst of the waterfaring stone. On the top

of the foliage you will see an eagle perched, and a well-made bowl. From the flaming tree fire selfmade spits out wonderful sparks, and the glow devours the olive tree all round but consumes it not. A snake writhes round the tree with its highlifted leaves, increasing the wonder both for eyes and for ears. For the serpent does not creep silently to the eagle flying on high, and throw itself at him from one side with a threatening sweep to envelop him, nor spits deadly poison from his teeth and swallows the bird in his jaws; the eagle himself does not seize in his talons that crawler with many curling coils and carry him off high through the air, nor will he wound him with sharptoothed beak; the flame does not spread over the branches of the tall trunk and devour the olive tree, which cannot be destroyed, nor withers the scales of the twining snake, so close a neighbour, nor does the leaping flame catch even the bird's interlaced feathers. No—the fire keeps to the middle of the tree and sends out a friendly glow: the bowl remains aloft, immovable though the clusters are shaken in the wind, and does not slip and fall."

"You must catch this wise bird, the highflying eagle agemate of the olive, and sacrifice him to Seabluehair. Pour out his blood on the sea-wandering cliffs to Zeus and the Blessed. Then the rock wanders no longer driven over the waters; but it is fixed upon immovable foundations and unites itself bound to the free rock. Found upon both rocks a builded city, with quays on two seas, on both sides."

Such was my prophetic message. The Earthborn awaking were stirred, and the divine message of the unerring dreams still rang in the ears of each. I showed yet another marvel after the winged dreams to these troubled ones, indulging my mood of founding cities, myself destined to be City-holder: out of the sea popped a nautilus fish, perfect image of what I meant and shaped like a ship, sailing on its voyage selftaught. Thus observing this creature so like a ship of the sea, they learnt without trouble how to make a voyage, they built a craft like to a fish of the deep and imitated its navigation of the sea. Then came a voyage: with four stones of an equal weight they trusted their balanced navigation to the sea,[178] imitating the steady flight of the crane; for she carries a ballast-stone in her mouth to help her course, lest the wind should beat her light wings aside as she flies. They went on until they saw that place, where the rocks were driven by the gales to navigate by themselves.

There they stayed their craft beside the seagirt isle, and climbed the cliffs where the tree of Athena stood. When they tried to catch the eagle which was at home on the olive tree, he flew down willingly and awaited his fate. The Earthborn took their winged prey inspired, and drawing the head backwards they stretched out the neck free and bare, they sacrificed with the knife that selfsurrendered eagle to Zeus and the Lord of the waters. As the sage bird was sacrificed, the blood of prophecy gushed from the throat newly cut, and with those divine drops rooted the seafaring rocks at the bottom near to Tyre on the sea; and upon those unassailable rocks the Earthborn built up their deepbreasted nurse.

SUMMARY

A novel hypothesis validates its own utility by enabling new connections to be made in previously unconnected material; its tenets ought to lead to solutions of long-standing problems; and the model should be able to predict the appearance of new facts and data.

In this chapter a solution was proposed on the basis of the Replacement Paradigm for a knotty problem in Indo-European semantics. Words in the daughter languages having to do with the hammer and the mill exhibit striking polysemantic meanings. The etymon reflected in English *hammer* has a range of meanings from "stone" to "divine weapon" and from "sharp stone axe" to "anvil" and "lightning." In other languages the reflex from which English *mill* derives have ranges of meanings from "Thor's hammer-weapon" to "sharp" and from "mill" to "lightning." Why does *mill* mean "hammer" and *hammer* mean "anvil?" And why do both mean "lightning?" The solution can be had from the paradigm. After the invention of the mill for grinding grain, a metaphor was developed whereby the operation of the universe is seen to be like the operation of a mill—a slow turning on the axis which may grind out not flour but good luck or bad luck. This metaphor is quite explicitly presented in "The Mill Song" and in the "Amritamanthana," studied in chapter 3. Before the invention of the mill, there was another machine requiring rotary motion which led to the establishment of a similar metaphor—the bowdrill. The bowdrill was used for several purposes, including making fire and drilling holes, especially haft-holes in the culture's ubiquitous stone axes. Earthly fire is made from a churning motion motivated by human action; lightning is made from the churning of the heavens motivated by divine action. Drilling produces a stone axe for humans; rotation produces a fire weapon for the gods. The several different kinds of fire in the Indo-European tra-

dition are classified according to whether they are created from earthbound or heavenly friction. This complex of ideas, explicable through
the paradigm, joins the complex typified by the Latin *glans* and the
Greek *balanos* set forth in a previous chapter.

The heavenly mill can grind out bad luck as well as good luck and
the juice of immortality. Mills can break and then grind out salt instead
of gold. Chariot wheels can come off in mid-career destroying the
driver and sometimes the world itself. Kings and dynasties, human and
divine, are liable to fall. We know that the mundane matters of wealth
or woe have a celestial model—the good- or the ill-running of the
heavenly mill. Is there a celestial archetype for Frodi's broken mill? I
have suggested in this chapter that the precession of the equinoxes is
the only possibility. The pole shifts from one pole star to another, and
in between there is no marker. This fact represents the eon of anarchy.
Likewise, the equinoctial point may be marked by one star and then
another, but for hundreds of years in between there is no harbinger.
One king died, another will replace him, and in the interim there is
anarchy.

In far antiquity the small asterism we call the Pleiades after its Greek
name served as a harbinger of the spring equinox. Numbering six stars,
the Pleiades were almost universally counted as seven, and just-so
stories were told to explain how the seven sisters came to be six. In this
chapter I proposed that the six were supplemented to seven on the
model of the two northern constellations known variously as the Dippers or the Bears, each of which has seven bright stars. This fact is
paramount in their Persian name: Haptoiringa. Throughout antiquity
and into the present, these constellations have guarded the pole between them, and once in a while, as now with Polaris, one of their stars
has marked the pole itself.

The etymology of the Pleiades asterism in several daughter languages
and the meanings of the names of some of the stars preserved for us
corroborate the original role of the constellation as an equinox marker
and adumbrate the precession-caused lapse from this role. The etymology of the name in several languages (likely changed by folk etymology), involving the root *ple-*, is probably from an Indo-European
form meaning "first." Their heliacal rising was the first of the year as

marked from the spring equinox. They led the "circling of the stars." This contention is supported by an Avestan phrase for the Pleiades in the *Tishtar Yasht: purviyoni,* "primordial womb." In the Vedas, Krittikas is the word for the Pleiades, a name with an etymology rooted in agriculture and fertility.

After the heliacal rising of the Pleiades ceased to be important for the determination of the spring equinox, other asterisms supplanted them. Prior to the advent of the Pleiades' importance, there were other important asterisms which they supplanted. In the Greek tradition there seems to be no recollection of the latter occurrence, but in the Vedas there is evidence for the whole gamut of facts wrought by the precessional shift of the equinoxes in the sky. For the most part, however, the calendrical facts were tied to the heavens not through the use of heliacal risings and settings, as in the Greek systems, but by the twenty-seven or twenty-eight asterisms that formed the stations of the moon during its monthly circuit through the sky. These moon-station asterisms were called Nakshatras. Frozen in the names of some of these Nakshatras are facts that reflect the calendar of ages gone by—perhaps to a time some 7,000 years ago. One of the Nakshatras is called Punarvasu, "the Doublegood Pair," which corresponds to our Gemini, made up of the two bright stars Castor and Pollux (the Dioscuri in Greek tradition). In about 4500 B.C. the equinox lay in this constellation. Hence when the full moon occurred near to Castor and Pollux, it was the autumn equinox, and when the full moon occurred near Antares (180° away from Gemini), it was the spring equinox. The "regent" star of Punarvasu was named Aditi, "Mother of the Gods," in whom all sacrifice must begin and end. This means that the ritual (equinoctial) calendar began and ended with Aditi. Circumstantial evidence allows the inference that Aditi corresponds to our Antares. A full moon far enough east of Antares so as to allow its visibility was the Nakshatra indication of the equinox (in Punarvasu), as occurred exactly in the year 4501 B.C. In turn, the leading stars of other Nakshatras became signs of the equinox: Rudra-Betelgeuse, Mriga-lambda Orionis, Manu-Aldebaran, and the Kritikkas-Pleiades.

When the Pleiades began to outlive their utility as an equinox marker, their inexorable slipping into the sun at the time of the equinox gave rise to stories, epithets, and names. The story of the seven Heliades weeping amber tears for the fallen Phaethon on the banks of a river, for example, is likely rooted in these astronomical facts. The river is to be equated with the western sky, and the color of the amber confirms this; the name of one of the Pleiades, Electra, means "amber." This name is to be contrasted with that of her sister, Maia, "Midwife," whose name reflects the function of the Pleiades during their period of ascendancy as harbingers of the equinox. The name for the Pleiades in Latin also refers to their slipping—Vergiliae, which derives from the Latin verb *vergere*.

The Dipper constellations of the northern sky lent to the Pleiades their number seven. In turn, the Pleiades' number and setting led to the Indic plan for the world's geography of seven regions, six arranged around a central seventh. The Dvipas of the Vedic tradition and the Karshvares of the Avesta are connected with stories about epochal battles. Tishtrya (the star Sirius) battles Apaosha, the serpentine Daeva of drought. In its several extant versions, the story is paradigmatic and involves not merely the releasing of fertilizing rain to break the long drought but also the possession of the equinoctial point, with its implications for the good running of the universe (Huyairya) or its ill running (Duzyairya). Apaosha and Aharman himself are conceived of as dragons that issue from the underworld through a hole encircling the world tree and destroying it. Vritra, the drought dragon in the Vedic tradition, is also thought to be involved in an epic battle with Indra for control of the world. The story is repeated in a version called the Descent of the Ganges. The seven streams of the river represent both the order implicit in the number seven, the flood that has inundated the celestial sign, which must then "float" to a new home, and the Milky Way, which is both an upper road to life and light and a lower road to the "other" ocean in hell.

The dragon of disorder is ambiguous. The infernal dragon is sometimes seen as the guardian of the sacred mountain (the world's pivot), the world tree, or the pole. The Greek Ladon is a case in point. Guardian of the apples of the Hesperides, Ladon is an opponent of Herakles. Yet Ladon was put up in the northern sky as Draco, the constellation that encircles and guards the only point in the northern sky that is free of precession. Draco as Ladon was put in charge of the world order (the apple tree), but because he does not guard it well enough, the world goes awry (precession disturbs the sense of regularity); so the serpent becomes a figure of evil.

In sum, I refer to a myth not treated here: Rheingold left its home and was forged into a ring, which the giant Fafnir earned by his creative acts (constructing Valhalla); in the form of a serpent he guarded it, now a figure of evil. Siegfried takes the ring away, but it continues to be an object whose possession is disputed. At last it returns to its old and now newly established home with the Rhinemaidens—the center (and source) of the Rhine's flood of waters.

CHAPTER VII

CONCLUSION

G rand myths such as the "Amritamanthana" display an underlying
structure that is as sweeping as their content. Dumézil saw here
evidence for an underlying structure: the production of a magic drink,
its subsequent theft, and as a consequence of its loss, mortality. In this
book I have demonstrated that Dumézil's structure, based on recurrent
motifs, gives an inadequate account of the myths' complexities.

Motif analysis looks at recurrent themes: a myth would not belong
to this archetype, which Dumézil called the Ambrosia Cycle, unless it
contained the theme of the magic drink. If one restricts an analysis only
to those stories that contain this motif, a grander level of unity is
missed. The drink of immortality is of a type with, for example, the
cornucopia, porridge produced from a magic pot, gold ground from a
mill or spun from straw, and immortality itself, gained or lost by whatever means. These common themes fit together better if they are taken
as variant elements in a not-so-apparent category: the Golden Age,
which itself is just one structural feature of a larger design that has been
set forth here and called the Myth of Replacement.

Identifiable by the recurrence of ideas rather than motifs, this entity
is discoverable using structural techniques. By using methodologies set
forth by Lévi-Strauss and honed by other structuralists, this analysis
discovers unities on a much higher level of abstraction than those iden-

tified by Dumézil. Nine groups of recurrent "bundles" constitute the complete paradigm for the Myth of Replacement. These groups include not only the Golden Age mentioned above but also the circular motion used to brew or express Dumézil's magic drink, the etymological importance of words significant to churning and milling, and the proper names of mythological characters, a feature from which all comparative mythology, Dumezilian or Müllerian, takes its departure.

Putting comparative mythology into a structuralist's mold has empowered it with functionalist powers. It helps ally myth to ritual; it makes myth more generalizing by lending it cross-cultural applications; it discovers constellations of hidden unities in the cultural milieus of the daughter Indo-European societies—unities expressed not merely in myth and ritual but in the very vocabularies of the relevant cultures—and it gives us some evidence for the ultimate extracultural factors that disposed peoples, both related and unrelated, to compose myths expressing the idea of Replacement.

The function of myth and ritual belong to the larger field of defense in the cultural panoply. Arms and armor protect a society against the physical incursions of alien tribes, thus maintaining those cultural imperatives by which a society defines itself as "we, the people." It became clear in our examination of South-American myth that the same thinking is applied to sets of nonhuman aliens—groups of animals, the stars, and so on. Some of these alien groups are too powerful simply to oppose and thus end them. Rendering them harmless entails adopting them into the group. Myths fashion an account of extracultural entities behaving as if they were members, while ritual enforces upon them the regularities that a culture imposes on all its members. Myth and ritual, then, defend a culture in all its regularity from unpredictable, alien nonhuman phenomena, first by personalizing them and then by making them behave as if bound or conditioned by cultural rules. The disturbing observation that the "rules" of seasonal succession gradually fail, that old signs drift out of "synch" through precession, leads to the creation of a story of dynastic succession in which the old king, whose reign is marked by the milling of gold, falls when the mill breaks, when salt becomes the grist instead of gold. Then a new king comes to replace the old. Famine (which comes irregularly) is an old hag who refuses bread to a group of seven boys; they begin to dance in a circle, rising gradually to the sky. The hag runs up to offer them bread, but too late; they have ascended into the sky, where their dance has created the regularity of the seasons, and they are transmogrified into the Pleiades—all of this with the implication that heavenly order, derived from cultural ritual, will overwhelm and control the disorder of sporadic famine.

In stories of dynastic replacement, the mill (whole and then broken) has clear parallels first in the rituals of right running, which are found throughout the areas where Indo-European languages are spoken. In myth its parallels lie in the story of the Churning of Ocean, which produces the drink of immortality, an object of contention by the several dynasties of gods. Other parallels lie in myths about a charioteer, heavenly or earthly, who (bound to replace or to be replaced) goes on a disastrous, careening ride, which, in its heavenly type, threatens the regularity of the sky's order. These myths, in turn, can be associated with others involving dynastic displacement, in which the element of right running takes a form different from a wheel or a churn. Other myths involve not dynasties of gods but wars between human generations: Theseus vs. Minos, for example. There are stories about dynastic wars between Zeus and his relatives. Other stories about the enmity between Zeus and Typhon, Ixion, Tantalus, Sisyphus, and Prometheus involve the possession of an Earth-mother goddess. A taboo has been broken; Earth has been raped (plowed) and an object forbidden to mortals has been produced (divine food, agricultural plenty, fire), which the opponent threatens to give to humans. Humans, who used to live in a Golden Age, forfeit this (divine) status for the forbidden good. They are condemned to mortality, to work, to begetting children to care for them in their old age and to carry on their generation, and to acts of sacrifice.

Two semantic complexes that pervade the Indo-European languages were found to be resolvable by means of the considerations set forth here. The castration of Ouranos and the hiding of the Olympians in Kronos's maw were seen to be parallel instances of the bundle of hiding. The latter is like hiding the seed in Mother Earth, which is parallel to death. Seed is hidden in a seed hole in a furrow; death is the passage through the gates of the sun into the realm of the unseen, where Kronos-Hades is king. The expression of this bundle in castration involves the complex of terms acorn-genital. Castration is at once the stripping of the fruit from the great tree when the world is out of synch and the sowing of the seed from that fruit to make a new generation. The complex has celestial connections, for the Greek word belonging to this complex, *balanos,* means pivot point. The other complex involves reflexes of the reconstructed Indo-European forms *Haekmon* (*akmon*) and *mel*. Both terms exhibit striking polysemy whose universes overlap on each other. Each term can mean "lightning" in several of its reflexes. Each can refer to a hammer- or axe-like weapon. They overlap because each refers to a universe involving a tool that is in rotary motion, the first to a bowdrill, the second to the mill. The working of the sky is like a great bowdrill or mill, and its product is not fire but lightning, not flour but the plenty associated with continued right running. Lightning is the gods' weapon, and human stone axes are produced by bowdrilling a hole for the haft.

Ultimately this question will occur: If myth serves as a defense against the irregular and alien, and if a huge corpus of myths can be interrelated into a paradigm through structural considerations, what irregularity in nature does this paradigmatic myth serve to answer? The closing chapter of the book proposes that the cyclical wobbling of the earth on its axis over a period of 26,000 years, a phenomenon called precession, is the only celestial anomaly that could account for the production of this corpus of myth. Precession causes the pole to move among the stars. Polaris was not a polestar a thousand years ago, nor will it be a thousand years from now. Once it no longer serves, there will be no polestar. The universe will be without a regent, in a state of anarchy—Duzyairya. When the pole drifts into the region of another star, the universe will acquire a new regent. Dynastic change has been effected; all is again in order—Huyairya. In actual fact, however, most myths we encounter are not about polar phenomena at all. The great bulk of the myths are based on parallel phenomena that take place at the equinoctial points. These, like the poles, shift among the stars as precession turns them. The one-time regent of the spring equinox ceases to be. The old rules no longer hold. Then a new regent is located and all is well again. Right now, for example, the sign is moving out of the constellation Pisces, where it has lodged for 2,000 years (compare the Christian emblem of the Fish and the medieval Jewish good-luck charm and Yiddish name *Fischl*) and is moving into the constellation of the Water Carrier—the age of Aquarius is upon us. Prior to being in Pisces, the point was located in Aries the Ram (compare the good-luck signs cornucopia and *shofar*), in Taurus (compare the ignominious Golden Bullock, the Mithraic bull, and the Minotaur) with its Pleiades (stories about seven sisters such as the Heliades weeping on the banks of a river and the Hesperides guarding golden apples), and Gemini.

Certainly myths about the Pleiades do involve this connection between that asterism and its regency of the equinoctial point, as the etymologies of their several names and their roles in stories exhibit. Precession drove the Pleiades behind the sun at the equinox and then into the evening sky, where they reappeared as equinoctial denizens of the west: the Hesperides. Vedic sources may preserve myths that have to do with equinoctial regents even prior to the regency of the Pleiades, as distant in time as the regency of Gemini—Punarvasu in Sanskrit.

APPENDIX

THE REPLACEMENT PARADIGM

A. Confrontation, war, deadly social or family conflict.
   1. Father and son, opposing generations or kinds of people or gods.
   2. Twins, brothers, an impaired pair.
   3. The numbers three, nine, nine hundred.
   4. Something that changes ownership.
   5. A place of battle.
   6. Help given to one side or the other by a trickster and/or by a divine lady, often in disguise.
B. Incest, adultery, or other illicit sexual activity.
   1. A central female figure, often a spouse, usually disloyal.
C. Symbols of sexual intercourse: female element predominant.
   1. A socket: millstone, container, well, whirlpool.
   2. A vehicle: ship, shoe, chariot.
   3. Circular jewelry: necklace, ring, crown.
   4. A bow, a bridge.
   5. A devourer: wolf's mouth, eagle, a coiled serpent, a detached head.
   6. A residence, throne.
   7. Sun, moon.
D. Symbols of sexual intercourse, male element predominant.
   1. A rod: axle, stirring rod, spear, arrow, tree, mountain, rock, fish hook, hammer, horn, pillar, fishing line, structural members, other weapons.
   2. Teeth, beak.

    3. Sun or moon.

    4. Trickery.

C-D. Fulfilled sexual activity, right running, clockwise motion about an axis.

    1. The churning of the mill, the stirring of a cauldron, the brewing of beer, boring holes, wrenching off heads by the horns, rowing, winding and unwinding twine, production of fire.

    2. Swallowing, devouring.

    3. Tying a boat to shore, bringing booty to the house.

    4. Hitting the target.

    5. Due season.

C/D. The abrogation of sexual activity, wrong running.

    1. The mill breaking down, pillars breaking, a weapon missing.

    2. Regurgitation.

    3. Theft, loss of mooring.

  E. Hiding, encirclement, disappearance into the dark or into the bright sky.

    1. Capture, detainment.

    2. Drowning, sinking, bathing.

    3. Spattering the sky with blood or poison (bloody branches, golden boughs).

    4. Swallowing whole.

    5. Hell (the ultimate meaning of which is "to cover").

    6. Where the sky ends.

    7. Abnormal sleep or late return.

    8. The number twelve, the number forty.

    9. Transfiguration, disguise.

    10. Amphibianism.

  F. Destruction, death, human sacrifice, the loss of order, damnation.

    1. Earthquake, skyquake, mountain quake, the shattering of bonds and props; flood; general catastrophe.

    2. Monsters on the loose, the devouring of stabilizing elements; cannibalism.

    3. Conflagration.

    4. Sun, moon, and stars dark or off their path.

    5. Breaking of bones, laming.

    6. Loss of nourishment or fertility; plague; lack.

    7. Destruction of mankind; human sacrifice.

    8. Distortion or obscuring of truth.

    9. Curse.

    10. Impossible or difficult task.

  G. The Golden Age, return to normalcy, restoration.

    1. Gold, precious objects.

2. Abundance, fertility restored, hunt successful.
3. A magic drink brewed or recovered: ambrosia, beer, dew.
4. Birth, salvation, or rebirth of gods and men; release of captives.
5. The sun restored to its path.
6. New cosmological, natural, or civil order.
7. Weapons restored, machinery restored to working.
8. Feasting, plenty, song.
9. Truth revealed or discovered or the future foretold.
10. Thirty years, nine hundred years, or some other large number of years; numbers divisible by three.
11. Restoration of moral order.

H. Etymological significance: names of persons, things, places.
I. Cosmological significance: world beginning or ending; the structure or operation of the heavens.

1. The number seven.

NOTES

Chapter 1. METHODOLOGIES

1. This paragraph and many others that follow in this synopsis owe a great deal to a book-length recapitulation of myth criticism, Richard V. Chase's *The Quest for Myth* (Baton Rouge: Louisiana State University Press, 1949).

2. J. A. Wolf, in *Ueber die Encyclopaedie der Altertumswissenschaft*, as paraphrased in Chase, *Quest*, 38, from a citation by K. Hildebrand in *Histoire de la Litterature Grecque*, 1:45n.

3. Quoted and translated by Chase, *Quest*, 40, from the letters of the philologist K. F. Hermann to Friedrich Creuzer (*Briefe von Hermann und Creuzer* [Heidelberg, 1818], 15–16]). See Chase, *Quest*, 139n.8, for a bibliography of the controversy raging in Germany at this time between the Romantic interpreters of myth and the philologists.

4. See the bibliography for a list of Müller's works on mythology. Müller's theories have often been misunderstood and misrepresented, probably because he himself never bothered to condense his ideas into one succinct volume. He is almost universally lambasted for "flawed etymologies." In my view, this complaint is not only ill-founded but is also a sure sign that the critic has not examined Müller's own work. It is true that his methods were seldom in accord with today's established practice, but strong arguments still can be made for many of his results. A sympathetic view of Müller's work and its place in the history of myth criticism, with a bibliography, can be found in Richard Dorson, ed., *Peasant Customs and Savage Myths*, 2 vols. (Chicago: University of Chicago Press, 1968). An essay germane to the discussion of Müller in this book can be found in Dorson's "The Eclipse of Solar Mythology," in Thomas Sebeok, ed., *Myth: A Symposium* (1955; reprint, Bloomington: Indiana University Press, 1958).

5. Andrew Lang's output was voluminous. The title of his magnum opus, *Modern Mythology* (London, 1897), seems in itself to be a polemic against what he considered to be the outmoded methodologies of the philological approach. For a bibliography of Lang's work vis-à-vis his dispute with Müller, see Richard Dorson's works cited in the previous note.

6. Sir Edward B. Tylor's *Primitive Culture: Researches into the Development of Mythology, Philosophy, Religion, Language, Art and Custom* (London, 1871) was preceded by two earlier works, *Anahuac; or, Mexico and the Mexicans Ancient and Modern* (London, 1861), which grew out of a sojourn in America during which he met an ethnologist named Henry Christie, with whom he traveled in Mexico, and *Researches into the Early History of Mankind* (London, 1865).

7. Its position as a precursor can be seen from the title of Lang's other great work, in two volumes, *Myth, Ritual and Religion* (London, 1913).

8. Sigmund Freud, *The Basic Writings,* ed. and trans. A. A. Brill (New York: Modern Library, 1938), 929.

9. See especially Leo Frobenius, *Paideuma: Umrisse einer Kultur- und Seelenlehre* (Munich, 1921).

10. George Cox, *The Mythology of the Aryan Nations* (London, 1870), 1:68. The reference is taken from the second edition, of 1882.

11. Von Hahn, *Sagwissenschaftliche Studien* (Jena, 1876); Lord Raglan, *The Hero: A Study in Tradition, Myth, and Drama* (1936; reprint, New York: Random House, 1956).

12. Stith Thompson, *The Folktale* (1946; reprint, New York: Holt Rinehart and Winston, 1960).

13. Vladimir Propp, *Morphology of the Folktale,* trans. Laurence Scott (1928; reprint, Austin: University of Texas Press, 1968).

14. C. Scott Littleton, *The New Comparative Mythology,* 3d ed. (Los Angeles: University of California Press, 1983).

15. "Flamen-Brahman," *Annales du Musée Guimet, Biblioteque de Vulgarisation,* vol. 31.

16. Formal rules permit the cognate relationship. Difficulties of semantics, however, argue against the admission of the relationship. For a précis of these considerations, see Emile Benveniste, *Indo-European Language and Society,* trans. Elizabeth Palmer, Miami Linguistics Series no. 12 (Miami, Fla.: University of Miami Press, 1973), 229.

17. It is hazardous at best to attempt to recapitulate Lévi-Strauss's work and his theories, a hazard not eased by the difficulty of his style and the rarity of his comments on his own voluminous oeuvre. For such comments as there are, see G. Charbonnier, *Conversations with Claude Lévi-Strauss,* trans. John and Doreen Weightman, (1961; reprint, New York: Grossman, 1969). For a sympathetic synopsis, see Edmund Leach, *Claude Lévi-Strauss* (New York: Viking, 1970). Criticisms of the method may be found in Michael Lane, ed., *Structuralism: A Reader* (New York: Basic Books, 1970), especially Edmund Leach's "On the Legitimacy of Solomon"; and Peter Munz, *When the Golden Bough Breaks: Structuralism or Typology?* (London: Routledge and Kegan Paul, 1973).

18. Henri Frankfort et al., *Before Philosophy: The Intellectual Adventure of*

Ancient Man; An Essay on Speculative Thought in the Ancient Near East (1946; reprint, Baltimore: Penguin, 1949), 12–15.

Chapter II. THE RITUAL OF RIGHT RUNNING

1. William Simpson, *The Buddhist Praying-Wheel: A Collection of Material Bearing on the Symbolism of the Wheel and Circular Movements in Custom and Religious Ritual* (London: Macmillan and Co., 1896), 80.

2. Ibid., 81–82, quoting Rajendralala Mitra, *The Antiquities of Orissa,* 2:60.

3. Simpson, *Praying-Wheel,* 29–39.

4. Ibid., 10, and in general, 7–27.

5. Ibid., 69–70, quoting Julius Eggeling, ed. and trans., *Satapatha-Brahmana,* Sacred Books of the East, vol. 41 (Oxford: Clarendon Press, 1884), 22–23.

6. Eggeling, *Satapatha-Brahmana,* 23.

7. Simpson, *Praying-Wheel,* 42, fig. 10. The origins of this image are Hindu. In *Satapatha-Brahmana* 6.7.2.8 an altar is described as having been constructed in the form of a wheel.

8. Simpson, *Praying-Wheel,* 46–47, citing *Hiuen Tsiang,* translated by Beal.

9. Ibid., 15, with fig. 3.

10. Ibid., 50, citing Cunningham, *The Bhilsa Topes,* 352; also found in John Dowson, *A Classical Dictionary of Hindu Mythology, and Religion, Geography, History, and Literature,* 11th ed. (London: Routledge and Kegan Paul, 1968), 65, under "Chakra-Varti."

11. Dowson, *Hindu Mythology,* 65, under "Chakra-Varti," attributing the idea to Wilson.

12. Simpson, *Praying-Wheel,* 42, fig. 11.

13. Ibid., 276, citing Alex K. Forbes, *Ras Mala: or, Hindoo Annals of the Province of Goozerat,* 2:315.

14. It also requires moving to the right; see Eggeling, *Satapatha-Brahmana* 2.6.2.15. For a complete discussion of rita in the Vedas, see Jeanine Miller, *The Vision of Cosmic Order in the Vedas* (London: Routledge and Kegan Paul, 1985), esp. chap. 2.

15. *Rig Veda* 6.51.1.

16. Müller, *Lectures on the Origin and Growth of Religion* . . . (London: Longmans, Green, and Co., 1878), 239–244.

17. F.K.D. Bosch, *Golden Germ,* 59: "When the principle of creation, unmanifested, omnipresent, and all-pervading, consisting of pure breath, light and mind, personified as god Prajapati and acting as the masculine element in the process of creation, penetrates the female substance embodied in the obscure, inert, primeval waters, it manifests itself as Hiranyagarbha, the golden germ of life which is essentially one with the golden god of fire, Agni."

18. *Satapatha-Brahmana* 11.1.6.24, translated by Bosch, *Golden Germ,* 122.

19. Heinrich Zimmer, *Myths and Symbols in Indian Art and Civilization,* ed. Joseph Campbell, Bollingen Series 6 (Princeton, N.J.: Princeton University Press, 1972), 23–24, 91–92, quoting the Vedic *Khila,* no. 8.

20. *Rig Veda* 10.82.5–6, translated by Bosch, *Golden Germ*, 55.

21. *Atharva Veda* 10.21.19–33, translated by Bosch, *Golden Germ*, 54. Vedic Brahman is akin in conception to the later Vishnu; it is absolute and undifferentiated, the source of every form and quality. This neuter noun is not to be confused with the later Brahma, the masculine deity.

22. This is the very thesis of Bosch's extremely well documented book.

23. *Mahabharata* 14.47.12, translated by Bosch, *Golden Germ*, 67.

24. Bosch, *Golden Germ*, 93–94.

25. Ibid., 154.

26. Cited by Simpson, *Praying-Wheel*, 187.

27. Cited by Simpson, *Praying-Wheel*, 193.

28. Ibid., 183–184, citing from Orwell, *The Bishop's Walk and the Bishop's Times*, 122.

29. Simpson, *Praying-Wheel*, 188–189, citing several sources, including Lachlan Shaw, *History of Moray*, and Forbes Leslie, *The Early Races of Scotland and Their Monuments*.

30. Simpson, *Praying-Wheel*, 191, citing William Reeves, *Life of Saint Columba*.

31. Ibid., 193.

32. Ibid., 194.

33. Ibid., 291, citing James M. Maclinlay, *Folklore of Scottish Lochs and Springs*, 141.

34. Simpson's sketch, *Praying-Wheel*, 244, fig. 37. The same figure is reproduced as the frontispiece in M. J. Green, *The Wheel as a Cult Symbol in the Romano-Celtic World*, Collection Latomus, vol. 83 (Brussels: Revue d'Études Latines, 1984).

35. Simpson, *Praying-Wheel*, 247, fig. 40.

36. Campbell, *Creative Mythology*, 417–419.

37. Sir James G. Frazer, *The New Golden Bough*, ed. Theodore H. Gaster (New York: Doubleday and Co., 1961), 354, quoting John Ramsay. The agaric referred to was probably *Amanita muscaria*, Fly Agaric. Compare Soma-Agni. Soma has been identified as a drink made from this same mushroom.

38. The relationship between thunderbolts and fire is discussed in chapter 6.

39. Simpson, *Praying-Wheel*, 78–79, quoting from Eggeling, *Satapatha-Brahmana*, Sacred Books of the East, vol. 12, 41.

40. Simpson, *Praying-Wheel*, 198, citing M. Gaidoz, *Le Dieu Galois du Soleil, et le Symbolisme de la Roue*, 21. Drilling for sacrificial fire with a bow drill is a rite well-attested in Hindu and Roman practice, as when the sacred fires of Vesta were extinguished. The Romans also approached divinity toward the right (see Plautus *Curculio* 70), and a part of the marriage ceremony, *dextratio*, involved a movement to the right for luck and fertility (Solinus, 45.15). Yet I can find no evidence that the Romans produced fire by turning a wheel clockwise, enlisting participants by threes.

41. Simpson, *Praying-Wheel*, 211–212, citing Grimm, *Teutonic Mythology*, 12:611–612.

42. Simpson, *Praying-Wheel*, 207, citing Gordon Cumming, *From the Heb-*

rides to the Himalayas, 1:245–246. This constraint regarding the hammer may have its roots in deepest antiquity. See the discussion of **Haekmon* in chapter 6.

43. Sir James G. Frazer, *The New Golden Bough,* 352.

44. Simpson, *Praying-Wheel,* 217, citing John Beleth, *Summa de divinis officiis* (Paris, ca. 1152), Latin translated by the author. Unless otherwise noted, all other translations appearing in this book are the author's own.

45. Simpson, *Praying-Wheel,* 212, citing H. Mayhew, *German Life and Manners,* 2:371.

46. Simpson, *Praying-Wheel,* 201, citing Hone's *Every-Day Booke,* 1:845.

Chapter III. MYTHS EXHIBITING THE AMBROSIA CYCLE

1. Except in titles of works, no attempt will be made to reproduce the diacriticals sometimes used in Romanized transliterations of the Devanagari script.

2. Snorri Sterluson, *The Prose Edda of Snorri Sterluson: Tales from Norse Mythology,* trans. Jean I. Young (1954; reprint, Berkeley: University of California Press, 1964), 118. Some sources claim that only Menja sang the lay. See Giorgio de Santillana and Hertha von Dechend, *Hamlet's Mill: An Essay on Myth and the Frame of Time* (Boston: Gambit, 1969), 88. In this book I have opted for the simplest English transliteration of Norse names, following the system employed by H. R. Ellis Davidson in *Gods and Myths of Northern Europe* (Harmondsworth, Eng.: Penguin, 1964).

3. The poem is called "Grottasongr," also translated "The Lay of Grotti." Though this poem belongs properly to the *Poetic Edda,* it is extant only in a copy made in a manuscript of Snorri's *Prose Edda* (*Regius 2367*). Some readings are therefore doubtful. The translation is the author's; the proper names may may be transliterated differently elsewhere. Quotation marks are used only to set off passages in which Frodi's words address the sisters, where their address to him is made personal by the vocative, and where the two sisters are engaged in dialogue.

4. One feature of twins in Indo-European belief is that they bear etymologically or phonologically similar names. See Donald Ward, *The Divine Twins: An Indo-European Myth in Germanic Tradition,* University of California Publications, Folklore Studies, vol. 19 (Berkeley: University of California Press, 1968), 6.

5. *Skáldskaparmál,* chap. 42 in *The Prose Edda by Snorri Sterluson,* trans. Arthur Gilchrist Brodeur (New York: American Scandanavian Foundation, 1929), 161ff. Significantly for this discussion, the name Frodi is related etymologically to a root that means legend, lore, history, or knowledge.

6. Ibid.

7. Ibid.

8. Ibid.

9. *Skáldskaparmál,* chap. 43, in Brodeur, *Prose Edda,* 169.

10. Saxo Grammaticus, *The First Nine Books of the Danish History of Saxo*

Grammaticus, trans. Oliver Elton (1905; reprint; Nendeln, Lichtenstein: Kraus, 1967), 376.

11. Ibid., 335.

12. Significantly for the point that follows, Od in Icelandic means "point."

13. Summarized from Elton, *First Nine Books,* 273–285.

14. The ox is named Sky Bellower, as translated by Young in Sterluson, *Prose Edda,* 79. A different version of the confrontation between Thor and Hymir is presented here in "The Deluding of Gylfi."

15. In Snorri Sterluson's version, the serpent spat poison; see Sterluson, *Prose Edda,* 80.

16. In the episode of Utgard-Loki from "The Deluding of Gylfi," Thor raised the Midgard serpent to the *sky*; Sterluson, *Prose Edda,* 78.

17. Summarized from Terry, *Poems of the Vikings,* 69–74; Lee Hollander, *The Poetic Edda* (Austin: University of Texas Press, 1928), 97–104; and Lawrence S. Thompson, ed., *Norse Mythology: The Elder Edda in Prose Translation* [by Gudbrand Vigfnsson and F. York Powell] (Hamden, Conn.: Archon Books, 1974), 40–42.

18. As described in "The Deluding of Gylfi"; Sterluson, *Prose Edda,* 45.

19. The serpent is not always known by the name Fenrir, which is also the name of the monstrous wolf that will break free come Ragnarok. Jormungand is a name applied to the Midgard serpent in the "The Deluding of Gylfi" (see Sterluson, *Prose Edda,* 56), a sibling of Fenrir, whose other brother was Hel, all of whom were the children of Angrboda (Boder-of-Sorrow). It is clear from the account given earlier, in the *Sibyl's Vision,* that a doublet of Fenrir is Mánagarm (Moon's Dog) in that he eats the flesh of all the dead and will someday swallow the moon and spatter the sky and air with blood. The *Sibyl's Vision* at this point sounds like Ragnarok, *fimbulvetr* and all. Sterluson, *Prose Edda,* 39.

20. Summarized from the closing chapters of "The Deluding of Gylfi"; Sterluson, *Prose Edda,* 88–93.

21. The Indo-European base *kel-²* (see *AHD,* appendix) also yields Latin *color,* which we borrow unchanged. It also yields the German adjective *hell,* "bright, light in color, yellow-gold." I explore the connections among these ideas in "The Idea of 'Sky' in Archaic Greek Poetry," *Glotta* 66 (1988): 1–19.

22. Joseph Campbell, *The Hero with a Thousand Faces,* 2d ed., Bollingen Series 17 (Princeton, N.J.: Princeton University Press, 1968), 19.

23. Ibid., 15.

24. Ibid.

25. At the close of an eight-year period—i.e., after 99 lunations (2,921 days)—the octaeteris, a period almost equally divisible by an integral number of months and of years (8). This statement about the great year is given in Plutarch *Theseus* 15 and Diodorus Siculus 4.61.3.

26. *The Mahabharata of Krishna-Duaipayana Vyasa,* trans. Pratap Chandra Roy, 2d ed., 12 vols. (Calcutta, n.d.). This is the main source for this synopsis. Its chapter-reference numbers are given in brackets.

27. In one variant the gods mistake him for Agni and so worship him.

28. The variant to be summarized is a conflation from several versions, but it follows mainly that of the *Mahâbhârata,* as cited above.

29. Mt. Meru and Mt. Mandara make up a significant pair (A2).

30. Has the elixir appeared or not? The discrepancy is in the text, not in my summary. One must allow a few inconsistencies in these immense and detailed narratives.

Chapter IV. MYTHS FROM SOUTH AMERICA TO GREECE

1. Both the criticisms and the translated quotation from Lévi-Strauss, *Le Cru et le cuit,* 346, are from Geoffry S. Kirk, *Myth: Its Meaning and Function in Ancient and Other Cultures,* Sather Classical Lectures, vol. 40 (Berkeley: University of Califorina Press, 1970), 59.

2. Lévi-Strauss, *The Raw and the Cooked,* trans. John and Doreen Weightman (New York: Harper and Row/Harper Colophon Books, 1975), 250–251. Since a myth's item number is always given, a note with page reference to the *Raw and the Cooked* is not always given with the citation for a myth.

3. Add to FI of the paradigm: flood.

4. Add II to the paradigm: the number seven. Compare Minos's sacrifice by sevens every great year.

5. Add E9 to the paradigm: transfiguration, disguise.

6. Add GII to the paradigm: restoration of the moral order.

7. Lévi-Strauss, *The Raw and the Cooked,* 243–244.

8. Add to F2 of the paradigm: cannibalism.

9. Lévi-Strauss, *The Raw and the Cooked,* 244.

10. Ibid., 218.

11. Lévi-Strauss deals with this disparity by calling up two "codes," the aquatic, in which "viscera are congruous with fish and marsh plants," and the celestial, in which they are congruous with stars, especially the Pleiades (*The Raw and the Cooked,* 244). The explanation given here finds the interrelationship between aquatic and celestial beings harmonized in the myth through the ubiquitous, mediating amphibious being.

12. Add EIO to the paradigm: amphibianism.

13. All hole-dwelling rodents, especially those that also frequent the water, would be amphibians.

14. Lévi-Strauss, *The Raw and the Cooked,* 125–127.

15. Add to E2 of the paradigm: bathing.

16. For a discussion of native beliefs about the opossum, see Lévi-Strauss, *The Raw and the Cooked,* 171.

17. Add FIO to the paradigm: impossible or difficult task.

18. Lévi-Strauss, *The Raw and the Cooked,* 165–166.

19. Ibid., 166–167.

20. Add C-D5 to the paradigm: due season.

21. Lévi-Strauss, *The Raw and the Cooked,* 126.

22. Ibid.

23. Ibid., 140.

24. It even goes into the water to fetch one of its favorite prey, the turtle, and it is also known to fish.

25. Lévi-Strauss, *The Raw and the Cooked*, 156.

26. Ibid., 155.

27. These ideas are universal. In a Trobriand myth recounted by Malinowski, we learn that people used to live underground, where they grew old and gray, but they were able in those days to rejuvenate themselves by sloughing off their skins. Even when they came to the surface, they continued to possess this power. But one day an old woman lost her skin, which she had taken off to bathe; it floated away on the tide. In her rejuvenated form, the old woman was not recognized by her granddaughter. She had to put her old skin (mortality) back on to be recognized. From that day on men have had to die. Bronislaw Malinowski, *Magic, Science, and Religion and Other Essays* (Garden City, N.Y.: Doubleday, 1954), 127.

28. Lévi-Strauss, *The Raw and the Cooked*, 124.

29. Ibid.

30. Ibid., 156.

31. Compare M_1, the Bororo song that Lévi-Strauss gives as his key myth, is to be found in *The Raw and the Cooked*, 35.

32. Nur Yalman, "'The Raw:The Cooked::Nature:Culture': Observations on *le Cru et le cuit*," in *The Structural Study of Myth and Totemism*, ed. Edmund Leach (London: Tavistock, 1967), 77.

33. Lévi-Strauss, *The Raw and the Cooked*, 104–105 (M_{27}).

34. Facts of the myth and ritual from "Hunters of the Dugong," no. 105 of the series "Living Wild," narrated by David Attenborough for the BBC.

35. From now on, unless the particular variant being used is cited in a special footnote or in the text, lack of space will restrict our retelling of the stories to conflation of the sort to be found in dictionaries and handbooks of myth. The particular source for the variants as given can be found by resorting to such ready sources.

36. *Fabulae*, 152A. All translations from Hyginus are taken from *The Myths of Hyginus*, ed. and trans. Mary Grant, University of Kansas Publications, Humanistic Studies, no. 34 (Lawrence, 1960). Fabula 152A is on pp. 123–124.

37. *Myths of Hyginus*, 124–125. The learned Hyginus was a turn-of-the-era author, a friend of Ovid, and a freedman of the emperor Augustus. He wrote extensively as part of Augustus's program exalting old and local Roman values. His *Urbes Italiae* has been lost; his lost commentary on Virgil is quoted here and there by others. Under his name (his authorship of them is very doubtful) survive the two works we will quote from here, the *Fabulae*, a corpus of general mythology, and *De Astronomia*, a compilation of myths having to do with the constellations and other celestial events. Despite their lack of authority and their occasional blunders, these two works (which themselves may not have been penned by the same hand) preserve unique and valid variants of the myths under discussion.

38. *IG* I 928 III, cited by Otto Gruppe, *Die griechischen Kulte und Mythos in ihren Beziehungen zu den orientalischen Religionen* (1887; reprint, New York: Georg Olms, 1973), 1:266; Nonnos *Dionysiaca* 6.76, etc.; *Il.* 11.735; *Od.* 5.479, etc.; *Theogony* 760; Soph. *El.* 824.

39. Schol. E. *Phoen.* 3, where he is paired with Lampon. Is Phaethon the type or the antitype of the stray horse that brings the chariot to ruin? In *Phaedrus* 246B, Plato's image of the chariot of the soul seems to be modeled on the solar chariot, and there one of the horses is good, the other wayward.

40. Hyginus, *Poetic Astronomy*, 242; contrast Cicero *ND* 2.20.

41. Gruppe, *Kulte und Mythos*, 266, uncharacteristically without citation. Compare the story of Joseph and his brethren.

42. Manilius *Astronomica* 1.730.

43. Aratus *Phaenomena*, 328; compare Nonnos *Dionysiaca* 38.424–31.

44. Ovid *Metamorphoses* trans. Rolfe Humphries (Bloomington: Indiana University Press, 1955), 2.381–388.

45. The same word refers to the pale yellow alloy of gold and silver; compare êlektôr, "the beaming sun."

46. As seen on a vase painting reported by Karoli Kerenyi, *The Heroes of the Greeks*, trans. H. J. Rose (1959; reprint, New York: Grove Press, 1960), 65. This is the wrong color (F8) ram to offer to Zeus.

47. The idea that there may be paronomasia in this name is taken from Graves, *Greek Myths*, 2:39. Compare Pausanias 7.14.12.

48. Pausanias 5.20.6.

49. Schol. E. *Phoen.* 26, cited in Kerenyi, *Heroes of the Greeks*, 93 n.493.

50. Ibid.

51. Hesychius, under *kedalon*

52. Hyginus, in *Poetic Astronomy* 2.21, preserves a tradition that the name of the mother of the Pleiades and Hyades was one and the same (Atlas being their father), namely, Aithra.

53. Bellerephon was in exile for having killed his brother (A2), who bore the name Bellerus (whence the etymology of Bellerephon might be taken as Bellerus-Murderer); his second name was Hipponoos (Horsesense).

54. Artemidorus *Onirocriticus* 2.12, cited in Kerenyi, *Heroes of the Greeks*, 216n.396.

55. Compare the sentiments of the chorus about Oedipus's origin in Sophocles' *Oedipus Rex* 1085ff.

56. Our source is Pausanias 2.33.1. His reason for telling the story is to give the etiology of the current name of the island, Holy Island. Because she lay with the god Poseidon while on a mission of obeisance to the hero Sphairos, Aethra founded a shrine to Deceitful Athena (the goddess had sent the dream that urged her on one mission only to find a rendezvous of a different kind awaiting her). Concurrently, Aethra changed the name of the island to Holy Island and established a ritual for Troizenian virgins to dedicate their girdles to the Deceitful Aphrodite before marriage. At 5.10.7, Pausanias mentions a group of statues on the front pediment of the temple to Zeus at Olympia; the group represents the race between Pelops and Oenomaus at its beginning. Myrtilus is

mentioned by name as the driver of Oenomaus, but though a figure of Pelops's driver is in the group, Pausanias does not mention the name Sphairos.

57. Gruppe, *Kulte und Mythos,* 191, argues that the Hippolytus legend arose from a conflation of the Phaethon and Adonis stories and that Phaedra is a name likely taken from a list of the Heliades. He points out that Helios Eleutherios was worshiped in Troezen from the earliest times.

58. Pausanias 2.32.1; compare Hyginus *Poetic Astronomy* 2.13, and Nonnos *Dionysiaca* 38.424–431.

Chapter V. ZEUS AND HIS OPPONENTS

1. Aeschylus *Coephoroe* 314.

2. Hesiod *Theogony* 126–127ff. Hesiod's text is the basis for the synopsis that follows.

3. Zeno said that "*ouranos* is the edge (or limit) of the *aither,* from which and in which all things are manifest, for all things revolve except it"; Hans Friedrich August von Arnim, ed., *Stoicorum veterum fragmenta* (Stuttgart: Teubner, 1964), 1:33, 28; compare 2:198, 11. For Ouranos as Colored-Sky, see my "Ideas of 'Sky' in Archaic Greek Poetry," *Glotta* 66 (1988): 1–19.

4. E. A. Wallis Budge, *The Gods of the Egyptians; or, Studies in Egyptian Mythology* (1904; reprint, New York: Dover Publications, 1969), 2:102, 104, with the illustration on p. 101. Compare Eusebius, *Praeperationis evangelicae,* in *Opera,* 1:10, 29, where, referring to Philo of Byblus, he says that there is a spring whose waters are tainted by the blood of Ouranos (spring = dayspring) as a result of his having been castrated by El-Kronos.

5. Hesiod *Theogony* 156–166.

6. For the Lithuanian and Slavic material, see Gimbutas, "Perkunas/Perun: The Thunder-God of the Balts and Slavs," *Journal of Indo-European Studies* 1 (1973): 473.

7. The Delphic stone was anointed with oil (G) and dressed with unspun wool; Pausanias 10.24.5.

8. Hyginus *Poetic Astronomy* 2.13.

9. Hesiod *Theogony* 620–626ff. The account of the Titanomachy to follow is derived mainly from Hesiod's text.

10. Ibid., 376: *dia theaôn.*

11. Ibid., 644: *aglaa.*

12. Ibid., 670, 123, 721.

13. Ibid., 653: *hypo zophou eeroentos.*

14. Ibid., 729.

15. Homer *Iliad* 20.611–665.

16. This logic is not a priori but rather is supplied by the syntax of the passage.

17. Hesiod *Theogony* 720–725.

18. Homer *Iliad* 8.478–481; *neiata* is ambiguous, for it could also mean "deepest." But since "deep" (*bathus*) Tartarus is on both sides (*amphis*), we take the meaning "outermost" to be the one intended.

19. Aeschylus *Persians* 839.

20. Hence Pindar's *cheimerios zophos* in *Isthmians* 430.

21. Homer *Odyssey* 3.329, 335.

22. Ibid., 10.190.

23. Ibid., 24.9–14.

24. Bright and golden Dawn gives birth to bright gods: Heosphoros and the shining stars to Astraeus, and Phaethon to Kephalos (*Theogony* 378–382, 984–991). Perhaps the most elaborated image derived from this model is Aphrodite Anadyomene (The Birth of Venus), rising up into life from the drowned genitals of Ouranos as if from the bath.

25. Homer *Iliad* 8.476–481.

26. Described in Homer *Odyssey* 4.563–569, without mention of Kronos, and in Hesiod *Works and Days* 109–120, and 168–173, and in Pindar *Olympians* 2.61–284, and *Threnoi* 129–130.

27. (*Neiata*) *peirata gaiês* or *eschata gaiês*; Hesiod *Theogony* 622, 731, 738, and the Homeric and Hesiodic passages cited in the previous note.

28. Hesiod *Theogony* 745–819. See my discussion of this passage in "Ideas of 'Sky' in Archaic Greek Poetry," 13–15.

29. Pindar *Threnoi* 129–130 (95).

30. Pauly-Wissowa, *Realenkyklopädie des Klassischen Altertumswissenschaft* Stuttgart: J. B. Metzler, 1963), under "Kronos."

31. Pindar *Olympians* 2.68–72.

32. The daffodil (cf. Middle English *affodil*). Asphodel probably derives from **hasphodelos*, an intensive form of *sphodelos* (variant of *spodelos**), from *spodos*, "ash"; so the name would mean "emberflower," probably from its gray foliage and yellow flower. Compare *anthrax*, a red boil with a blackened eschar which resembles a burning coal covered by ash. The association of asphodel with the underworld is problematic. A resemblance to the color of the evening sky is a possible connection. The flower was also used as a cure for snakebite and as a remedy against sorcery, but did these medicinal uses precede or follow the hellish associations? The Greeks seem to have extended the infernal associations of this flower to other Lilaceae—for example, to the narcissus. According to Pamphos, it was not a violet but a narcissus which distracted Persephone just before her abduction to the underworld (cited in Pausanias 9.31.6). The Hesperides are called lily-like in Quintus Smyrnaeus 2.14. Lily-like is a traditional epithet applied to the voice of the cicada. The insect itself is infernal, living underground for many years, pupating briefly, and then shedding its skin, leaving a perfect cast of itself before it takes to its life of singing. Likewise, the flowers of the lily family live dormant underground as bulbs before coming up with the warmth and moisture of spring to flower gloriously.

33. Elysium is probably related to *eilyô*, "to cover" (base + primary suffix *-sio*), the place curtained from view by the horizon.

34. The same verb, *embasileuô*, is used by Hesiod to describe Kronos's sway in Olympus during the Golden Age and in the Isles of the Blessed; *Works and Days* 111, 169 (the latter verse being preserved only in Proclus's commentary).

35. If the passage cited above from the *Iliad* (8.476–481) seems out of keeping with this conclusion in its insistence that neither sun nor breezes are to be

found at the underworld seat of Iapetus and Kronos, let us notice that it says Helios-*Hyper*ion sheds no ray there. Of course not, but Helios-*Kat*ion (i.e., Helios-katachthonios, the underworld sun) may have.

36. There were three statues to Zeus in the marketplace of Corinth, one nameless, one to Zeus Chthonios, and one to Zeus Hypsistos, as reported in Pausanias 2.2.7.

37. Minos, Rhadymanthes, and a third brother, Sarpedon, were involved in their own dispute about sovereignty (A1) involving not a girl (A4) but a boy (Atymnius or Miletus). Minos got the kingdom and exiled his brothers. Compare Zeus, Hades, Poseidon.

38. See Charles Daremberg and Edmund Saglio, eds., *Dictionnaire des antiquites grecques et romaines, d'apres les textes et les monuments* (1877–1919; reprint, Graz: Akademische Druck- und Verlaganstalt, 1963), under "Kronos."

39. Pindar *Olympians* 3.41.

40. The golden dog of Zeus, stolen by Pandareos (F) and concealed by Tantalus (E), is emblematic of the Golden Age (G) and is a precursor in the dynasty of Pelops to the golden ram of Atreus. Hence, its theft is parallel to the theft of ambrosia and nectar and constitutes one of Tantalus's parallel crimes.

41. The motif of eating forbidden food occurs again in Persephone's consumption of the fatal pomegranate seed, which kept her in Hades.

42. Whatever the etymology of the Greek word for ivory (*elephas*), its compounds with -*phanes* and -*chros* make it clear that ivory was prized for its gleaming white color. Compare the name Glaucus and other names referring to color and visual value discussed above in chapter 4.

43. Various etymologies for the several forms of this goddess's name have been proposed, but there is no consensus. Pronunciation of the name engendered fear (Plato *Cratylus* 404 c–d), and it seems likely, therefore, that the several forms arose owing to taboo deformation. Compare the Homeric epithet for Persephone: *epainê*, "awesome." There are some clues, however, that the name may be a term referring to brightness in the dark (contrast the meaning of Hades, "unseen," "unseeable"). In most common forms of the name, the first element is *perse*-. In itself this etymon is a name, Perse, daughter of Ocean, wife of Helios, mother of Aëtes, Circe, and Perses. Another Perses, son of the Titan Krios, was married to Asteria (Starlady), who bore a daughter Hecate. Hecate is often confused with Persephone; she was a goddess both of the light and of the dark. One of her names was Perseis. All of these are good indications that *perse*- is the aboriginal first element in Persephone and that it has to do with light or brightness. As to the correct aboriginal form of the second element of the name, I adduce the fact that Perse, wife of Helios, was also said to be the mother of Pasiphae (All Shining, Evident to All); the second element of this name is to be derived from the verb base *pha*- "to appear, to shine." Although no such adjective is extant, Greek could well have admitted of the adjective forms *phaeis, phaessa, phaen*, of which the feminine form contracted would yield **phâssa*. An extant form of Persephone is Phersephaassa (with the *a* vowel doubled). Under this explanation, the name would mean "bright shining." It is interesting that a cult title of Aphrodite preserved by Hesychius is Persithea (Bright? Goddess). An etymology for the name Pelops is developed below.

44. The name of Tantalus's town was Sipylos (Pindar *Olympians* 1.38). Pausanias 7.24.7 reports that a city on the flanks of Mount Sipylos disappeared into a chasm, and water gushed from the place at which it disappeared. This seems to be a myth, not a fact. The connection between Tantalus's city, Sipylos, and the city mentioned here is by inference.

45. This rivalry may be extended, too, to the third brother, Poseidon, who is supposed to have raped Demeter in the form of a stallion.

46. The etymology of this name is not certain; it may refer to the mania generated in certain feverish illnesses (hence Typhus) and/or it may refer to whirling motion (C-D), especially that created by the smoke column from a fire or the dust column of a dust devil. Typhöeus, already mentioned, and Typhaon are alternate forms of this name.

47. The name Typhon refers in one context to Ursa Major or to a part of it. See LSJ under "*typhôn*."

48. "Lame Mountain" (F5). See LSJ under "*nysos*."

49. In a variant story, we find evidence of a variant in which Typhon was Zeus's twin (A2). A scholium to Homer (*Iliad* 2.782–783) reports that Typhon was conceived from two eggs smeared with Kronos's semen. Hera buried these eggs underground for incubation (compare Vinata's two eggs, one yielding Aruna, the other Garuda). The *Homeric Hymn to Apollo* (3.305ff.) says that Hera bore Typhaon parthenogenically in response to and out of revenge for Zeus's production of Athena. She prays to Earth and the Titans below to offer her help in producing "a son outstanding among the immortal gods" (327), one "nothing less in strength than him [Zeus]—let him be even mightier by as much as far-seeing Zeus is mightier than Kronos" (338–339). Like Zeus, Typhon was raised in a cave (E), and when Zeus's hiding place was penetrated by Kronos, Zeus took on a serpentine form (see Graves, *Greek Myths*, 7.c). The similarities between Zeus and his archenemy are astounding.

The Typhon myth is treated in detail by Joseph Fontenrose in *Python: A Study of the Delphic Myth and Its Origins* (Berkeley: University of California Press, 1959). There Fontenrose develops an elaborate paradigm of the combat myth which bears some coincidental resemblances to the paradigm developed here.

50. Another Atlas (named after the Titan?) is discussed below. This Atlas, son of Poseidon, figured in his own story as builder and master of Atlantis, a paradise (G) named after him. Atlantis was drowned (E2, F). The fabulous city, surrounded by concentric belts (C-D) of water, suffered a great earthquake (F1) as well. The city and its relationship to the Titanic Atlas and to Tantalus are discussed below.

51. Hyginus *Poetic Astronomy* 2.42.

52. *De Natura Deorum* 2.20. In the face of Cicero's evidence, are we to suppose alternatively that Heraclides Ponticus made an error here, or that Hyginus wrongly reported his source? This is unlikely, for Hyginus reported this second tradition and traced its source to Eratosthenes.

53. For a summary of the evidence on this point, see Franz Cumont, "Les Noms des planètes et l'astrolatrie chez les Grecs," *L'Antiquité Classique* 4 (1935): 18–22.

54. *Homeric Hymn* 5, 202–217.

55. These are proximate constellations.

56. Hyginus *Poetic Astronomy* 2.29, citing Hegesianax.

57. Hyginus *Poetic Astronomy* 2.16.

58. Ibid., 2.16.

59. Ibid., 2.15. The eagle is an amphibian (air, land, and for fishing eagles, water); hence this is the proper bird to snatch Ganymede from his terrestrial domain and transport him to Zeus's celestial one.

60. Hyginus *Fabulae* 31.

61. The proper name is masculine, is identical with the name for the bird, and is necessarily of the same etymology. Merope is the feminine name made on the same etymon. An etymology for this name is developed below.

62. *Aeneid* 1.394.

63. *Ankylomêtês* at *Theogony* 546.

64. Pausanias 9.25.6.

65. Scholium to Virgil's *Eclogues* 6.42.

66. Since Euhemerus got it backward—that is, myths about gods do not, as he says, develop from legends about human beings, but rather myths about heroes and humans were once told of the gods—I propose that we honor the name Euhemerus for his noticing the operation of similar typologies in stories of men and gods but that we acknowledge the process as it actually occurs—in the direction opposite to that proposed by Euhemerus—by coining the words *dyshemerize* and *dyshemerization*.

67. *The Suida,* under "Eurybatos." For citations and a discussion of the traditions about the Kerkopes, see Otto Gruppe, *Die grieschischen Kulte und Mythos in ihren Beziehungen zu den orientalishcen Religionen* (1887; reprint, New York: Georg Olms, 1973), 1:419n.2, 487n.2.

68. *The Suida,* under "Kerkopes." The text used here is from Hesiod, *Hesiod: The Homeric Hymns and Homerica,* ed. and trans. Hugh G. Evelyn-White (London and New York: Loeb Classical Library, 1920), 538–539.

69. Ibid.

70. Appianus *Bella Civilia* 5.69, cited in Kerenyi, *Heroes of the Greeks,* 195n.224.

71. Herodotus *Histories* 7.216, the passage describing the secret path above Thermopylae.

72. See Emile Benveniste, "Arménien *aregakan* 'soleil,' et la formation du nominal en *-akn*," *Revue des Études Armeniennes,* n.s., 2 (1965): 5–19, where he demonstrates the etymology of Armenian *-akn* (from I.E. *-okw*; cf. Greek *-opê*) is not "eye," but "spring"; hence, *asteropê* means something like "star opening." See Calvert Watkins, "I-E. 'star'," *Sprache* 20 (1974): 10. Now we may hazard an etymology for Merope as well: "thigh opening." The shortening of the vowel of *mêr-,* "thigh," in the compound is due to the well-attested folk etymology that derived *merop-* from *meromai,* "to divide," and *-opê,* "voice." Hesychius (17), A 2455, reports the gloss: *akmona. aletibanon* (pestle). *Kyprioi.*

73. *Passalos* means *membrum virile* according to one citation by LSJ. Herakles was known as the Tirynthian Akmon (Callimachus *Hymn to Artemis* 146).

Akmones in Homer and Hesiod are often celestial, suspended from Olympus by a golden cord.

74. *Theogony* 561–612; *Works and Days* 60–68.

75. Sexist bias like Hesiod's occurs in other traditions as well. In one Babylonian creation myth, the advent of female gods means a lessened food supply in heaven. Enki's solution was the creation of mankind, whose sacrificial offerings would supply the deficit. In another myth there is an adumbration of creation based upon the division of labor: both male and female protohumans, Uligarra and Zalgarra, have names with similar meanings, "Establisher of Plenty," and "Establisher of Abundance," which is typical of names for twins. In this story the craftsman gods (Lamga) are destroyed to provide the raw material for the creation of mankind. Can we extrapolate from this that the created people will be divided as to occupation, as were the gods who provided the stuff for their making? In *Genesis,* Eve's creation is sexist, both on the basis of her origin from Adam's rib and on the basis of the division of labor (she was to be Adam's helpmate).

76. Scholium to Apollonius Rhodius *Argonautica* 2.1249, cited in Robert Graves, *The Greek Myths,* rev. ed. (New York: Penguin, 1955), 1:145n.8 (Graves, §39.i).

77. I take the shortening of eta to epsilon (*pêlos* = "mud") in the name Pelops to be due to taboo deformation. Persephaasa was altered into several competing forms, thus concealing the etymology. Merope was likely altered from Mêrope.

78. Planting is culture given up to the whims of nature. Sacrifice is culture attempting to bend the will of nature.

79. For a summary of the evidence, see Fred W. Householder and Gregory Nagy, *Greek: A Survey of Recent Work* (The Hague: Mouton, 1972), 52–53.

80. Homer *Odyssey* 15.403–411.

81. Ibid., 343–344.

82. Ibid., 371–373; cf. 14.65–66.

83. Ibid., 14.444–445; cf. Hesiod *Works and Days* 3–8.

84. Homer *Odyssey* 14.41–42.

85. Homer *Odyssey* 22.19, 74.

86. Homer *Odyssey* 14.110.

87. Homer *Odyssey* 15.488–492.

88. In Homer the first is solid, the second liquid; see *Odyssey* 5.93, for example.

89. Early Greek had no strictly secular word to refer to slaughter, but the alternative verb *sphazô,* while being ritual is not dedicatory and does not appear in the passages cited. See Jean Casabona, *Recherches sur le vocabulaire du sacrifice en grec, des origines à l'époque classique.* Publications des Annales de la Faculté des Lettres, n.s., vol. 56 (Aix-en-Provence, 1966), as cited in Vernant, "Sacrificial and Alimentary Codes in Hesiod," 61, 274.

90. Babrius, 58; see Denison B. Hull, ed. and trans., *Aesop's Fables Told by Valerius Babrius* (Chicago: University of Chicago Press, 1960).

91. **egnis* and **pur* respectively.

92. The Latin term for this wood is *felix arbor, felix materies* (*mater-* = "mother").

93. The Sanskrit term for this fire, from which comes rain, is *parjanyah*.

94. For an authoritative discussion of the Vedic evidence upon which this discussion rests, together with semantic, linguistic, and formal links between Roman, Greek, Vedic, and Avestan materials, see Gregory Nagy, "Patroklos, Concepts of the Afterlife, and the Indic Triple Fire," *Arethusa* 13 (1980): 161–195.

95. See under "Vesta" in Pauly-Wissowa; and Charles V. Daremberg and Edmund Saglio, eds., *Dictionnaire des antiquites grecques et romaines, d'apres les textes et les monuments* (1877–1919, reprint; Graz: Akademische Druck- und Verlaganstalt, 1963.

96. The withholding of fire by Zeus from the Melian race (*Theogony* 563) is parallel to the keeping of ambrosia and nectar from mankind.

97. Hesiod *Works and Days* 57. Zeus says that he will give men an evil (Pandora) in place of (or as the price for) fire (*anti pyros*), as though they are equal or parallel (cf. *Theogony* 570).

98. Is it possible that the empty facsimile set next to the *pignus* represents the ambiguity found in food that is taboo as food?

99. Hesiod *Theogony* 555–556. The sequel, too, is etiological (how mankind got fire, the origin of evil, and why Prometheus was punished) but quite illogical: how could men burn bones if, as Hesiod tells it, Zeus's first and prior punishment for them was the withholding of fire?

100. Ibid., 538.

101. Nagy, "Patroklos," 172.

102. Ibid., 168.

103. Ibid., 173.

104. Ibid., 174. The root etymon of the name *vas-* means "shine" and is cognate with Vesta.

105. Ibid., 176.

106. Ibid., 180. Nagy calls him a "specialized multiform" of Vivasvat. In some variants he is the son of Vivasvat, and he shares the epithet Vaisvata with Vivasvat's other son, Yama. In the *Rig Veda,* Manu was given Agni by Matarisvan, and Agni continues to abide among Manu's offspring.

107. Aeschylus *Prometheus* 86 and Pindar *Olympians* 7.80, for example.

108. Adalbert Kuhn, *Die Herabkunft des Feuers und des Gottertranks* (Berlin, 1859).

109. See Pauly-Wissowa, 23:1, 689.

110. Pierre Chantraine, *Dictionnaire etymologique de la langue grecque: Histoire des mots.* (Paris: Editions Klincksieck, 1968–), under *"manthano, promêthes."*

111. Julius J. Pokorny, *Indogermanisches etymologisches Wörterbuch* (Bern: Francke Verlag, 1959–60), 1:727.

112. Nagy, "Patroklos," 180. Bruce Lincoln avers that Manu is to be derived from I.-E. **man-¹,* "man, human being"; "The Indo-European Myth of Creation," *History of Religions* 15 (1975): 134. Perhaps future work will reveal that **men-³* and **man-¹* are identical in ultimate origin.

113. Lincoln, "Myth of Creation," 129. Yama had a twin sister, Yamî or

Yamuna, and they are given in some sources as the Adam and Eve of Hindu mythology.

114. Pauly-Wissowa, 23.1, 689.

115. Scholium to Lykophron, 537 (Tzetzes).

116. Pauly-Wissowa, 23.1, 646. The *pro-* in Prometheus is taken to be emphatic, leaving *-mêtheus* as equivalent to Menzana.

117. Or **man-²* "to have in mind"; see Nagy, "Patroklos," 180.

118. Ibid., 182.

Chapter VI. PRECESSION

1. Manilius, *Astronomica,* 1.730–734.

2. The Brahman achieves the world of the gods in the singing of the Saman, discussed in chapter 2.

3. Brihaspati is the "name of a deity in whom the action of the worshipper upon the gods is personified," in this instance the diety of right impulsion. Brihaspati is also the name of the regent of the planet Jupiter in Hindu astronomy; the name is then often used as the name of the planet itself. See John Dowson, *A Classical Dictionary of Hindu Mythology and Religion, Geography, History, and Literature,* 11th ed. (London: Routledge and Kegan Paul, 1968), under "Brihaspati."

4. See chap. 2, nn. 5, 6.

5. *Rig Veda* 10.82, 10.121.

6. *Atharva Veda* 10.7.38.

7. See *AHD* under *nebh.* Even more interesting is the etymology of the second part of the word, *-heim* from Indo-European **kei-¹* (see *AHD* under "*kei-¹*"), "to lie down; bed, couch." One of the Sanskrit reflexes of this etymon yields the name of the god Shiva, the ultimate etymology of whose name, therefore, is connected semantically with his second name, *nabhoyoni,* "sky vagina."

8. Recall that Ocean and Sky, at least at the horizon, are the same: as Savitri, the heavenly fire is reborn every morning from the grandfather of the waters, Apam Napat.

9. The wheel was not used as a model by these peoples for obvious reasons: prior to contact with European cultures, they were unacquainted with large-scale, functioning wheels.

10. Gregory Nagy, "Patroklos, Concepts of the Afterlife, and the Indic Triple Fire," *Arethusa* 13 (1980): 175.

11. Ibid.

12. Nagy, "Patroklos," 177.

13. Ibid., 178.

14. Ibid., called *ojas,* "power," in the *Rig Veda* 10.65.2; but the word *ojas* is cognate with *vajra.*

15. Nagy, "Patroklos," 179. The reference is to the *Rig Veda* 10.52.5. A common epithet for Indra and Indragni alike is *vajra-bahu,* "he who has the vajra in his arms."

16. The author is not competent to judge between the various forms which

have been proposed for the etymon, i.e., whether *ak-men with the metathetic variant *ka-men is sufficient or whether one must resort to laryngeal theory to account for all the reflexes. All experts seem to agree that they may be referred to a suffixed aboriginal form containing an unvoiced palatal stop with the basic meaning "sharp."

17. Most recently Peter J. Maher, "Hae'kmon: '(Stone) Axe' and 'Sky' in I.E./Battle-Axe Culture," *Journal of Indo-European Studies* 1 (1973): 441–465. See also F. Crevatin, "Un problem di antichita' indeuropee. Il cuneo del fulmine," *Incontri Linguistici* 1 (1974): 61–68, and 2 (1975): 47–59.

18. For the most recent and revolutionary reevaluation of the evidence, see Colin Renfrew, *Archaeology and Language: The Puzzle of Indo-European Origins* (London: Jonathan Cape, 1987). The central thesis of Renfrew's book is that no single culture whose material remains are found in prehistoric Europe can unequivocally be identified as speakers of Indo-European-derived languages, nor can their locations be ascribed with certainty to massive migration from any of the supposed Indo-European homelands, no matter where they were located. The best model for the final distribution of peoples speaking Indo-European languages and for the phonetic and semantic evolution that characterizes the language of these peoples lies in the gradual transformation of language with their migration and their assimilation of (and into) aboriginal cultures under the impetus of the advent of agricultural technology, which originated roughly at the same time (before 6000 B.C.) in the three centers in the Fertile Crescent: one in Anatolia at Çatal Hüyük (which center likely gave rise to the diaspora of Indo-European-speaking farmers), one at Jericho that was the ancestor of Hamitic-Arabic speaking farmers, and one at Ali Kosh.

19. Marija Gimbutas, "Kurgan Axes: An Archaeological Note," *Journal of Indo-European Studies* 1 (1973): 463–465.

20. Marija Gimbutas, "Perkunas/Perun: The Thunder-God of the Balts and Slavs," *Journal of Indo-European Studies* 1 (1973): 466–478.

21. The idea that certain myths "preserve" traditional knowledge about precession is not original with this author. The latest of the century-old literature on the subject was Giorgio de Santillana and Hertha von Dechend, *Hamlet's Mill: An Essay on Myth and the Frame of Time* (Boston: Gambit, 1969).

22. A case can be made also for winter from *ghei yielding Latin *hiems* and *hibernus*, and Old Irish *gaim*, Greek *chiôn*, and Avestan *zya*. See *AHD* under "*ghei-²*."

23. See LSJ under "ear."

24. Not in Homer with the meaning "rise" of the sun—or at least not overtly: at *Iliad* 5.777 the celestial horses (dawn's horses?) are let (*aneteile*) to pasture on ambrosia where the two rivers Simoeis and Scamander meet.

25. *Homeric Hymn to Hermes*, 542.

26. See Norman Austin, "Odysseus Polytropos: Man of Many Minds," *Arche* 6 (1981): 40–52.

27. Cited by *OED* under "spring."

28. For the most comprehensive bibliography on the subject of archaeoastronomy to the early 1970s, see Elizabeth Chesley Baity, "Archaeoastronomy and Ethnoastronomy So Far," *Current Anthropology* 14 (1973): 389–449.

29. The language here suggests a celestial phenomenon: *ôrto chelidôn es phaos anthrôpois earos neon histamenoio.* But we know of no asterism named "swallow" (*chelidôn*) whose heliacal rising could be the subject of this reference. In Hesiod's era, the heliacal rising of Aries marked the equinox.

30. May 11 and October 31, according to the refined calculations of M. L. West in his edition of Hesiod, *Works and Days* (Oxford: Clarendon, 1978), notes to lines 383–384.

31. Some scholars are reluctant to give hypothetical dates but place the date of the spread of the Kurgan Cultures (ca. 2500 B.C.) as much too late; see Calvert Watkins's conclusion to his essay "Indo-European and the Indo-Europeans" in *AHD*, 1502. Colin Renfrew, at the extreme, would see the beginning emigration of language and technology from the Anatolian agricultural locus at ca. 6500 B.C.; see *Archaeology and Language.* Renfrew abridged this book into a serviceable article, "The Origins of the Indo-European Languages," *Scientific American* 261 (October 1989): 106–114. In the abridgement, however, one misses his devastating argument against the hypothesis of Dumézil.

32. Compare the societal-linguistic complexes explored by Emile Benveniste in *Indo-European Language and Society,* summaries, table, and index by Jean Lallot, trans. Elizabeth Palmer, Miami Linguistics Series no. 12 (Miami, Fla.: University of Miami Press, 1973).

33. Hence the several spellings in Greek: Plêiades, with long *ê* for metrical reasons, and Peleiades, which form makes transparent a derivation from *peleia,* "dove," an ancient idea supported by some modern scholars. Some have attempted to derive the name from the verb *pleô,* "set sail," since Hesiod says that good and bad sailing weathers are concurrent with the phases of this asterism. The name of the mother of the Pleiades, Pleione, retains the correct etymon.

34. Variously from *AHD*; Pierre Chantraine, *Dictionnaire etymologique de la langue grecque: Histoire des mots* (Paris: Klincksieck, 1968); Hjalmar Frisk, *Griechisches etymologisches Wörterbuch* (Heidelberg: Carl Winter, 1973); Julius Pokorny, *Indogermanisches etymologisches Wörterbuch* (Bern-Munich: Francke Verlag, 1959–60). The latter three cite the Iranian forms as parallel to the Greek; Chantraine and Frisk derive the constellation names from "first," but the semantic connection between this and Greek *pleio-* is my own.

35. Herman Lömmel, ed. and trans., *Die Yasts des Awesta* (Göttingen: Vandenhoeck and Ruprecht, 1927), 51: " . . . die weibliche Ersten (*purviyoni*)" which he glosses with "die Pleijaden."

36. The charts dealing with precession that appear in some books (e.g., de Santillana and von Dechend, *Hamlet's Mill*) are misleading in that they show the date when a given asterism was located *at* the equinoctial point. This was true for the Pleiades about 2000 B.C. But under such conditions they could not serve as equinoctial markers at their heliacal rising, because the sun, also located at the equinox, would keep them from being visible. It has been calculated (see Hesiod, *Works and Days,* notes to lines 383–384) that the sun must be 16° below the horizon for the Pleiades to be visible. It would take on the order of 1500 years for precession to move the asterism from visibility to the equinoctial point.

37. Apollonius Rhodius 4.598ff. I do not mean to suggest that every instance

of the drowning motif in myth was inspired by a shifted sign. The disappearance of any star or planet at its setting was thought to be "similar" to drowning.

38. Hyginus, *Poetic Astronomy,* in *The Myths of Hyginus,* 2.21, italics mine. "After" indicates that they have failed as a marker of the *onset* of spring.

39. Ibid. The facts presented by Hyginus are true only in the loosest sense. Only now, two thousand years later, is the heliacal rising of this asterism a sign of the summer solstice. Compare Varro, *Res Rustica* 2.164, and Columella 11.2.77 for other notices of the seasonal importance of the Pleiades to the Romans.

40. *AHD* under "*wer-*³."

41. *OED* under "weird."

42. LSJ under "*rhombos.*"

43. Only six Pleiades are visible to the unaided eye. The seventh Pleiad is discussed below.

44. Ganga and Parvati come together in mythology, for both are daughters of Himavat, the latter girl usually being called by the name Uma, "light." Maha-Devi has many by-names, often contradictory; e.g., Gauri, "yellow, brilliant"; Kali, "black"; Jagau-mata, "mother of the world"; Tara, "star"; and Durga, "the inaccessible." As Kali, she is represented as a hideous face, dripping blood and surrounded by snakes hung round with skulls. Compare Fenrir and the Midgard serpent in the description of Ragnarok.

45. Manfred Mayerhoffer, *Kurzgefasstes etymologisches Wörterbuch des Altindischen: A Concise Etymological Sanskrit Dictionary* (Heidelberg: Carl Winter, 1956–80), under "*krittikas.*"

46. G. E. Stechert, *Star Names: Their Lore and Meaning* (New York: Dover, 1963), 393. This is an unabridged, corrected, and translated republication of G. E. Stechert, *Star Names and Their Meanings* (1899).

47. See Ralph L. Turner, *A Comparative Dictionary of the Indo-Aryan Languages* (London: Oxford University Press, 1966), and Mayerhoffer, *Wörterbuch des Altindischen,* under "*kr-*" and "*krs-.*"

48. Other characters in Hindu mythology named Taraka show similar histories. One was carried off by Soma, the moon, which led to a great war between the gods and the Asuras. The other was a female Daitya on the bank of the Ganges at its confluence with the Sarju; there she ravaged the countryside. A contract was let for her murder, but Rama-chandra, being reluctant to kill a woman, maimed her by cutting off her arms (F5). Lakshmana then cut off her ears and nose. She assailed her attackers with showers of stones (cf. *as'man*), and Rama was finally forced to kill her with a well-aimed arrow. This myth is discussed in the text below. The summary evidence here and the summaries of stories from Hindu mythology to follow are taken from John Dowson, *Classical Dictionary of Hindu Mythology.*

49. Qanirac, comparable to Jambu-Dvipa.

50. Gâh 5.5, translated "seven-fold earth" in L. H. Mills, ed. and trans., *The Zend Avesta,* Part 3: *The Yasna, Visparad, Afrînagân, Gâhs, and Miscellaneous Fragments,* Sacred Books of the East, vol. 31 (Oxford: Clarendon Press, 1887). Parsi mythology knows of seven heavens as well; see James Darmesteter, ed. and trans., *The Zend Avesta,* Part 1: *The Vendidad,* Sacred Books of the East, vol. 4. (Oxford: Clarendon Press, 1880), lix n.4.

51. *Bundehesh* (also *Bundahis*) 11.2, as paginated by E. W. West, ed. and trans., *Pahlavi Texts,* Part 1: *The Bundahis, Bahman Yast, and Shâyast Lâ-Shâyast,* Sacred Books of the East, vol. 5 (Oxford: Clarendon Press, 1880); Ferdinand Justi paginates this selection 20.9; *Handbuch der Zendsprache: Altbactrisches Wörterbuch, Grammatik, Chrestomathie* (Wiesbaden: Sändig, 1969).

52. Also *Yasht*[*Yast*] 8.

53. *De Iside et Osiride* 47.

54. *Bundehesh* 7.1.

55. Compare the contrasting phases of Maha-Devi (Parvati): light (Uma or Gauri) and dark (Kali). Compare as well the contest of the two wives of Kashyapa, Kadru and Vinata, both daughters of Daksha, to determine whether the color of the horse Uccaihshravas (just churned from Ocean) was white or black. Compare, too, the motif of the alternation of white and black found in the Greek myths studied in chapter 3.

56. *Tir Yasht* 8.20–22.

57. Ibid., 24–29.

58. This is a paraphrase of chapters 1–17 only. Selections from the *Zâd-Sparam* are translated in West, *Pahlavi Texts.*

59. In the *Bundehesh,* Aharman is usually referred to only by circumlocution so that his presence as primal opponent in chapter 7 is lost sight of beside the explicit mention of Apaosha.

60. *Zâd-Sparam* 1.4–5.

61. Ibid., 1.11.

62. Ibid., 1.22. If the *nabhoyoni* is equivalent to the equinoctial point, as I argue above, this text corroborates in sum the argument of this book: for 3,000 years the navels were not disturbed, and the sun, moon, and stars stood still (i.e., were not subject to unpredictable extravagation). The "mischievous incursion" would then refer to the errant motion of the *nabhoyoni* from one sign into another. In astronomical fact, the equinoctial point is resident within one zodiacal sign for very nearly 2,200 years, an eon. This figure, of course, would have been impossible for the ancients to arrive at with any precision; they knew it was a long time, but just why they chose to round it off to 3,000 is a subject of investigation beyond the scope of this book.

63. *Zorvân* is the Avestan word.

64. *Zâd-Sparam* 1.26.

65. Ibid., 1.28.

66. See E. W. West's note (*Pahlavi Texts*) to *Bundehesh* 3.12, and compare *Bundehesh* 25.7.

67. On the phrase "a sheep trembles at a wolf," compare Fenrir.

68. *Bundehesh* 7.6, 7.11.

69. There is a genealogical connection between the main character of this story and the Pleiades, for in one variant Ganga is the mother of Karttikeya.

70. Other variants say that the enemies were holy men or harassing demons.

71. In this particular, Visvamitra is curiously similar to Vaisvata (Sun-born), a member of the Kshatriya by race, who became one of the seven Manus, i.e., leaders of an eon. Vaisvata's son was Nabhanedistha (Navel Neighbor), who was deprived of his inheritance by his father (or by his brothers) (A).

72. These are the same demons warded off by Agastya. In other tales the Rakshasas are malevolent deities comparable to the Titans.

73. Compare this with the source of the Ganges in Vishnu's toe. The god's foot (c) is at once the source of plenty in the form of water and of ruin in the form of demons. The flood motif in many stories (E) underlines the fact that water had destructive as well as constructive aspects.

74. Treta is the second *maha-yuga* (eon), so named (its etymology is "three") because it is 3,000 years long and its "dawn" and "dusk" are each 300 years long.

75. The same Taraka whose other name is Krauncha. The planetary star Kart-tikeya was pitted against Krauncha. Now we learn that Agastya-Canopus was also pitted against a sidereal opponent, Taraka. Rama (Bala-Rama), who also meets this Taraka in battle, is brightness incarnate from the hair of Vishnu; he was born of the mother Rohini, while his dark half-brother Krishna was born of Devaki (cf. Devi).

76. Urvasi was the celestial incarnation of the lotus.

77. Compare Aphrodite Anadyomene.

78. In the *Puranas* they are enumerated into seven or fourteen classes. Some say they were created by the seven Manus.

79. Compare the seed of Ouranos falling into the water or onto the ground. Shall we continue to believe the comparative linguists who of late insist, contrary to Kühn, that Ouranos and Varuna have no etymological connection?

80. In the sequel, Urvasi incurs the anger of Mitra and Varuna and is forced to marry Puru-Ravas, a hero of the sun and dawn who lives in miduniverse. The two are the subject of a drama that is patently celestial in origin, involving her twin rams, which were stolen by the Gandharvas (sky-dwelling deities who knew and revealed the secrets of the heavens).

81. This sounds like a repetition of the motif of Brahman against Kshatriya and vice versa.

82. Pisces replaced Aries as the locus of the equinox at the beginning of the Christian era and as the sign of the equinox by its heliacal rising somewhat earlier. The text of the *Ramayana* was formed in the last few centuries B.C. By this time the Hindu astronomers had been influenced by the Greeks, but the old Hindu and Tamil names for the constellations seem to have referred to these animals anyway. See Allen, *Star Names,* under "Aries" and "Pisces." Owing to the Hindus' use of the Nakshatras rather than heliacal risings (to be explained below), the date of the formation of the text of the *Ramayana* coincides with the replacement of the Ram by the Fishes as the equinoctial marker. See p. 215.

83. It is interesting that the nakshatra (the lunar station as opposed to the zodiacal sign) in the constellation Pisces (compare Agastya) is named Revati (Abundance). Revati was the *nabhoyoni* of the eon, as can be seen from the myth about a mortal named Revati who was so beautiful that her father thought no mortal husband could be her match. He went to the heaven of Brahma to seek advice and was told of a mortal incarnation of a portion of Vishnu named Bala-Rama. When he returned to earth, the father found that eons had gone by while he was on his mission and that the race of men were reduced in vigor, stature, and intellect (F). He gave Revati (G) to Bala-Rama,

but the husband found his bride exceedingly tall (D) for him, so he shortened her with the end of his plowshare (D, G) and made her his wife (C-D). Rama's wife in the *Ramayana* was named Sita (Furrow).

84. Again the story revolves around the conflict between Brahman and king (Kshatriya) (A).

85. For Manu as meaning "primordial man" and "man of the eon," compare the etymology of the English word "world" in *AHD*.

86. The commentator says this means Himalaya; in the celestial sense, the north pole is meant.

87. Manu's displaced son (A) was named Nabhanedistha (Navel Neighbor), whereby we can see that this theme is reminiscent of Yggdrasil's root in Niflheim.

88. Compare the evil maid Manthara.

89. Compare the hole made in Krauncha.

90. Sairibha, Misraka-vana, Tavisha, Tridivam, Tri-pishtapam, and Urdhwa-loka. See Dowson, *Hindu Mythology,* under "Swarga."

91. Su-meru, Hemadri, Ratna-sanu, Karnikachala, Amaradri, and Deva-parvata. See Dowson, *Hindu Mythology,* under "Meru."

92. Dowson, *Hindu Mythology,* under "Sapta-sindhava," citing al Biruni.

93. The river itself was the channel of communication. Compare the name Sagara (Ocean), which is attached both to the Ganges and to the hole into the underworld.

94. At times, St. James is supposed to appear descending the Milky Way. The idea must come from Jacob's Ladder (Jacob is James's Old-Testament namesake), which is still the name for the Milky Way in some German-speaking traditions. See Allen, *Star Names,* under "The Galaxy."

95. The pagan origin of the latter two names is patent. Waetla's giant sons are supposed to have made Watling Street as they strode across Britain. Iring is supposedly a descendant of Waetla. See Allen, *Star Names,* under "The Galaxy," where he quotes from Anglo-Saxon glossaries.

96. An idea recapitulated in the *Divine Comedy.* In Langland's *Vision Concerning Piers Plowman,* the Milky Way is the heavenly path to the Virgin's succor; the earthly way was the road to her shrine in Norfolk. See Allen, *Star Names,* under "The Galaxy."

97. Called *sukram arnah*; *Rig Veda* 5.45.10.

98. *Rig Veda* 2.23.18.

99. In keeping with the contrast between the day river and the night river, the word "Ocean" appears in the dual *samadrau* in one place, *Rig Veda* 10.136.5. Oceans are said to be on "this side" (*avara*) and the "other side" (*para*) in *Rig Veda* 7.6.7. "Ocean beyond" (*paravati samudre*) occurs at *Rig Veda* 8.12.17; it must be analogous to the third sky of Agni.

100. *Rig Veda* 8.69.12, 7.49.2.

101. *Rig Veda* 7.47.3; compare the aerial-watery pathway of the Sun, a path made by Mazda, a watery pathway opened by the gods in *Zend Avesta, Vendidad* 21.4–5.

102. Compare the anvil thrown from heaven.

103. Hyginus *Poetic Astronomy* 2.21; Apollodorus 2.7.5–8, 3.12.1; Lycophron 72ff., with Tzetzes's commentary.

104. Electra's departure and Sterope's blushing for having married a mere mortal, both of which are used as just-so stories to account for the "missing" Pleiad, are variants: acknowledgment that the slipping of the Pleiades back into the dawn (Electra means "amber") renders them mortal (they are "drowning"), i.e., they no longer serve as markers of the divine equinoctial point at their heliacal rising.

105. *Minokhired* 49.12, cited by Darmesteter, *Zend Avesta* 2.105, in his note (3) to *Tir Yasht* 13. Darmesteter and West (note to *Bundehesh* 2.7) propose that Vanant (Smiter) be identified with the star Fomalhaut. The arguments are unconvincing. It seems better to identify it with Canopus, making Vanant parallel with Canopus's Vedic avatar, Agastya, who commanded the Vindhya mountains to become lower (Smiter?) and then guarded them as Vanant does Mount Alborz.

106. The same collocation of names—minus Verethragna but with the addition of Satavaesa—is made in *Sirozah* 1.13, 2.13. West, *Pahlavi Texts, Bundehesh* 2.7n, identifies Satavaesa with Antares, which may be correct. Then the equation Mars-Antares (Verethragna-Satavaesa) was not just a Greek invention.

107. See previous note with reference to West, *Pahlavi Texts.*

108. Another connection between Verethragna and Karttikeya is that both were said to have subdued great demons. Verethragna overcame Vritra (cf. the Vedic battle between Indra and Vritra), and Karttikeya overcame Taraka.

109. *Tir Yasht* 8.

110. Ibid., 9.

111. Persian Haptok-ring (other forms are Hafturengh, Heft Averengh, and Heft Reng), which in folk practice are invoked as protectors against demons, witches, and wizards.

112. The latter part of the name Saptarshi is interesting: *riksha,* "the bear star," may have been confused phonetically with *rishi,* "sage"; the seven great Rishis were represented in the sky by the seven stars of the Great Bear, and as such they are called Riksha. See Dowson, *Hindu Mythology,* under "Saptarshi" and "Rishi." Al Biruni reports that these were later called Saptar Shayar, "the seven anchorites." They were raised by Dharma to the highest elevation among the stars. As if in keeping with the concept of the *nabhoyoni* developed here, al Biruni goes on to quote from Varaha Mihura: "The northern region is adorned with these stars as a beautiful woman is adorned with a collar of pearls strung together and a necklace of white lotus flowers, a handsomely arranged one. Thus adorned, they are all like maidens who dance and revolve round the pole as the pole orders them." See Allen, *Star Names,* 435.

113. The brightness of the two Ursae is to be contrasted. The brightest seven stars of Ursa Major are magnitude 2.5 or brighter, while the eighth is of magnitude 3.5. Ursa Minor's brightest star is magnitude 2.2, and the seventh is 4.3. A yet dimmer star (designated *b*) lies outside the dipper shape but was at one time noticeable even though it is but magnitude 5 because it was close to the pole (4° away in Hipparchus's time and likely the star that he claimed with

two others [Beta and Zeta] made a quadrilateral with the vacant location of the pole).

114. *Phenomena*, 42; because it circles (the pole) in a tighter circle.

115. Homer mentions Arktos, also called Hamaxa (Wagon), twice in nearly identical passages, *Iliad* 18.487 and *Odyssey* 5.273: It "peruses [*dokeuei*] Orion and never bathes in Ocean." Were it not for a later tradition that it was Thales who formulated the constellation Ursa Minor, by which the Phoenicians navigate (Callimachus, fragment 94), we would not know for certain to which of the two Ursae Homer referred, since the phenomena described fit Ursa Minor as well as or better than Ursa Major. In any case, both were later called both *arktoi* and *hamaxai* (Aratus, 27). The larger is called Helice (Revolver), while the smaller has the name Cynosura (Aratus, 37).

116. *Surya Siddhanta*, trans. Ebenezer Burgess, revised by P. Gangooly, with an introduction by P. Sengupta (Calcutta: University of Calcutta Press, 1935), 12.34.

117. With paronomasia on *-bjorn*, "bear?" Bifröst (Rainbow) is also called Asgard Bridge, a name that is itself applied to the Milky Way.

118. Allen, *Star Names*, 452, 454.

119. Hyginus *Poetic Astronomy* 2.3, quoting Pherecydes, 2.6. Also Pseudo-Eratosthenes *Catasterismoi* 3–4. Apollonius Rhodius 4.1396ff. identifies the serpent as Ladon in a passage that describes the serpent's death at Herakles's hands.

120. Hyginus *Poetic Astronomy* 2.3.

121. This is a variant of the story of Prometheus bound.

122. Or is the etymology to be reckoned as from *ha-* + *tla-*, "great sufferer?"

123. This tryst between Atlas and Heracles probably reflects the Titanomachy. A fragment of the cyclical poem *Titanomachy* (in Philodemus, *On Piety*) says that the author of *Titanomachy* claims that "the apples of the Hesperides were guarded." In no other sources do the apples or the Hesperides play a role in the Titanomachy, and here alone, therefore, is recorded a variant of the primordial battle in which the world-tree and its guardians (or thieves) play a role as they do in the *Amritamanthana*.

124. Ladon, which is also a name given to a river in Arcadia.

125. *Yasht* 19.47–52.

126. Atar is both a thing (a weapon of Ahura) and a person (Ahura's son), so the fire of heaven is conceived as being flung from it or born from it; see Darmesteter, *Zend Avesta*, lxii.

127. Darmesteter, *Zend Avesta*, lxiii.

128. In Hindu belief, as discussed above, Apam Napat is sky-ocean, Ocean-skywater, from whom (with the sacrifice of a horse at dawn) the sun is induced to be reborn. Hvareno's flight to the waters and capture by Apam Napat indicates that Hvareno is a phenomenon of sky-ocean too, to be seen at dawn near the ecliptic.

129. Also called the *Hom Yasht*.

130. In this source Threataona is said to be son of Athwya. Elsewhere they are one and the same.

131. His Vedic counterpart is Vivasvat.

132. *Yasna* 9.4–5.

133. *Zamyad Yasht* 31–34, in James Darmesteter, ed. and trans., *Zend Avesta*, pt. 2, Sacred Books of the East, vol. 23 (Oxford, 1883).

134. *Zamyad Yasht* 36.

135. *Zamyad Yasht* 22–23.

136. Also called *Zand of the Vohuman Yasht*; see West, *Pahlavi Texts*, l–lix.

137. Compare Herakles and Ladon. Victors use clubs against the serpents in other variants and versions of the epochal battle as well.

138. *Zâd Sparam* 2.1, in West, *Pahlavi Texts*, 153–188.

139. In the Avestan variant, this failure is attributed to Yima's shortcomings. In one version of the story about the Hesperides, they, who are usually guardians of Hera's (or Atlas's) garden, become purloiners of the fruit, which fact occasions the recruitment of Ladon to guard them thereafter.

140. Reduced to 1,000 in the *Bahman Yasht*. In post-Vedic sources the Hindus counted the number of Ages as four; the length of each, their phases, their relationships to the ages of the Brahma, and other aspects are all highly technical and combine into an elaborate system of chronology. The Golden Age is preserved in Krita Yuga, and the present evil age is the age of dissolution, Kali Yuga. In between are two ages whose names, ostensibly referring to their length of 3,000 and 2,000 years, may preserve an aboriginal system of three: Treta Yuga (Threefold Conjunction) and Dwapara (Two-Chief [Age]).

141. *Rig Veda* 1.158.5, 10.99.6.

142. Could the ambiguous nature of the guardian have contributed to the confusion between names for good deities and bad in the Indo-European tradition? Asuras are either good or bad in the Vedas. In the Avesta the supreme deity, Ahura (cognate with Asura), is always good, while the Daevas are always evil demons. Perhaps the very dualism of Mazdaism has its roots in this ambiguity.

143. This was their last appearance in the evening sky before disappearing into the sun. Hesiod does not mention this apparition of the Pleiades. Hesiod refers to their *cosmic* setting; *Works and Days*, 619–622.

144. Apollonius Rhodius *Argonautica* 4.1407ff.

145. The time at which the Pleiades would appear last just after sunset at the vernal equinox would be about 1250 B.C. The myth of the Hesperides is late in comparison with that of the Pleiades, but their stories are interconnected not merely by this celestial dependency but also by the name- and myth-typology discussed in chapter 3.

146. See David Ulansey, "Mithraic Studies: A Paradigm Shift?" *Religious Studies Review* 13 (April 1987): 104–110; and *The Origins of the Mithraic Mysteries* (Oxford: Oxford University Press, 1989), condensed in "The Mithraic Mysteries," *Scientific American* 261 (December 1989): 130–135.

147. Ulansey, "Mithraic Mysteries," 133.

148. Actually, Capella and Hamal (the brightest star in Aries) are never exactly *paranatellonta* (the technical term for bodies that rise at the same time), but at some point they would become visible at the same time, Capella at a

lesser elevation but considerably to the north of the sun and brighter, with Hamal at an elevation of 13.5° at sunrise but dimmer and right above (east of) the sun's rising point.

149. See Dowson, *Hindu Mythology,* under "Aditi." Varuna is the chief son. Some variants report an eighth son invisible to mortals because he remains near the central mountain of the universe (Meru). He not only illuminates that region but also sheds light from which the other seven derive their brilliance. His name was Kashyapa (Tortoise) which is reminiscent of the tortoise that served as the pivot point in the *Amritamanthana.*

150. See S. B. Roy, *Prehistoric Lunar Astronomy, 19,000–3100* B.C. (New Delhi: Institute of Chronology, 1976), with reference to Yaska, *Nirukta* 4.4.22.1.

151. For a parallel explanation, see Bal Gangadhar Tilak, *Orion; or, Researches into the Antiquity of the Vedas* (Bombay, 1893), 81.

152. This system has gone out of "synch" since its institution, but religious conservatism keeps it in place despite the fact that it no longer works.

153. *Taittriya Sanhita* 7.4.8; see also Tilak, *Orion,* 44 and passim.

154. Tilak, *Orion,* 205.

155. Ibid.

156. Ibid., 201, paraphrasing *Aittareya Brahmana* 1.7.

157. Further evidence is supplied by the fact that Punarvasu was called Yamakau (Twin Yamas). In 4500 B.C. Punarvasu was at one time the focus of the equinox—that is, the point where the ecliptic and the equator intersect. This was therefore the place where the circle of the Nakshatras began, fourteen of them north of the equator and fourteen south. Those south belonged to the underworld (Yama), and those north to the upperworld (Deva). At each of the two intersections, one marked by Punarvasu rising (the vernal equinox), the other by the full moon near Punarvasu (the autumnal equinox), lay a way down to the underworld (Yama), whence the title Twin Yamas.

158. *Atharva Veda* 7.6.1.

159. Tilak, *Orion,* 203.

160. *Satapatha-Brahmana* 2.4.4.2; *vasishtha* means "the best."

161. Somadeva Bhatta, *Katha Sarit Sagara; or, Ocean of the Streams of Story,* trans. Charles Henry Tawney, 2d ed. (reprint; Delhi: Motilal Banarsidass, 1968), 1.5.

162. *Rig Veda* 1.114.5, 2.33.8.

163. Ibid., 1.43.5.

164. Ibid., 5.46.2.

165. Compare this with the name Punarvasu (Doublegood Pair, or perhaps better, Pair Made Good Again). It is difficult to see how Betelgeuse could function as an equinox marker except during a two-hundred-year period (3750–3550 B.C.) when its heliacal setting occurred on or within a day or two of the equinox.

166. *Satapatha-Brahmana* 10.4.2.1.

167. Ibid., 10.4.4.2.

168. *Rig Veda* 10.62.11.

169. Recall that in the Nakshatra system the equinox and the star coincide; hence, this datum does not conflict with the use of the heliacal rising of the Pleiades during the same eon.

170. Some of the content and most of the conceptual framework of the above argument is owed to S. B. Roy, *Prehistoric Lunar Astronomy,* chaps. 3, 4. The idea that Mriga contained the vernal equinox, which then shifted to the Krittikas, was first published by Tilak in *Orion;* S. B. Roy, in *Prehistoric Lunar Astronomy,* argues a parallel case.

171. *Aittareya Brahmana* 3.33.

172. Roy, *Lunar Astronomy,* chap. 4, p. 167. The two brighter stars are separated by one hour and twenty minutes of right ascension. This is too far apart. Ideally the Nakshatras would be placed equidistantly along the zodiac at roughly seven-eighths of an hour angle apart (24 hours divided by 27.3).

173. *Satapatha-Brahmana* 2.1.2.8–10.

174. Ibid., 1.7.4.5.

175. Ibid., 1.7.4.4, alluded to in *Rig Veda* 10.62.5–8; see also *Aitareya Brahmana* 3.34.

176. Roy, *Lunar Astronomy,* 43, but without references.

177. Nonnos, *Dionysiaca,* trans. W.H.D. Rouse (Cambridge, Mass.: Loeb Classical Library, 1942), 40.423–534.

178. Dardanus, son of the Pleiad Electra, ballasted the goatskin coracle on which he sailed from Samothrace to Troy. The goatskin recalls the guide star Capella and the four stones of equal weight, the (roughly) equally dim stars of the onetime equinoctial constellation Aries.

BIBLIOGRAPHY

ABBREVIATIONS

AHD   *The American Heritage Dictionary of the English Language,* 1st ed.

LSJ   Liddell, Henry George, and Robert Scott. *A Greek-English Lexicon.* Revised by Henry Stuart Jones, Roderick McKenzie, et al.

OED   *Oxford English Dictionary.* Compact edition.

Pauly-Wissowa   *Realenkyklopädie der Altertumswissenschaft.* Edited by Pauly, Wissowa, and Kroll.

AESCHYLUS. *Septem quae supersunt Tragoedias.* Edited by Denys Page. Oxford: Oxford University Press, 1972.

AESOP. See Hull, D.

Aitareya Brahmana. See Keith, A. B.

The American Heritage Dictionary of the English Language. Edited by William Morris. Boston: Houghton Mifflin, 1968.

The Ancient Near East: An Anthology of Texts and Pictures. Edited by James B. Pritchard. Princeton, N.J.: Princeton University Press, 1958.

APOLLODORUS. *The Library.* See Simpson, Michael.

APOLLONIUS RHODIUS. *Argonautica.* Translated by R. C. Seaton. The Loeb Classical Library. Cambridge: Harvard University Press, 1967.

ARATUS. *Phaenomena.* Translated by G. R. Mair. The Loeb Classical Library. Cambridge, Mass.: Harvard University Press, 1921.

ARNIM, HANS FRIEDRICH AUGUST VON, ed. *Stoicorum veterum fragmenta.* 4 vols. Stuttgart: Teubner, 1964.

Atharva-Veda. See Bloomfield, M.

Atharva-Veda Samhita. Translated by William Dwight Whitney. Delhi: Motilal Banarsidass, 1962.

AUSTIN, NORMAN. "Odysseus Polytropos: Man of Many Minds." *Arche* 6 (1981): 40–52.

AVENI, ANTHONY F. "Old and New World Naked-Eye Astronomy." In *Astronomy of the Ancients,* edited by Michael Feiertag and Kenneth Brecher, 39–60. Cambridge, Mass.: MIT Press, 1979.

BAITY, ELIZABETH CHESLEY. "Archaeoastronomy and Ethnoastronomy So Far." *Current Anthropology* 14 (1973): 389–449.

BALDRY, H. C. "Who Invented the Golden Age?" *Classical Quarterly,* n.s., 2 (1952): 83–92.

BASHAM, ARTHUR LLEWELYN. *The Wonder That Was India: A Survey of the Culture of the Indian Sub-Continent Before the Coming of the Muslims.* New York: Grove Press, 1959.

BEGLEY, W. E. *Visnu's Flaming Wheel: The Iconography of the Sudarsana-Cakra.* New York: New York University Press, for the College Art Association of America, 1973.

BENVENISTE, EMILE. "Arménien *aregakan* 'soleil,' et la formation du nominal en *-akn.*" *Revue des Etudes Arméeniennes,* n.s., 2 (1965): 5–19.

———. *Indo-European Language and Society.* Summaries, table, and index by Jean Lallot. Translated by Elizabeth Palmer. Miami Linguistics Series no. 12. Miami: University of Miami Press, 1973.

BERNHARD, HERBERT J., DOROTHY A. BENNET, and HUGH S. RICE. *New Handbook of the Heavens.* New York: Signet, 1941.

BLOOMFIELD, MAURICE. *A Vedic Concordance.* 1906. Reprint. Delhi: Motilal Banarsidass, 1964.

———, ed. and trans. *Atharva-Veda, Together with Extracts from the Ritual Books and the Commentaries.* Sacred Books of the East, vol. 42. Oxford: Clarendon Press, 1897.

BOLL, FRANZ. *Kleinschriften.* Edited by Viktor Stegemann. Leipzig: Koehler and Amelang, 1950.

BOSCH, F.K.D. *The Golden Germ: An Introduction to Indian Symbolism.* Indo-Iranian Monographs, vol. 2. The Hague: Mouton and Co., 1960.

BOSWELL, FRED. *What Men or Gods Are These? A Geneological Approach to Classical Myth.* Metuchen: Scarecrow, 1976.

BOYANCÉ, PIERRE. "La religion astral de Platon à Ciceron." *Revue des Etudes Grecques* 65 (1952): 312–350.

BRENNAND, W. *Hindu Astronomy.* London: C. Straker, 1896.

BRODEUR, ARTHUR GILCHRIST, trans. *The Prose Edda by Snorri Sterluson.* New York: American Scandanavian Foundation, 1929.

BROWN, NORMAN O. *Hermes the Thief: The Evolution of a Myth*. Madison: University of Wisconsin Press, 1947.

BUCK, CARL D. *A Dictionary of Selected Synonyms in the Principal Indo-European Languages: A Contribution to the History of Ideas*. Chicago: University of Chicago Press, 1949.

BUDGE, E. A. WALLIS. *The Gods of the Egyptians; or, Studies in Egyptian Mythology*. 2 vols. 1904. Reprint. New York: Dover, 1969.

BURGESS, EBENEZER, trans. *Surya-Siddhanta, with Notes and an Appendix*. 6 vols. Reprint. San Diego: Wizard's Bookshelf, 1978.

BURKERT, WALTER. *Structure and History in Greek Mythology and Ritual*. Berkeley: University of California Press, 1979.

BUTTERWORTH, E.A.S. *The Tree at the Navel of the Earth*. Berlin: De Gruyter, 1970.

Callimachus. Edited by Rudolfus Pfeiffer. 2 vols. Oxford: Clarendon Press, 1949–53.

CAMPBELL, JOHN F. *The Celtic Dragon Myth*. Edinburgh: J. S. Grant, 1911.

CAMPBELL, JOSEPH. *The Hero with a Thousand Faces*. 2d ed. Bollingen Series 17. Princeton, N.J.: Princeton University Press, 1968.

———. *The Masks of God*. 4 vols. New York: Viking Press, 1959.

———. *The Mythic Image*. Princeton, N.J.: Princeton University Press, 1974.

———. *Myths to Live By*. Princeton, N.J.: Princeton University Press, 1972.

CARLSON, JOHN B. "The Double-Headed Dragon and the Sky: A Pervasive Cosmological Symbol." In *Ethnoastronomy and Archaeoastronomy in the American Tropics,* edited by Arthur F. Aveni and Gary Urton. New York Academy of Sciences, no. 385. New York, 1982.

CARPENTER, RHYS. *Folk-Tale, Fiction and Saga in the Homeric Epics*. Berkeley: University of California Press, 1946.

CHANTRAINE, PIERRE. *Dictionnaire etymologique de la langue grecque: Histoire des mots*. 3 vols. to date. Paris: Editions Klincksieck, 1968–.

CHARBONNIER, G. *Conversations with Claude Lévi-Strauss*. Translated by John and Doreen Weightman. 1961. Reprint. New York: Grossman, 1969.

CHASE, RICHARD V. *The Quest for Myth*. Baton Rouge: Louisiana State University Press, 1949.

COLEBROOKE, HENRY T. *Essays on History, Literature and Religions in Ancient India*. Reprint. New Delhi: Cosmo Publications, 1977.

COLPE, CARSTEN. "Altiranische und zoroastrische Mythologie." In *Wörterbuch der Mythologie,* edited by P. Haussig. Suttgart: E. Klett, 1965.

COOK, ARTHUR B. *Zeus: A Study in Ancient Religion*. 3 vols. Cambridge: Cambridge University Press, 1914–40.

COX, GEORGE. *Mythology of the Aryan Nations*. 2 vols. 2d ed. London, 1882.

CREVATIN, F. "Un problem di antichita' indeuropee: Il cuneo del fulmine, I." *Incontri Linguistici* 1 (1974): 61–68.

CROCKER, J. CHRISTOPHER. *Vital Souls: Bororo Cosmology, Natural Symbolism, and Shamanism.* Tucson: University of Arizona Press, 1985.

CUMONT, FRANZ. "Les Noms des planètes et l'astrolatrie chez les Grecs," *L'Antiquité Classique* 4 (1935): 18–22.

DAREMBERG, CHARLES V., and EDMUND SAGLIO, eds. *Dictionnaire des antiquites grecques et romaines, d'apres les textes et les monuments.* 1877–1919. Reprint. Graz: Akademische Druck- und Verlaganstalt, 1963.

DARMESTETER, JAMES, ed. and trans. *The Zend Avesta.* Parts 1 and 2. Sacred Books of the East, vols. 4 and 23. Oxford: Clarendon, 1880–83.

DAVIDSON, H. R. ELLIS. *Gods and Myths of Northern Europe* (Harmondsworth, Eng.: Penguin, 1964).

DEMETRAKOS, ed. *Lexicon holês tês Hellênikês Glossês.* Athens: Hellenike Paideia, 1964.

DE SANTILLANA, GIORGIO, AND HERTHA VON DECHEND. *Hamlet's Mill: An Essay on Myth and the Frame of Time.* Boston: Gambit, 1969.

DE SAUSSURE, LEOPOLD. *Les origines de l'astronomie chinoise.* Rev. ed. Taipei: Ch'eng-Wen Publishing Co., 1967.

DICKS, D. R. *Early Greek Astronomy to Aristotle.* Ithaca, N.Y.: Cornell University Press, 1970.

DORSON, RICHARD, ed. *Peasant Customs and Savage Myths.* 2 vols. Chicago: University of Chicago Press, 1968.

DOWSON, JOHN. *A Classical Dictionary of Hindu Mythology and Religion, Geography, History, and Literature.* 11th ed. London: Routeledge and Kegan Paul, 1968.

DUCHESNE-GUILLEMIN, J. "Fire in Iran and Greece." *East and West,* n.s., 13 (1962): 198–206.

DUMÉZIL, GEORGES. *The Destiny of the Warrior King.* Translated by Alf Hiltbeitel. Chicago: University of Chicago Press, 1970.

———. *Le Festin d'immortalité: Étude de mythologie comparée indo-européenne.* Annales du Musée Guimet, vol. 34. Paris: Bibliothèque d'Études.

———. *Ouranos-Varuna: Étude de mythologie comparée indo-européenne.* Paris: Librairie d'Amérique et d'Orient, 1934.

EGGELING, JULIUS, ed. and trans. *Satapatha-Brahmana.* Sacred Books of the East, vol. 41. Oxford: Clarendon Press, 1884.

ELIADE, MIRCEA. *Cosmos and History: The Myth of the Eternal Return.* Translated by Willard R. Trask. New York: Harper, 1959.

———. *The Forge and the Crucible.* Translated by Stephen Corrin. New York: Harper, 1962.

Eusebii Caesariensis Opera. Edited by Wilhelm Dinsdorf. 4 vols. Leipzig: Teubner, 1867–90.

FARNELL, L. R. *The Cults of the Greek States.* 5 vols. Oxford: Clarendon Press, 1896–1909.

FAUTH, W. "Widder, Schlange und Vogel am heiligen Baum: Zur Iko-
nographie einer anatolisch-mediterranean Symbolkonstellation." *Anatolica* 6
(1977–78): 129–157.

FONTENROSE, JOSEPH E. "The Cult and Myth of Pyrros at Delphi." In
University of California Publications in Classical Archaeology 4: 191–266. Berkeley: University of California Press, 1960.

———. *Orion: The Myth of the Hunter and Huntress*. University of California
Publications in Classical Studies no. 23. Berkeley: University of California
Press, 1981.

———. *Python: A Study of the Delphic Myth and Its Origins*. Berkeley: University of California Press, 1959.

———. "The Spring Telphousa." *Transactions and Proceedings of the American
Philological Association* 100 (1969): 119–130.

FRAME, DOUGLAS. *The Myth of the Return in Early Greek Epic*. New Haven:
Yale University Press, 1978.

FRANKFORT, HENRY. *Kingship and the Gods*. Chicago: University of Chicago
Press, 1946.

FRANKFORT, HENRI, H. A. FRANKFORT, J. A. WILSON, and THORKILD
JACOBSEN. *Before Philosophy: The Intellectual Adventure of Ancient Man; An
Essay on Speculative Thought in the Ancient Near East*. Chicago: University of
Chicago Press, 1946. Reprint. Baltimore: Penguin, 1949.

FRAZER, SIR JAMES G. *The Golden Bough: A Study in Magic and Religion*.
Abridged ed. New York: Macmillan, 1922.

———. *The New Golden Bough*. Edited by Theodor H. Gaster. New York:
Doubleday and Co., 1961.

FREUD, SIGMUND. *The Basic Writings*. Edited and translated by A. A. Brill.
New York: Modern Library, 1938.

FRISK, HJALMAR. *Grieschisches etymologisches Wörterbuch*. Heidelberg: Carl
Winter, 1973.

FROBENIUS, LEO. *Paideuma: Umrisse einer Kultur- und Seelenlehre*. Munich,
1921.

FURLEY, WILLIAM D. *Studies in the Use of Fire in Ancient Greek Religion*.
New York: Arno, 1981.

GASTER, THEODOR H. *Thespis: Ritual, Myth and Drama in the Ancient Near
East*. New York: Henry Schuman, 1950.

GELLING, PETER and H. R. ELLIS DAVIDSON. *The Chariot of the Sun and
Other Rites and Symbols of the Northern Bronze Age*. New York: Praeger, 1969.

GILGAMESH. See Sandars, N. K.

GIMBUTAS, MARIJA. "Kurgan Axes: An Archaeological Note." *Journal of
Indo-European Studies* 1 (1973): 463–465.

———. "Perkunas/Perun: The Thunder-God of the Balts and Slavs." *Journal
of Indo-European Studies* 1 (1973): 466–478.

GLENN, J. "The Polyphemus Myth: Its Origin and Interpretation." *Greece and Rome* 25 (1978): 141–155.

GLOECKNER, H. *Himmelsrichtung-Himmelsgewölbe: Versuch einer indogermanischen Einordnung.* Waldorfhaslich Selbstverlag, 1979.

GOODENOUGH, WARD H. "The Evolution of Pastoralism and Indo-European Origins." In *Indo-European and Indo-Europeans,* edited by George Cardona, Henry M. Hoenigswald, and Alfred Senn. Philadelphia: University of Pennsylvania Press, 1970.

GRAVES, ROBERT. *The Greek Myths.* 2 vols. Baltimore: Penguin Books, 1955.

Great Folktales of Old Ireland. Compiled by Mary McGarry. New York: Bell Publishing Co., n.d.

GREEN, M. J. *The Wheel as a Cult Symbol in the Romano-Celtic World.* Collection Latomus, vol. 83. Brussels: Revue des Études Latines, 1984.

GREPPIN, JOHN. "Xvarena as a Transfunctional Figure." *Journal of Indo-European Studies* 1 (1973): 232–242.

GRIAULE, MARCEL. *Conversations with Ogotemmeli: An Introduction to Dogon Religious Ideas.* Oxford: Oxford University Press, for the International African Institute, 1965.

Griechisch-Deutsches Wörterbuch Über die Gedichte des Homeros und der Homeriden. Edited by E. E. Seiler. 8th ed. Leipzig: Hahnsche, 1878.

GRUPPE, OTTO. *Die griechischen Kulte und Mythos in ihren Beziehungen zu den orientalischen Religionen.* 2 vols. 1887. Reprint. New York: Georg Olms, 1973.

GUNDEL, H. G. "Zodiakos: Der Tierkreis in der Antiken Literatur und Kunst." In *Realenkyklopädie der Altertumswissenschaft,* edited by Pauly, Wissowa, and Kroll. Vol. 2. Suppl. 19 (1972), 462–709.

HALLO, WILLIAM, and J.J.A. VAN DIJK. *The Exaltation of Inanna.* New Haven: Yale University Press, 1968.

HAUDRY, J. "Les trois cieux." *Études indo-européen* 1 (1978): 23–48.

HERODOTUS. *Herodotus, with an English Translation.* Edited and translated by A. D. Godley. The Loeb Classical Library. Reprint. Cambridge: Cambridge University Press, 1971.

HERZFELD, ERNST. *Zoroaster and His World.* 2 vols. Princeton, N.J.: Princeton University Press, 1947.

HESIOD. *Carmina.* Edited by Aloisius Rzach. Stuttgart: Teubner, 1958.

———. *Hesiod: The Homeric Hymns and Homerica.* Edited and translated by Hugh G. Evelyn-White. London and New York: The Loeb Classical Library, 1920.

———. *Works and Days.* Edited by M. L. West. Oxford: Clarendon Press, 1978.

HODSON, F. R., ed. *The Place of Astronomy in the Ancient World.* Joint Symposium of the Royal Society and the British Academy. London: Oxford University Press, 1974.

HOFFMAN, E.T.A. *The Best Tales of Hoffman.* Edited by E. F. Bleiler. New York: Dover Publications, 1967.

HOLLANDER, LEE. *The Poetic Edda.* Austin: University of Texas Press, 1928.

HOMER. *Iliad.* Edited by Walter Leaf and M. A. Bayfield. 2 vols. London: Macmillan and Co., 1888.

———. *Odyssey.* Edited by Walter Merry and James Riddel. 2d ed. Oxford: Oxford University Press, 1886.

———. *Odyssey.* Edited by W. B. Stanford. 2 vols. London: Macmillan Co., 1959.

———. *Opera et Reliquiae.* Edited by D. B. Munro. Oxford, 1881.

HOOKE, S. H., ed. *Myth and Ritual.* London: Oxford University Press, 1933.

HOUSEHOLDER, FRED. W., and GREGORY NAGY. *Greek: A Survey of Recent Work.* The Hague: Mouton, 1972.

HUDSON, TRAVIS, and ERNEST UNDERHAY. *Crystals in the Sky: An Intellectual Odyssey Involving Chumash Astronomy, Cosmology and Rock Art.* Socorro, N.Mex.: Baleena Press, 1978.

HULL, DENISON B., ed. and trans. *Aesop's Fables Told by Valerius Babrius.* Chicago: University of Chicago Press, 1960.

"Hunters of the Dugong." *Living Wild,* no. 105. Narrated by David Attenborough. PBS.

HYGINUS. *The Myths of Hyginus.* Edited and translated by Mary Grant. University of Kansas Publications, Humanistic Studies, no. 34. Lawrence, 1960.

INGERSOLL, ERNEST. *Dragons and Dragon Lore.* New York: Payson and Clark, 1928.

JUSTI, FERDINAND. *Handbuch der Zendsprache: Altbactrisches Wörterbuch, Grammatik, Chrestomathie.* Wiesbaden: Sändig, 1969.

Kalevala, or Poems of the Kalevala District. Compiled by Elias Lönrott. Translated by Francis Peabody Magoun. Cambridge, Mass.: Harvard University Press, 1963.

KEITH, ARTHUR BERRIEDALE, trans. *Aitareya Brahmana.* In *Rig Veda Brahmanas.* Harvard Oriental Series, vol. 25. Reprint. Delhi: Motial Banarsidass, 1971.

KEITH, ARTHUR BERRIEDALE, and ARTHUR A. MACDONELL. *Vedic Index of Names and Subjects.* 2 vols. Reprint. Delhi: Motilal Banarsidass, 1967.

KERENYI, KAROLY. *Goddesses of the Sun and Moon: Circe, Aphrodite, Medea, Nike.* Translated by Murray Stein. Irving, Tex.: Spiro Publications, 1979.

———. *The Gods of the Greeks.* Translated by Norman Cameron. 1951. Reprint. New York: Grove Press, 1960.

———. *The Heroes of the Greeks.* Translated by H. J. Rose. 1959. Reprint. New York: Grove Press, 1960.

———. *Zeus and Hera: Archetypal Image of Father, Husband and Wife.* Translated by Christopher Holme. The Bollingen Series, vol. 65. Princeton, N.J.: Princeton University Press, 1975.

KIRK, GEOFFRY S. *Myth: Its Meaning and Function in Ancient and Other Cultures.* Sather Classical Lectures, vol. 40. Berkeley: University of California Press, 1970.

————. *The Nature of Greek Myths.* Harmondsworth, Eng.: Penguin, 1974.

KRUPP, EDWIN C. *Echoes of Ancient Skies: The Astronomy of Lost Civilizations.* New York: Harper and Row, 1983.

————, ed. *In Search of Ancient Astronomies.* Garden City, N.Y.: Doubleday, 1978.

KUHN, ADALBERT. *Die Herabkunft des Feuers und des Gottertranks.* Berlin, 1859.

LANE, MICHAEL, ed. *Structuralism: A Reader.* New York: Basic Books, 1970.

LANG, ANDREW. *Modern Mythology.* London, 1897.

————. *Myth, Ritual and Religion.* 2 vols. London, 1913.

LANTERMAN, RAY, and WILL KYSELKA. *North Star to Southern Cross.* Honolulu: University of Hawaii Press, 1976.

Laws of Manu. Translated by Georg Buehler. Sacred Books of the East, vol. 25. Oxford: Clarendon Press, 1886.

LEACH, EDMUND. *Claude Lévi-Strauss.* New York: Viking, 1970.

LENOWITZ, HARRIS, and CHARLES DORIA, eds. *Origins: Creation Texts from the Ancient Mediterranean.* New York: Anchor, 1976.

LÉVI-STRAUSS, CLAUDE. *The Raw and the Cooked.* Translated by John and Doreen Weightman. New York: Harper, 1975.

LIDDELL, HENRY G., and ROBERT SCOTT. *A Greek-English Lexicon.* Revised by Henry Jones, Roderick McKenzie, et al. Oxford: Oxford University Press, 1968.

LINCOLN, BRUCE. "Death and Resurrection in Indo-European Thought." *Journal of Indo-European Studies* 5 (1977): 247–264.

————. "The Indo-European Cattle-Raiding Myth." *History of Religions* 16 (1976): 42–65.

————. "The Indo-European Myth of Creation." *History of Religions* 15 (1975): 121–157.

LITTLETON, C. SCOTT. *The New Comparative Mythology.* 3d ed. Los Angeles: University of California Press, 1983.

LÖMMEL, HERMAN, ed. and trans. *Die Yasts des Awesta.* Göttingen: Vandenhoeck and Ruprecht, 1927.

LONG, CHARLES. *Alpha: The Myths of Creation.* New York: George Brazillier, 1963.

MCGUIRE, J. D. *Primitive Methods of Drilling.* Annual Report of the U.S. National Museum. Washington, D.C.: Smithsonian Institution Press, 1894.

MACLAGAN, DAVID. *Creation Myths: Man's Introduction to the World.* London: Thames and Hudson, 1977.

MACROBIUS. *The Saturnalia*. Translated by Percival Vaughn Davies. New York: Columbia University Press, 1964.

The Mahabharata of Krishna-Duaipayana Vyasa. Translated by Pratap Chandra Roy. 2d ed. 12 vols. Calcutta, n.d.

MAHER, PETER J. "Haékmon: '(Stone) Axe' and 'Sky' in I.E./Battle-Axe Culture." *Journal of Indo-European Studies* I (1973): 441–465.

MALINOWSKI, BRONISLAW. *Magic, Science, and Religion and Other Essays*. Garden City, N.Y.: Doubleday, 1954.

MALLORY, J. P. "The Chronology of the Early Kurgan Tradition." *Journal of Indo-European Studies* 4 (1976): 257–294 and 5 (1977): 339–378.

MANILIUS. *Astronomica*. Translated by G. P. Goold. Cambridge, Mass.: Loeb Classical Library, 1977.

MARINGER, JOHANNES. "Fire in Prehistoric Indo-European Europe." *Journal of Indo-European Studies* 4 (1976): 161–186.

MARTIN, ERNEST L. *New Star Over Bethlehem*. Pasadena: fbr publications, 1980.

MAYERHOFFER, MANFRED. *Kurzgefasstes etymologisches Wörterbuch des Altindischen: A Concise Sanskrit Dictionary*. Heidelberg: Carl Winter, 1956–80.

MILLER, JEANINE. *The Vision of Cosmic Order in the Vedas*. London: Routledge and Kegan Paul, 1985.

MILLS, LAWRENCE H. *A Dictionary of the Gathic Language of the Zend Avesta*. Reprint. New York: AMS Press, 1977.

——, ed. and trans. *The Zend Avesta*. Part 3 (*The Yasna, Visparad, Afrînagân, Gâhs and Miscellaneous Fragments*). Sacred Books of the East, vol. 31. Oxford: Clarendon Press, 1887.

MONIER-WILLIAMS, MONIER. *A Sanskrit-English Dictionary Etymologically and Philologically Arranged*. Oxford: Clarendon Press, 1899.

MOUNTFORD, CHARLES PEARCY, and AINSLEE ROBERTS. *The Dreamtime: Australian Aboriginal Myths in Paintings by Ainslee Roberts, with text by Charles P. Mountford*. Adelaide, Aust.: Rigby, 1965.

MÜLLER, FRIEDRICH M. *Chips from a German Workshop*. 2 vols. London, 1867.

——. *Comparative Mythology*. Edited by A. Smythe Palmer. London, 1909.

——. *A History of Ancient Sanskrit Literature so far as It Illustrated the Primitive Religion of the Brahmans*. Rev. ed. Chowkamba Sanskrit Series, vol. 15. Varanasi, India: Chowkamba Sanskrit Series Office, 1968.

——. *Lectures on the Origin and Growth of Religion as Illustrated by the Religions of India*. Hibbert Lecture for 1878. London: Longmans, Green, and Co., 1878.

——. *Lectures on the Science of Language*. Delivered at the Royal Institution of Great Britain in 1861 and 1863. New York: Charles Scribner, 1870.

MUNZ, PETER. *When the Golden Bough Breaks: Structuralism or Typology?* London: Routledge and Kegan Paul, 1973.

NAGY, GREGORY. "Patroklos, Concepts of the Afterlife, and the Indic Triple Fire." *Arethusa* 13 (1980): 161–195.

NILSSON, MATIN P. *Primitive Time-Reckoning: A Study in the Origins and First Development of the Art of Counting Time Among the Primitive and Early Culture Peoples.* 2d ed. Malmö: Nya Litografen, 1960.

NONNOS. *Dionysiaca.* Translated by W.H.D. Rouse. Annotated by H. J. Rose. The Loeb Classical Library. Cambridge, Mass.: Harvard University Press, 1940–42.

O'BRIEN, STEPHEN. "Indo-European Eschatology: A Model." *Journal of Indo-European Studies* 4 (1976): 295–320.

OVID. *Metamorphoses.* Translated by Rolfe Humphries. Bloomington: Indiana University Press, 1955.

Oxford English Dictionary. Edited by Sir James A. H. Murray et al. Compact ed. Oxford: Oxford University Press, 1971.

Oxford Latin Dictionary. Edited by P.G.W. Glare. Oxford: Oxford University Press, 1982.

PAGE, DENYS. *The Homeric Odyssey.* Oxford: Oxford University Press, 1955.

PANOFSKY, DORA, and ERWIN PANOSFSKY. *Pandora: The Changing Aspects of a Mythical Symbol.* New York: Pantheon Books, 1956.

PARKER, RICHARD A. "Ancient Egyptian Astronomy." In *The Place of Astronomy in the Ancient World,* edited by F. R. Hodson. Joint Symposium of the Royal Society and the British Academy. London: Oxford University Press, 1974.

PARKER, RICHARD A., and OTTO NEUGEBAUER. *Egyptian Astronomical Texts.* 2 vols. Providence, R.I.: Brown University Press, 1969.

PAULY, AUGUST FRIEDRICH VON, ed. *Realencyclopädie der classischen Altertumswissenschaft.* Revised by Georg Wissowa, Wilhelm Kroll, and Kurt Witters. Reprint. Stuttgart: J. B. Metzler, 1963.

PAUSANIAS. *Description of Greece.* Translated by W.H.S. Jones and H. A. Ormerod. 2 vols. The Loeb Classical Library. Reprint. Cambridge: Harvard University Press, 1979.

———. *Guide to Greece.* Translated by Peter Levi. 2 vols. Harmondsworth, Eng.: Penguin Books, 1971.

PINDAR. *Carmina.* Edited by W. Christ. Leipzig: Teubner, 1904.

———. *Epinicia.* Edited by Bruno Snell. Leipzig: Teubner, 1959.

PLATO. *The Collected Dialogues of Plato, Including the Letters.* Edited by Edith Hamilton and Huntington Cairns, with translations by various authorities. Bollingen Series, no. 11. New York: Pantheon Press, 1961.

———. *Opera.* Edited by John Burnet. 5 vols. Oxford: Clarendon Press, 1902.

PLAUTUS. *Curculio.* Edited by John Wright. Chico, Calif.: Scholar's Press, 1981.

PLINY. *The Natural History.* Translated by H. Rackham and W.H.S. Jones.

10 vols. The Loeb Classical Library. Cambridge: Harvard University Press, 1938.

PLUTARCH. *Plutarch's de Iside et Osiride.* Edited and translated by John Gwyn Griffiths. Cardiff: University of Wales Press, 1970.

POCOCK, LEWIS G. *Odyssean Essays.* Oxford: B. Blackwell, 1965.

POKORNY, JULIUS J. *Indogermanisches etymologisches Wörterbuch.* 2 vols. Bern-Munich: Francke Verlag, 1959–60.

PROPP, VLADIMIR. *Morphology of the Folktale.* Translated by Laurence Scott. Austin: University of Texas Press, 1968.

RAGLAN, LORD. *The Hero: A Study in Tradition, Myth and Drama.* 1936. Reprint. New York: Random House, 1956.

RENFREW, COLIN. *Archaeology and Language: The Puzzle of Indo-European Origins.* London: Jonathan Cape, 1987.

———. "The Origins of the Indo-European Languages." *Scientific American* 261 (October 1989): 106–114.

Der Rig Veda. Translated by Karl Friedrich Geldner. Harvard Oriental Series, vols. 33–35. Cambridge: Harvard University Press, 1951.

Rig-Veda Sanhita: A Collection of Ancient Hindu Hymns of the Rig-Veda. Translated by H. H. Wilson. Reprint. New Delhi: Cosmo, 1977.

ROSE, HERBERT J. *A Handbook of Greek Mythology, Including an Extension to Rome.* New York: Dutton, 1959.

ROUSE, W.H.D. *Greek Votive Offerings: An Essay in the History of Greek Religion.* Cambridge: Cambridge University Press, 1902.

ROY, S. B. *Prehistoric Lunar Astronomy, 19,000–3100 B.C.* New Delhi: Institute of Chronology, 1976.

SANDARS, N. K., ed. and trans. *The Epic of Gilgamesh.* Baltimore: Penguin Books, 1960.

SAXO GRAMMATICUS, *The First Nine Books of the Danish History of Saxo Grammaticus.* Translated by Oliver Elton. Folk-Lore Society Publication 33. 1894. Reprint. Nendeln, Lichtenstein: Kraus, 1967.

SAYCE, ARCHIBALD H. *Lectures on the Origin and Growth of Religion as Illustrated by the Religion of the Ancient Babylonians.* 2d ed. Reprint. New York: AMS Press, 1980.

SCHMIDT, H. H. *Gerichtigkeit als Weltordnung.* Tubingen, 1968.

SCHNABEL, P. "Kidenas, Hipparch und die Entdeckung der Präzession." *Zeitschrift für Assyriologie* 37 (1926): 1–60.

SEBOEK, THOMAS, ed. *Myth: A Symposium.* 1955. Reprint. Bloomington: Indiana University Press, 1965.

SEN, P. R. "The Uranus Legend and Its Interpretation." *Calcutta Review* 66 (1938): 223–234.

SETHNA, TEHMURASP RUSTAMI. *Yashts in Roman Script with Translation.* Karachi: Sethna, 1976.

SIMPSON, MICHAEL, ed. and trans. *Gods and Heroes of the Greeks: The Library of Apollodorus*. Amherst: University of Massachusetts Press, 1976.

SIMPSON, WILLIAM. *The Buddhist Praying-Wheel: A Collection of Material Bearing on the Symbolism of the Wheel and Circular Movements in Custom and Religious Ritual*. London: Macmillan and Co., 1896.

SIVARANA MENON, CHERUBALA PATHAYPURA. *Early Astronomy and Cosmology: A Reconstruction of the Earliest Cosmic System*. London: Allen and Unwin, 1932.

SMITH, WILLIAM ROBERTSON. *Lectures on the Religion of the Semites: The Fundamental Institutions*. 3d ed. London: A. C. Black, 1927.

SOMADEVA BHATTA. *The Katha Sarit Sagara; or, Ocean of the Streams of Story*. Translated by Charles H. Tawney. 2d ed. 1923. Reprint. Delhi: Motilal Banarsidass, 1968.

SOMAYAJI, D. A. *A Critical Study of the Ancient Hindu Astronomy in the Light and Language of the Modern*. Dharwar, 1971.

SÖRENSON, S. *An Index to the Names in the Mahabaharata, with Short Explanation and a Concordance to the Bombay and Calcutta Editions and P. C. Roy's Translation*. Reprint. Delhi: Motilal Banarsidass, 1978.

SPEISER, E. A. "The Rivers of Paradise." In *Festschrift: Johannes Friedrich zum 65 Geburtstag*. Heidelberg: Carl Winter, 1965.

STECHERT, G. E. *Star Names: Their Lore and Meaning*. Translated and revised by Richard Hinckley Allen. New York: Dover, 1963.

STERLUSON, SNORRI. *The Prose Edda of Tales from Norse Mythology*. Translated by Jean I. Young. 1954. Reprint. Berkeley: University of California Press, 1964.

STRUTYNSKI, UDO. "Germanic Deities in Weekday Names." *Journal of Indo-European Studies* 3 (1975): 363–384.

STUTLEY, MARGARET, and JAMES STUTLEY. *A Dictionary of Hinduism: Its Mythology, Folklore, and Development, 1500 B.C.–1500 A.D.* London: Routledge and Kegan Paul, 1977.

Suidae Lexicon. Edited by Ada Adler. 5 vols. Leipzig: Teubner, 1928–38.

Surya-Siddhanta. Translated by Ebenezer Burgess. Revised by P. Gangooly. Calcutta: University of Calcutta Press, 1934.

SWARTZ, G. S. "Theogony 175; *Harpen Karcharodonta*: Why a Sickle?" *Revista di Studi Classici* 27 (1979): 177–188.

TEBBEN, JOSEPH R. *Hesiod-Konkordanz: A Computer Concordance to Hesiod*. New York: Georg Olms, 1977.

———. *Homer Kondordanz: A Computer Concordance to the Homeric Hymns*. New York: Georg Olms, 1977.

TERRY, PATRICIA, trans. *The Poems of the Vikings: The Elder Edda*. Indianapolis: Bobbs-Merrill, 1969.

THOMPSON, LAWRENCE S., ed. *Norse Mythology: The Elder Edda in Prose Translation*. Hamden, Conn.: Archon Books, 1974.

THOMPSON, STITH. *The Folktale*. 1946. Reprint. New York: Holt Rinehart and Winston, 1960.

TILAK, BAL GANGADHAR. *The Arctic Home in the Vedas, Being Also a New Key to the Interpretation of Many Vedic Texts and Legends*. Poona: Tilak Brothers, 1925.

———. *Orion; or, Researches into the Antiquity of the Vedas*. Bombay, 1893.

TURNER, RALPH L. *A Comparative Dictionary of the Indo-Aryan Languages*. London: Oxford University Press, 1966.

TYLOR, SIR EDWARD B. *Anahuac; or, Mexico and the Mexicans Ancient and Modern*. London, 1861.

———. *Primitive Culture: Researches into the Development of Mythology, Philosophy, Religion, Language, Art and Custom*. London, 1871.

———. *Researches into the Early History of Mankind*. London, 1865.

ULANSEY, DAVID. "The Mithraic Mysteries." *Scientific American* 261 (December 1989): 130–135.

———. "Mithraic Studies: A Paradigm Shift?" *Religious Studies Review* 13 (April 1987): 104–110.

———. *The Origins of the Mithraic Mysteries*. Oxford: Oxford University Press, 1989.

VAN DER WAERDEN, B. L. "The Great Year in Greek, Persian and Hindu Astronomy." *Archive for the History of the Exact Sciences* 18 (1977–78): 358–383.

Vedic Hymns. Translated by F. Max Müller. Sacred Books of the East, vol. 32. Oxford: Clarendon Press, 1891.

VERNANT, J. P. "Sacrificial and Alimentary Codes in Hesiod." In *Myth, Religion and Society*, edited by R. L. Gordon, 57–79. Cambridge: Cambridge University Press, 1981.

———. "The Myth of Prometheus in Hesiod." In *Myth, Religion and Society*, edited by R. L. Gordon, 43–56. Cambridge: Cambridge University Press, 1981.

VERNANT, J. P., and M. DETIENNE. *La Cuisine du sacrifice*. Paris: Éditions Gallimard, 1979.

VON DECHEND, HERTHA. "Bemerkungen zum Donnerkeil." In *Festschrift: W. Hartner*, edited by Y. von Maeyama and W. G. Slatzer. Wiesbaden: Steiner, 1977.

WALKER, BENJAMIN. *The Hindu World: An Encyclopedic Survey of Hinduism*. New York: Praeger, 1968.

WARD, DONALD. *The Divine Twins: An Indo-European Myth in Germanic Tradition*. University of California Publications, Folklore Studies, vol. 19. Berkeley: University of California Press, 1968.

WATKINS, CALVERT. "I-E 'Star'." *Sprache* 20 (1974): 10–14.

WEST, E. W., ed. and trans. *Pahlavi Texts*. Part 1: *The Bundahis, Bahman Yast and Shâyast Lâ-Shâyast*. Sacred Books of the East, vol. 5. Oxford: Clarendon Press, 1880.

WEST, M. L. *Hesiod's Theogony.* Oxford: Clarendon Press, 1966.

WIDENGREN, GEO. *The King and the Tree of Life in Ancient Near-Eastern Religion.* Uppsala universitets arskrift 1951:4. Uppsala: Lundequistska, 1951.

WIKANDER, STIG. "Histoire des Ouranides." *Cahiers du sud* 314 (1952): 9–17.

WINTERNITZ, MORITZ. *A Concise Dictionary of Eastern Religion, Being the Index Volume to The Sacred Books of the East.* Oxford: Clarendon Press, 1910.

WOLLEY, SIR LEONARD. "Stories of the Creation and the Flood." *Palestine Exploration Quarterly* 88 (1965): 14–21.

WORTHEN, THOMAS D. "The Idea of 'Sky' in Archaic Greek Poetry." *Glotta* 66 (1988): 1–19.

YALMAN, NUR. "'The Raw: the Cooked:: Nature: Culture.' Observations on *Le Cru et le cuit.*" In *The Structural Study of Myth and Totemism,* edited by Edmund Leach. London: Tavistock, 1967.

ZIMMER, HEINRICH. *Myths and Symbols in Indian Art and Civilization.* Edited by Joseph Campbell. The Bollingen Series 6. 1946. Reprint. Princeton, N.J.: Princeton University Press, 1972.

ZUIDEMA, R. T. "Catachillay: The Role of the Pleiades and of the Southern Cross and a and b Centauri in the Calendar of the Incas." In *Ethnoastronomy and Archaeoastronomy in the American Tropics,* edited by Gary Urton and Athony F. Aveni. New York Academy of Sciences, vol. 385. New York, 1982.

INDEX

About the Author

THOMAS WORTHEN is currently an associate professor of classics at the University of Arizona. His research has focused mainly on early Greek science. He has published papers and done scholarly work on Empedocles's theory of breathing, on the Thucydidean plague, on the body of lore surrounding the disease anthrax in ancient and medieval times, on the words for star and planet in the Indo-European language family, and on the idea of 'sky' as reflected in the Homeric vocabulary, in early Greek astronomical calendars, and in the star catalogue of Hipparchus and Ptolemy. This book grew out of the idea that in prehistory the ancients possessed a great deal of informal knowledge about the apparitions apparent to them in the heavens many centuries before the development of early science which, through observation and discussion, made that knowledge technical. This informal knowledge found expression in farmer's almanacs, lunisolar calendars, other systems of reckoning time, agonistic poetry (including drama), juridical astrology, and above all in the vast corpus of Greek and Hindu myth.